The Drama of Salvation

How God Rescues Us from Our Sins
and Brings Us to Eternal Life

JIMMY AKIN

The Drama of Salvation

How God Rescues Us from Our Sins
and Brings Us to Eternal Life

Published by Catholic Answers, Inc.
2020 Gillespie Way
El Cajon, California 92020
1-888-291-8000 orders
619-387-0042 fax
catholic.com

Printed in the United States of America

Cover design by Devin Schadt
Interior design by Sherry Russell

978-1-941663-12-7 hardcover
978-1-941663-13-4 paperback
978-1-941663-14-1 Kindle
978-1-941663-15-8 ePub

Contents

Preface

Good crystal gives off an unmistakable sound. If you strike it lightly with your forefinger, you'll hear the delicate *ping* that indicates: This is genuine; this is the real thing. But if the glass in your hand fails to make the telltale sound, you know that you're holding, at best, a glittering fake.

Something analogous happens in the world of the intellect. There are times when you just *know*, as if by instinct, and often before you're able to say exactly why, that an argument you're hearing is fatally flawed; it gives off something like the hollow *thunk* of cheap glass. But then there are those rare and precious times when you read a book or an article and—*ping!*—there's no mistaking: This is the real thing. At the banquet table of apologetics, Jimmy Akin's *The Drama of Salvation* is the finest of fine crystal.

Questions relating to salvation—especially faith versus works, but also penance, purgatory, and indulgences—have been neuralgic points in the dialogue between Catholics and Protestants. Serious people on every side have reasonably wondered whether dialogue can accomplish very much if anything, for what they have seen trumpeted as the fruit of ecumenical dialogue too often has involved falsification and betrayal of their respective traditions. This book should lay all such doubts to rest.

Mr. Akin knows and respects the Protestant tradition in which he was raised and the Catholicism he has come to embrace. He is not about to falsify either or to pretend that crucial differences do not exist. But he is also unwilling to allow theological slogans (like "faith alone") to distract us from significant points of agreement or to allow verbal formulae to ease away the tense paradoxes of faith and freedom. His method is to follow Scripture and Tradition wherever they lead, and he is formidably equipped for the task with honesty, clarity of mind, and a superabundance of logical rigor.

In apologetical circles, Mr. Akin was long ago nicknamed "The Terminator" precisely because of his logical skills and the remorseless way he can wield them. Those skills are on frequent display in *The Drama of Salvation*. Though the sharp blade of dialectic is always tempered with charity, it still cuts straight and deep. So, readers, be warned: Some cherished theological nostrums may be reduced to a mass of tatters by the time Mr. Akin is finished with them.

Here I include myself among the bereaved. For many years I toyed with a certain interpretation of the meaning in Romans of "works." Then I read Mr. Akin's chapter on "Faith, Works, and Boasting." Few things in philosophy or theology deserve to be called definitive, but the argument of that chapter is surely a plausible candidate. At the very least it is a powerfully compelling case for one view of Pauline soteriology, and it demands a serious response from anyone who might hope to hold a different view.

That, in fact, could be said of this book as a whole. It is a serious work by a serious and supremely gifted apologist on a topic of central concern for everyone. If it elicits the response it deserves, then all of us, whatever our confessional commitments, will at least be clearer about what really does divide us. And what does not. Some notions, after all, deserve to be terminated.

—*Ronald K. Tacelli, S.J.*
Boston College

Introduction

There are many books on the subject of salvation, and many of them share certain characteristics:

1. They focus exclusively on the subject of *eternal* salvation.
2. They focus in particular on the doctrine of justification.
3. They often ignore, in the interests of systematic theology, the way in which the Bible uses language.
4. They are often written in a polemical, hostile style.
5. Due to the authors' unfamiliarity with the way other groups of Christians express themselves, they mistakenly criticize views on which there is no disagreement in substance.

It is my hope that this book will be different. While it does discuss the subject of eternal salvation, it also seeks to show that the concept of salvation in the Bible is much broader than that. While it discusses the doctrine of justification, it also gives attention to other biblical themes relating to salvation. While it addresses concerns of systematic theology, it focuses significantly on the way the Bible talks about salvation—the kind of *language* Scripture uses when addressing it. While it takes a very definite position on many matters, it is not meant to be polemical or hostile toward those with other beliefs. Finally, while this book is critical of positions I believe to be in error, it takes great care to understand the ways in which different groups of Christians express themselves.

Tragically, Protestants and Catholics often talk past each other, failing to perceive the ways that the other uses words and phrases. I hope that this book will help both Catholics and Protestants "translate" the theological language of one group into the language of the other so that individuals on both sides can better understand what their partners in dialogue or controversy actually *mean*, not just what they *say*.

Often the two groups are led astray by terminology. They often perceive themselves to be in disagreement when actually they are not—or, at least, when the disagreement is not as sharp as they think. This is precisely the kind of situation that St. Paul was addressing when he warned about quarreling over words. He instructed St. Timothy to charge his flock "before the Lord to avoid disputing about words, which does no good, but only ruins the hearers" (2 Tim. 2:14).

Similarly, Paul said that a person who is quarrelsome about words is "puffed up with conceit, he knows nothing; he has a morbid craving for controversy and for disputes about words, which produce envy, dissension, slander, base suspicions, and wrangling among men who are depraved in mind and bereft of the truth, imagining that godliness is a means of gain" (1 Tim. 6:4–5).

Contemporary Christians of all persuasions need to take Paul's words to heart. My hope is that this book will help bring about a greater understanding of how Scripture treats the subject of salvation and how different groups of Christians understand it.

1

The Drama of Salvation

Something is desperately wrong with the world. We all sense it. With all of the wars, crimes, hatreds, and cruelties the world contains, something is definitely wrong. Mankind's catalogue of sin and vice is endless, and there seem to be new moral challenges every day. What's worse, the problem is not just in the world. It is within us. Each of us has done wrong in our lives. Sometimes we have done things that are *very* wrong. If we are lucky, we have enough conscience and courage to face our own misdeeds. But too often, we rationalize them away or we ignore them and pretend that they don't exist.

The fact that we realize there is something wrong with the world—and with ourselves—raises a set of questions: What will happen as a result of all the bad things that take place in the world? Will the innocent always suffer? Will the guilty always triumph? Will matters ever be put right? Is there justice in the world? And if there is, can that justice be tempered with mercy?

Religions and philosophies propose different answers to these questions. From the Christian point of view, there is ultimate justice. In the last day, God will judge the living and the dead. He will eventually right every wrong. He will console and compensate those who have suffered innocently. He will punish those who have done wrong. And he will be merciful to those who have sought his grace and forgiveness.

From the Christian point of view, all human beings will have one of two destinies: to be spiritually united with God in heaven or to be spiritually separated from God in hell. The former promises an eternity of happiness, the latter an eternity of anguish.

Obviously, one destiny is preferable to the other. The question is how to make sure you have the preferable one—or, to put it another way, how to make sure that you're saved.

Salvation is one of many terms the Bible uses to describe the way God works in our lives to deal with the effects of sin. The basic image is one of rescue. To save someone is to rescue him, as when a fireman saves someone from a burning building or one soldier saves another on the battlefield. Any time someone is saved, he is rescued from a perilous situation.

From what are we being rescued when God saves us? This can be understood in different ways. In one sense, we are being rescued from being eternally lost. That state, though, is a result of our sins, and so we can also think about salvation as being rescued from our sins. Sin entered the world through the agency of the devil, and so we can think of salvation in terms of being rescued from the powers of darkness as well.

In addition to conceiving of salvation as rescue *from* one state, it can also be understood as rescue *to* another, better state. In this sense, God can be understood as saving us *from* hell *to* heaven, *from* sin *to* holiness, and *from* the devil *to* God himself.

None of these understandings are exclusive. They are all compatible.

In addition to the concept of salvation, the Bible uses other images to describe the way God deals with sin in our lives. These include justification (being made righteous), sanctification (being made holy), and forgiveness (releasing of spiritual debt). All of these describe different aspects of what God does in our lives to deal with our sins.

These concepts are what this book is about. In the coming chapters, we will look at them and the rich and, at times, surprising ways that Scripture employs them. We will also look at the controversy that surrounds them. Unfortunately, not all Christians understand these concepts in the same way. The disagreement is particularly strong in the Protestant community, which is sharply divided on several points.

To set the stage for that discussion, we will begin by looking—in broad outlines—at the view that was common prior to the Protestant Reformation and that is still common among Catholics, Orthodox, and members of other historic churches.

It is a view that is rooted in the Bible.

I. SCRIPTURE ON SALVATION

As we will see in future chapters, the topic of salvation (and the related concepts of justification, sanctification, and forgiveness) is a very rich one, and Scripture has a great deal to say about it. However, in answering the basic question "How can I be saved?," there are only a few themes that the New Testament presents to us.

Repentance

The first of these is repentance from sin. If we wish to be saved from our sins, we need to turn our back on them. We need to resolve, by God's grace, to break with sin and to obey God's will instead.

The need for repentance was emphasized by Jesus from the very beginning of his earthly ministry. According to the Gospel of Mark:

> Now after John was arrested, Jesus came into Galilee, preaching the gospel of God, and saying, "The time is fulfilled, and the kingdom of God is at hand; repent, and believe in the gospel" (Mark 1:14–15).

Biblical repentance calls for not just a mental rejection of sin but also a practical one. John the Baptist emphasized this in a warning he gave the Pharisees and Sadducees:

> Bear fruit that befits repentance, and do not presume to say to yourselves, "We have Abraham as our father"; for I tell you, God is able from these stones to raise up children to Abraham. Even now the axe is laid to the root of the trees; every tree therefore that does not bear good fruit is cut down and thrown into the fire (Matt. 3:8–10).

Repentance involves a change of heart, but this change of

heart must result in a change of action. In John's words, it must "bear fruit."

This fruit involves turning away from sin and acting instead in a righteous manner. John emphasized this to groups of tax collectors and soldiers who wanted to know what implications repentance had for their lives:

> Tax collectors also came to be baptized, and said to him, "Teacher, what shall we do?" And he said to them, "Collect no more than is appointed you."
>
> Soldiers also asked him, "And we, what shall we do?" And he said to them, "Rob no one by violence or by false accusation, and be content with your wages" (Luke 3:12–14).

Tax collectors were infamous for collecting more than the amount they were supposed to, and soldiers were infamous for robbing people, either "by violence or by false accusation," and so John indicates to these groups that they must avoid the sins that they are known for and live righteously instead.

Repentance does not mean a commitment to live in sinless perfection, for, as the New Testament elsewhere tells us, "we all make many mistakes" (James 3:2), and "If we say we have no sin, we deceive ourselves, and the truth is not in us" (1 John 1:8). However, it does mean that we will to turn from sin and, by the grace of God, to break with it fundamentally, even if we must still wrestle with it during the course of this life.

Faith

The second element that the New Testament requires for salvation is faith. In the broadest sense, it requires faith in God. As the book of Hebrews states:

> Without faith it is impossible to please him. For whoever would draw near to God must believe that he exists and that he rewards those who seek him (Heb. 11:6).

The New Testament calls us to a more specific form of faith than just belief that God exists, though. You will notice that, at the beginning of his ministry, Jesus preached both that people should repent and that they should "believe in the gospel."

As we will see in a future chapter, "the gospel" is the good news that God has sent his Son into the world to make salvation possible. As Jesus himself puts it in the Gospel of John:

> God so loved the world that he gave his only Son, that whoever believes in him should not perish but have eternal life. For God sent the Son into the world, not to condemn the world, but that the world might be saved through him. He who believes in him is not condemned; he who does not believe is condemned already, because he has not believed in the name of the only Son of God (John 3:16–18).

As God revealed his plan progressively through the prophets, men were required to believe the new aspects of his message as they were disclosed. This meant that the requirements of faith took on a more definite shape through the ages. When he made the final revelation of his Son, belief in the Son and his saving mission was added to the deposit of faith that God had been building over the centuries. Again, to quote the book of Hebrews:

> In many and various ways God spoke of old to our fathers by the prophets; but in these last days he has spoken to us by a Son, whom he appointed the heir of all things, through whom also he created the world (Heb. 1:1–2).

Christian faith thus calls not just for faith in God in general but specifically for faith in Jesus Christ his Son.

Baptism

Human beings are both physical and spiritual creatures, composed of body and soul. As a result, God often gives us his grace through physical means. He did this at various points in the Old Testament, such as when he raised a man back to life after he came in contact with the bones of the prophet Elisha (2 Kings 13:21).

In the New Testament, God chose a number of outward, physical symbols to communicate his inward, spiritual graces. These are known as *sacraments*, and the first of these—which is the Christian rite of initiation and thus the gateway to all other sacraments—is baptism.

Jesus indicated that his disciples, no matter where they are in the world, are to be baptized, telling the apostles:

> Go therefore and make disciples of all nations, baptizing them in the name of the Father and of the Son and of the Holy Spirit (Matt. 28:19).

Baptism is not just a ritual. It communicates God's graces, such as the forgiveness of sins and the gift of the Holy Spirit. Thus St. Peter told the crowd on the day of Pentecost:

> Repent, and be baptized every one of you in the name of Jesus Christ for the forgiveness of your sins; and you shall receive the gift of the Holy Spirit (Acts 2:38).

Similarly, when he was converted to the Faith, St. Paul was told:

> Rise and be baptized, and wash away your sins, calling on his name (Acts 22:16).

In his letters, St. Peter explicitly connected baptism with salvation. Comparing the process of being baptized to how eight people were saved in Noah's Ark, he writes:

> Baptism, which corresponds to this, now saves you, not as a removal of dirt from the body but as an appeal to God for a clear conscience, through the resurrection of Jesus Christ (1 Pet. 3:21).

Baptism does not save because it makes us physically cleaner, he says. Rather it "now saves you" because it involves "an appeal to God for a clear conscience," which is granted to us "through the resurrection of Jesus Christ."

Baptism thus places us in the state of salvation and reconciliation with God.

Mortal Sin

The fact that we may have been reconciled with God through repentance, faith, and baptism does not mean that we no longer have free will. We do still have it, and we can choose to turn away from God—to fall back into sin, to "unrepent." We have already seen that the New Testament recognizes the ongoing struggle with sin in the Christian life and the fact that we all fall into it (James 3:2, 1 John 1:8).

But not all sins are the same. Some are worse than others. It is one thing to be unnecessarily rude to someone; it is quite another to knowingly and deliberately kill an innocent person. Jesus acknowledged that sins have different gravities when he told Pontius Pilate, "[H]e who delivered me to you has the greater sin" (John 19:11).

To recognize this difference, the Church has developed a special vocabulary. The lesser sins that we fall into daily are known as *venial* sins. They may impair our relationship with God, but they do not kill the spiritual life he has given us. The greater transgressions are known as *mortal* sins, because they *do* kill the spiritual life in our souls and deprive us of the state of salvation.

Jesus himself emphasizes the fact that some sins are capable of doing this. When asked how to inherit eternal life, Jesus replied: "If you would enter life, keep the commandments" (Matt. 19:17). He went on to specify some of these: "You shall not kill, You shall not commit adultery, You shall not steal, You shall not bear false witness, Honor your father and mother, and, You shall love your neighbor as yourself" (Matt. 19:18–19). Here he is drawing on the Ten Commandments (cf. Exod. 20:1–17, Deut. 5:6–21).

Elsewhere, he told his disciples, "If you keep my commandments, you will abide in my love, just as I have kept my Father's commandments and abide in his love." On that occasion, he identified love as the commandment he was most concerned about: "This is my commandment, that you love one another as I have loved you" (John 15:10, 12; cf. Mark 12:28–34). St. Paul was equally clear that some sins will cost people their salvation:

> Do you not know that the unrighteous will not inherit the kingdom of God? Do not be deceived; neither the immoral, nor idolaters, nor adulterers, nor homosexuals, nor thieves, nor the greedy, nor drunkards, nor revilers, nor robbers will inherit the kingdom of God (1 Cor. 6:9–10).

He is similarly direct in Galatians, where he tells his readers:

> Now the works of the flesh are plain: immorality, impurity, licentiousness, idolatry, sorcery, enmity, strife, jealousy, anger, selfishness, dissension, party spirit, envy, drunkenness, carousing, and the like. I warn you, as I warned you before, that those who do such things shall not inherit the kingdom of God (Gal. 5:19–21).

Confession

Fortunately, when we fall into sin—mortal or venial—forgiveness is available to us.

In the Lord's Prayer, the model of all Christian prayers, Jesus taught his disciples to pray "forgive us our debts, as we also have forgiven our debtors" (Matt. 6:12), or, in Luke's version, "forgive us our sins, for we ourselves forgive everyone who is indebted to us" (Luke 11:4).

This indicates that, just as sin is an ongoing possibility in the life of the Christian, so is forgiveness.

For venial sins—those that do not destroy the spiritual life within us—daily prayer of this sort is sufficient for them to be forgiven. But for mortal sins, something more is required—a sacrament, one of the physical symbols that God uses to convey his spiritual graces.

After he rose from the dead, Jesus came to the apostles and did something unexpected.

> Jesus said to them again, "Peace be with you. As the Father has sent me, even so I send you."
> And when he had said this, he breathed on them, and said to them, "Receive the Holy Spirit. If you forgive the sins of any, they are forgiven; if you retain the sins of any, they are retained" (John 20:21–23).

Jesus thus empowered his ministers with the Holy Spirit to forgive or retain sins. This was an extension of Jesus' own ministry of forgiveness, which he had exercised previously (cf. Matt. 9:1–8, Mark 2:1–12). He thus sends the disciples to forgive or retain sins, just as the Father had sent him to.

For one of Christ's ministers to know whether to forgive or retain a sin, he has to know about the sin and whether the person is genuinely repentant for it. This requires the penitent to reveal these facts, and so today this sacrament is often called *confession*, because this is one of the acts required by the penitent.

It should also be noted that this sacrament—which takes the place of baptism for those who have already been baptized—presupposes repentance and faith. After falling into mortal sin, one needs to turn away from sin again, just as one did before. Similarly, if one has allowed one's faith to lapse, it needs to be renewed through a new commitment to Jesus and the Christian faith that he proclaimed.

Summary

There is much more that can be said about the subject of salvation. Indeed, the rest of this book will be devoted to it, and even the coming chapters can only scratch the surface. However, the above represent the key things the New Testament presents to us as what we need to do in order to be saved: We need to repent, believe, and be baptized. If we fall into mortal sin, we need to repent, believe, and go to confession. It's that simple—at least when we keep it on the level of the basics.

There are, of course, many more advanced questions that can be asked. For example, what about those who—through no fault of their own—never hear the message of Jesus in a persuasive way and never have Christian faith? Or what about those who do but who do not have access to the sacraments?

The answer is that God can make provision for people in these cases, and they can be saved if they otherwise respond to the grace that they have been given. But the above represent the ordinary manner in which people are saved, and they represent—as the New Testament indicates—what we must do if we want to accept salvation on God's terms. If we can't, through no fault of our own, God will not hold it against us; but if we can and don't, he will (see chapter 9).

There are also many questions about the Christian life that flows from these initial elements: the living of a moral live, doing "good works" under the impulse of God's grace, receiving the other sacraments—particularly the Eucharist—and growing in God's grace.

However, the basic elements needed to enter a state of grace (salvation) under ordinary circumstances are repentance, faith, and baptism. Those needed to reenter it after a fall into mortal sin are repentance, faith, and confession.

II. The Church Fathers on Salvation

The understanding of salvation that we have sketched from the New Testament is not a recent invention. In fact, it was the understanding of the earliest Christians who lived during the age of the Church Fathers—the centuries immediately following the time of Christ.

The witness of the Church Fathers is particularly important, because their era connects the age of the New Testament to our age. They were closer to the world of the New Testament than we are, and they preserved the original Christian message as it was passed from one generation to another (cf. 2 Tim. 2:2).

As we will see, they shared the same view described in the previous section.

Repentance

From the beginning of Christian history the Church Fathers were clear about the need for repentance. For example, the first-century Father known as Clement of Rome (Pope St. Clement I) wrote:

Let us look steadfastly to the blood of Christ, and see how precious that blood is to God, which, having been shed for our salvation, has set the grace of repentance before the whole world. Let us turn to every age that has passed, and learn that, from generation to generation, the Lord has granted a place of repentance to all such as would be converted unto him (*Letter to the Corinthians* 7).

At the turn of the second century, St. Ignatius, the bishop of Antioch, told his readers:

And pray without ceasing in behalf of other men. For there is in them hope of repentance that they may attain to God (*Letter to the Ephesians* 10).

And, in the mid-second century, St. Justin Martyr wrote:

What shall I say, too, of the countless multitude of those who have reformed intemperate habits, and learned these things? For Christ called not the just nor the chaste to repentance, but the ungodly, and the licentious, and the unjust; his words being, "I came not to call the righteous, but sinners to repentance" [Matt. 9:13]. For the heavenly Father desires rather the repentance than the punishment of the sinner (*First Apology* 15).

Note that the repentance being spoken of is not just mental but also practical, for it involves the reform of "intemperate habits," and it leads to salvation, for the alternative to repentance is "the punishment of the sinner."

There are numerous quotations from Fathers in later centuries stressing these same themes.

Faith

Of course, the Fathers also recognized the need of Christian faith. To provide just a few early quotations to illustrate, we may turn first to St. Clement of Rome:

> And we, too, being called by His will in Christ Jesus, are not justified by ourselves, nor by our own wisdom, or understanding, or godliness, or works which we have wrought in holiness of heart; but by that faith through which, from the beginning, Almighty God has justified all men; to whom be glory for ever and ever (*Letter to the Corinthians* 32).

At the beginning of the second century, St. Ignatius of Antioch wrote:

> None of these things is hid from you, if you perfectly possess that faith and love towards Christ Jesus, which are the beginning and the end of life. For the beginning is faith, and the end is love. Now these two, being inseparably connected together, are of God, while all other things that are requisite for a holy life follow after them (*Letter to the Ephesians* 14).

Ignatius's contemporary, St. Polycarp, the bishop of Smyrna, wrote:

If we please Him in this present world, we shall receive also the future world, according as He has promised to us that He will raise us again from the dead, and that if we live worthily of Him, "we shall also reign together with Him" (2 Tim. 2:12), provided only we believe (*Letter to the Philippians* 5).

The importance of faith for salvation was clearly understood, as one would expect, by the early Church Fathers.

Baptism

The first Christians also recognized the importance of baptism. According to the first-century Church manual known as the *Didache* (DID-uh-KAY), it could be performed in several different manners, but it was such an important spiritual event that it was to be accompanied by fasting.

And concerning baptism, this is how you baptize: Having first said all these things, baptize into the name of the Father, and of the Son, and of the Holy Spirit, in living water. But if thou have not living water, baptize into other water; and if thou canst not in cold, in warm. But if thou have not either, pour out water thrice upon the head into the name of Father and Son and Holy Spirit. But before the baptism let the baptizer fast, and the baptized, and whatever others can; but thou shalt order the baptized to fast one or two days before (*Didache* 7).

The reason for its having such spiritual importance is that it was recognized as providing salvation for the recipient. Thus the first-century author Hermas of Rome reported:

And I said, "I heard, sir, some teachers say that there is no other repentance than what takes place when we descended into the water and received remission of our former sins." He said to me, "That was sound doctrine you heard; for that is really the case" (*The Shepherd* 2:4:3).

The mid-second century writer St. Justin Martyr emphasized the same, explaining:

> As many as are persuaded and believe that what we teach and say is true, and undertake to be able to live accordingly, and are instructed to pray and entreat God with fasting, for the remission of their past sins, we pray and fast with them. Then they are brought by us where there is water, and are regenerated in the same way we were ourselves regenerated. For, in the name of God, the Father and Lord of the universe, and of our Savior Jesus Christ, and of the Holy Spirit, they receive the washing with water. For Christ also said, "Unless you be born again, you shall not enter into the kingdom of heaven" [John 3:3] (*First Apology* 61).

To give a final early example, the late-second century author St. Theophilus of Antioch stated:

> Moreover, the things proceeding from the waters were blessed by God, that this also might be a sign of men being destined to receive repentance and remission of sins through the water and washing of regeneration, as many as come to the truth, and are born again, and receive blessing from God (*To Autolycus* 2:16).

The Church Fathers thus understood baptism not just as a symbolic rite but as a true sacrament conveying God's grace to us.

Mortal Sin

While it was clear to the Church Fathers (as it is clear in Scripture) that baptism communicates God's grace to us, and specifically the forgiveness of sins and salvation, it is also clear that at times the baptized commit mortal sins that would deprive them of heaven. Thus the Church Fathers also recognized the possibility of mortal sin.

In the first century, the *Didache* warned Christians:

Watch for your life's sake. Do not let your lamps be quenched, or your loins be unclothed; but be ready, for you know not the hour in which our Lord comes (Matt. 24:42). But often shall you come together, seeking the things that are befitting to your souls: for the whole time of your faith will not profit you, if you be not made perfect in the last time (*Didache* 16).

Also in the first century, St. Clement of Rome warned certain people at the church of Corinth that through sin they had lost the righteousness (justification) granted to them by God:

> For this reason, righteousness and peace are now far departed from you, inasmuch as everyone abandons the fear of God, and is become blind in his faith, neither walks in the ordinances of his appointment, nor acts a part becoming a Christian, but walks after his own wicked lusts, resuming the practice of an unrighteous and ungodly envy, by which death itself entered into the world (*Letter to the Corinthians* 3).

The anonymous first-century author of the document sometimes called "Second Clement" also stressed the need not to fall into mortal sin after baptism:

> For if we do the will of Christ, we shall find rest; otherwise, if we disobey his commandments, nothing shall deliver us from eternal punishment. . . . How can we hope to enter into the royal residence of God unless we keep our baptism holy and undefiled? Or who shall be our advocate, unless we are possessed of works of holiness and righteousness? (*Second Clement* 6).

At the beginning of the second century, St. Ignatius of Antioch acknowledged that people could fall into sin and then repent and return so that they might attain God:

> And pray without ceasing on behalf of other men. For there is in them hope of repentance that they may attain to God. For

cannot he that falls arise again, and he that goes astray return? (*Letter to the Ephesians* 10 [c. A.D. 110]).

Finally, the mid-second century author St. Justin Martyr warned:

Eternal fire was prepared for him who voluntarily departed from God and for all who, without repentance, persevere in apostasy (fragment in St. Irenaeus of Lyons, *Against Heresies* 5:26:2).

Fortunately, for those who committed mortal sin, there was still a way to be reconciled with God.

Confession

The sacrament of confession (also known as the sacrament of penance or reconciliation) was also practiced in the early Church as a remedy for sins committed after baptism. At times, the confession of sins was made publicly before the whole congregation; at other times, it was privately before the priest or bishop alone. Either way, it was seen as essential to the process of reconciliation. The first-century *Didache* stated:

In the church you shall acknowledge your transgressions, and you shall not come near for your prayer with an evil conscience. This is the way of life. . . . But every Lord's day gather yourselves together and break bread and give thanksgiving after having confessed your transgressions, that your sacrifice may be pure (*Didache* 4, 14).

At the beginning of the second century, St. Ignatius of Antioch stated:

To all those who repent, the Lord grants forgiveness, if they turn in penitence to the unity of God, and to communion with the bishop (*Letter to the Philadelphians* 8).

Later in the second century, St. Irenaeus of Lyons observed that some Christian sinners were reluctant to make the confession of their sins that would have allowed them to have life with God:

> Some of them, indeed, make a public confession of their sins; but others are ashamed to do this, and in a tacit kind of way, despairing of [attaining to] the life of God, have, some of them, apostatized altogether; while others hesitate between the two courses (*Against Heresies* 1:13:7).

Around the year 200, the North African writer Tertullian of Carthage compared the reluctance to go to confession to the reluctance of a person with a shameful disease to seek medical attention:

> Most men either shun this work [confession and reconciliation] as a public exposure of themselves, or else defer it from day to day. I presume [they are] more mindful of modesty than salvation; just like men who, having contracted some malady in the more private parts of the body, avoid the probing of physicians, and so perish of their own bashfulness (*Repentance* 10).

Picking up on the same comparison of the sacrament of confession to medicine, in the mid-200s, Origen of Alexandria noted that one of the ways to achieve forgiveness is:

> the remission of sins through penance, when the sinner washes his pillow in tears (Ps. 6:7), when his tears are his nourishment day and night (Ps. 41:4), and when he does not shrink from declaring his sin to a priest of the Lord and from seeking medicine (*Homilies on Leviticus* 2:4).

Another famous image used by the Church Fathers to illustrate the role of confession in the Christian life is that of a plank that a man floating in the sea may grab to save his life following a shipwreck. After the shipwreck of sin, a man might find salvation first by seizing the "plank" of baptism, and, if he was foolish enough to let go of the graces it provides, he might find salvation again by seizing upon confession as a second "plank" (Tertullian, *Repentance* 4, Jerome, *Letters* 130:9, cf. CCC 1446).

Summary

We have seen that the Church Fathers held the same view of the fundamentals of salvation that is found in Scripture: To be saved one must repent, have faith, and be baptized. If one commits mortal sin after baptism, one should again repent (and have faith if one has turned away from it) and go to confession.

This view continued to be held through the centuries, both by the Catholic Church and by other communions of Christians that came into existence, including the ancient churches of the East and the Eastern Orthodox. While there were varying emphases and theological elaborations of it, the basic core was universally understood for the first 1,500 years of Christian history.

Until the time of the Protestant Reformation.

III. The Protestant Reformation

Luther

It is commonly held that the Protestant Reformation began in 1517, when the Augustinian monk Martin Luther circulated a document known as the *Ninety-Five Theses*. This document represented a set of propositions that he was proposing for theological discussion. Although the document is commonly referred to by the number of propositions (theses) it contains, it is more formally known as the *Disputation of Doctor Martin Luther on the Power and Efficacy of Indulgences*.

Indulgences are a theological elaboration of the Church's teaching on penance (see chapters 4 and 5), but the theological debate that Luther sparked quickly broadened to include other topics. One of the most important, perhaps *the* most important, of these is a subject not even mentioned in the *Ninety-Five Theses*: the doctrine of justification.

The word *justification* comes from Latin roots that mean "to make just" or "to make righteous," though theologians of different persuasions disagree as to the kind of justice or righteousness we receive from God.

The concept is not prominent in the Gospels, being mentioned only seven times (Matt. 11:19, 12:37; Luke 7:29, 35, 10:29, 16:15, 18:14)—several of which do not refer to justification before God but before men. The concept is mentioned a few times in the letter of James (2:21, 24, 25), but it is prominent in the letters of St. Paul, where it is mentioned more than two dozen times, primarily in Romans and Galatians.

For Luther, this concept became central to his thinking about salvation. In particular, he popularized the expression that we are justified *sola fide* (Latin, "by faith alone"). In his German translation of the Bible, Luther even added the word "alone" (German, *allein*) to Romans 3:28 so that it stated, "So now we hold, that man is justified without the help of the works of the law, alone through faith."

The word *alone* is not in the Greek in this verse, and Luther defended himself for adding it by arguing that the German idiom required the word and that this was what St. Paul meant, even though it wasn't literally what he said. The phrase "by faith alone" came to be one of the main slogans of the emerging Protestant movement, and it was picked up by others, including non-Lutherans. It remains one of the most popular Protestant slogans today.

How far did Luther and Lutheranism's understanding of justification and salvation depart from the historic view that we explored above? Not as far as is often supposed. In the twentieth century, Lutheran and Catholic scholars conducted a series of dialogues in which they found that, although they used different vocabulary and emphasized different points, they had substantial agreement on many aspects of the doctrine of justification. This led, in 1999, to the signing of a *Joint Declaration on the Doctrine of Justification* by the Holy See and the Lutheran World Federation (see chapter 8).

This declaration did not cover all aspects of the doctrine of justification, and disagreements between the two groups remain. Luther himself disagreed with part of the historic understanding that we have considered in this chapter, but not as much as many suppose.

For example, Luther was emphatic about the fact that baptism is the sacramental means through which salvation comes to us. His *Small Catechism* contains the following questions and answers on baptism:

Q. *What does Baptism give? What good is it?*
A. It gives the forgiveness of sins, redeems from death and the Devil, gives eternal salvation to all who believe this, just as God's words and promises declare.

Q. *What are these words and promises of God?*
A. Our Lord Christ spoke one of them in the last chapter of Mark:
"Whoever believes and is baptized will be saved; but whoever does not believe will be damned" (Mark 16:16).

Q. *How can water do such great things?*
A. Water doesn't make these things happen, of course. It is God's Word, which is with and in the water. Because, without God's Word, the water is plain water and not baptism. But with God's Word it is a Baptism, a grace-filled water of life, a bath of new birth in the Holy Spirit, as St. Paul said to Titus in the third chapter:
"Through this bath of rebirth and renewal of the Holy Spirit, which He poured out on us abundantly through Jesus Christ, our Savior, that we, justified by the same grace are made heirs according to the hope of eternal life. This is a faithful saying" (Titus 3:5–8).

Luther did reject parts of the historic Christian understanding of salvation. He appeared to reduce mortal sin to the single sin of apostasy (total abandonment of the Christian faith), and he appeared to hold that those who apostatized were unable to regain salvation.

Later Developments

After Luther touched off the Protestant Reformation, the movement grew and developed in many directions. Now, five hundred years later, there is considerable diversity among Protestants on the question of salvation. It is not possible in a brief space to survey the history of how the doctrine of justification has developed in Protestant circles, or all of the variations on how it is understood today, but we can note some of the main variations.

On the subject of repentance from sin, many Protestants understand this to be a genuine turning away from sin that involves a change of behavior. Others, particularly in American Evangelicalism, understand repentance to involve merely a change of mind in which a person recognizes that he is a sinner. It may be natural for such a person, by God's grace, to change his behavior as a result of this; but, according to this view, a change of behavior is not necessary. It is sufficient to recognize one's sinfulness and turn to God in faith.

Advocates of this view often defend it by pointing out that the roots of the Greek word for repentance (*metanoia*) are *meta* ("beyond," "after") and *nous* ("mind"), signifying an afterthought or change of mind. However, the roots of a word are not always a reliable guide to its meaning (otherwise the word *nice*, which is derived from the Latin word *nescius*, would mean "ignorant"). The key to what a word means is how it is used, and, as we saw in the section on the biblical requirement of repentance for salvation, the word was used in a way that involved a change of behavior.

The requirement of faith also has been understood differently in various Protestant circles. Although in ordinary speech the term *can* refer simply to belief (mere intellectual assent), the great majority of Protestants recognize that merely assenting to the truths of theology does not save one (cf. James 2:19). Consequently, it is common to draw a distinction between this type of faith and "saving faith" or "justifying faith."

How precisely this form of faith is defined varies, but one of the most commonly cited elements is trust. Saving faith is thus often understood to include not only a recognition of some of the basic truths of theology (e.g., God exists, Jesus is the Son of God, Jesus died for my sins) but also a trust in God to provide salvation. The difference is between *believing that* Jesus died to save you and *trusting in* Jesus to save you.

Some go further and require that saving faith include recognition of Jesus' Lordship, so that he is viewed not only as Savior but also as Lord, with the ability to make moral claims on our lives. In some instances, repentance from sin is said to be part of saving faith.[1]

Including repentance within the definition of saving faith avoids a problem that could result from the "by faith alone" formula. If saving faith does not include repentance, and if justification is understood to be by faith alone in a strict sense, then repentance from sin—in the sense of turning away from it by an act of the will—is not necessary. Unfortunately, some in the Protestant community seem to hold precisely this view, as we will see.

A similar problem arises with the "by faith alone" formula and baptism. As we saw earlier, Martin Luther did not understand this formula to exclude the requirement of baptism for salvation. Modern Lutherans, Anglicans, Methodists, and—with qualifications that limit this effect to elect infants—many Calvinists similarly understand baptism as a means through which salvation is granted.

Some Protestants, however, deny this. In fact, some have charged that the claim that baptism is a means of salvation makes baptism a "good work," and since we are saved by faith alone, in contrast to good works, this claim amounts to a false gospel. It is somewhat surprising that many of the people who make this charge look up to and laud Martin Luther rather than denouncing him as a purveyor of a false gospel. Presumably, most are unaware of Luther's view.

The concept or at least the term *mortal sin* is not used in most Protestant circles, and there is a difference of opinion about whether it is possible to sin in such a way as to lose salvation after it has been received.

Some believe that it is possible for a Christian to lose salvation through sin, though they do not have a developed theology of precisely how. In general, they sense that not every sin would cost a Christian his salvation but that grave ones (like murder) could. In this, they have a view that somewhat approximates the Catholic understanding of the distinction between mortal and venial sin.

Others would reduce mortal sin to the single sin of apostasy, or the complete loss of faith. If we are saved "by faith alone," then losing faith could be understood as losing salvation as well.

Some, particularly in Calvinist circles, hold that the kinds of sins that the New Testament names as being incompatible with salvation *would* cost a Christian his salvation *if* he were to commit them, but that a true Christian will never commit these, because he is preserved by God from doing so. In other words, God prevents all true Christians from committing those sins that would result in their losing salvation.

Finally, particularly in non-Calvinist American Evangelical circles, it is common to find advocates of a "once saved, always saved" view that holds that a true Christian can commit any sin at all, no matter how grave, and it will not cost him his salvation.

For those in the Protestant community who do recognize the possibility of a Christian losing his salvation, there is the question of whether and how he can get it back. A few are of the view that, if a Christian loses salvation, he is simply unable to get it back. This appears to have been Luther's view. Most, however, have been of the opinion that God will be merciful and the repentant Christian can regain his salvation by repenting and renewing his faith in God and Christ.

Conclusion

There are many more questions about salvation that can be asked. In the Protestant community there is a great deal of diversity on how these questions are to be answered, and the literature on the subject is vast. Here we cannot do more than offer a basic summary of some of the major viewpoints.

Even this brief survey illustrates that one cannot speak of "the" Protestant position on any of these questions. While the Protestant community may be united in its use of the expression "by faith alone," that phrase is interpreted and applied in different ways by different groups.

As a result, one cannot batch all Protestants together and act as if they held a single, monolithic opinion. They don't, and when Catholics discuss the subject of salvation with their Protestant brethren, they must first inquire and listen in order to understand the particular views of their partners in dialogue or debate.

2

Salvation Past, Present, and Future

This is a question Protestants often pose when they are evangelizing. It's one that takes many people by surprise, including many Catholics. One reason for this is that Catholics tend to focus on salvation as a future event, something that has yet to happen. As a result, the question "Have you been saved?" can be confusing. It can even sound presumptuous. But the question sounds natural to Protestant ears, because Evangelicals tend to conceive of salvation as a past event, something that happened to the believer at the very beginning of his life as a Christian.

Both of these conceptions of salvation are found in Scripture. For example, Paul speaks of salvation as a past event a number of times:

[E]ven when we were dead through our trespasses, [God] made us alive together with Christ (by grace you *have been saved*) (Eph. 2:5).

For by grace you *have been saved* through faith; and this is not your own doing, it is the gift of God (Eph. 2:8).

Since these passages speak of salvation as a past event, as something that *has been done* to us, it is valid to conceive of salvation in this way. But this past aspect is only one dimension of salvation. There is an ongoing aspect to salvation as well, as is indicated in:

Without having seen [Jesus] you love him; though you do not now see him you believe in him and rejoice with unutterable and exalted joy. As the outcome of your faith you *obtain the salvation of your souls* (1 Pet. 1:8–9).

The Greek participle here translated as "obtain" is in the present tense, which in Greek suggests ongoing action.

The same idea of salvation as something that is taking place in the present is found in the writings of St. Paul. In Philippians, we read:

Therefore, my beloved, as you have always obeyed, so now, not only as in my presence but much more in my absence, *work out your own salvation* with fear and trembling (Phil. 2:12).

Salvation in the Bible is, therefore, also an ongoing process. And it has a future aspect as well. There is a sense in which we have not yet received salvation:

Besides this you know what hour it is, how it is full time now for you to wake from sleep. For *salvation is nearer to us now* than when we first believed (Rom. 13:11).

If any man's work is burned up, he will suffer loss, though he himself *will be saved*, but only as through fire (1 Cor. 3:15).

[Y]ou are to deliver this man to Satan for the destruction of the flesh, that his spirit may *be saved in the day of the Lord Jesus* (1 Cor. 5:5).

These verses all speak of salvation as something that will happen in the future.

We could summarize these past, present, and future dimensions of salvation something like this: "Salvation is a process that begins when a person first becomes a Christian, continues through the rest of his life, and is completed in the future." This summary allows us to do justice to all of the biblical data by embracing all three aspects of salvation.

OTHER ASPECTS OF SALVATION

In addition to salvation as a whole, Scripture also speaks of individual aspects of salvation, such as redemption, forgiveness, sanctification, and justification. These share the same past, present, and future dimensions that salvation as a whole does.

REDEMPTION

Redemption is sometimes spoken of as a present possession of believers, which suggests that they were redeemed sometime in the past.

> In him we *have redemption* through his blood, the forgiveness of our trespasses, according to the riches of his grace (Eph. 1:7).

> He has delivered us from the power of darkness and transferred us into the kingdom of his beloved Son, in whom we *have redemption*, the forgiveness of sins (Col. 1:13–14).

These verses indicate that redemption was given to the Christian at the beginning of his life with God, when he first entered Christ (*in* him and *in* whom we have redemption). But there is yet a future redemption awaiting us, for we also read in Scripture:

> And not only the creation, but we ourselves, who have the first fruits of the Spirit groan inwardly as we *wait for . . . the redemption* of our bodies (Rom. 8:23).

> [The Holy Spirit] is the first installment of our inheritance *toward redemption* as God's possession, to the praise of his glory (Eph. 1:14, NAB).

> And do not grieve the Holy Spirit of God, in whom you were sealed *for the day of redemption* (Eph. 4:30).

Therefore redemption, like salvation in general, is something that occurs at different points in the Christian's life. There are no references in Scripture to redemption as a continuing process, but given the past and future dimensions of redemption, one may allow a sense in which we can be said to be in the process of "being redeemed" throughout the Christian life.

FORGIVENESS

In numerous places, Scripture speaks of our forgiveness as something that has already occurred:

> In [Jesus Christ] we *have . . . the forgiveness of our trespasses*, according to the riches of his grace (Eph. 1:7).

> And be kind to one another, tenderhearted, forgiving one another, just as God in Christ also *forgave* you (Eph. 4:32).

> . . . in whom we *have . . . the forgiveness of sins* (Col. 1:14).

> . . . forbearing one another and, if one has a complaint against another, forgiving each other; as the Lord *has forgiven* you, so you also must forgive (Col. 3:13).

These passages show that forgiveness is something that has happened to us in the past, but the following passages are among those that speak of forgiveness as something that we must continue to appropriate. For example:

> And *forgive us our debts*, as we also have forgiven our debtors (Matt. 6:12).

> And the prayer of faith will save the sick man, and the Lord will raise him up; and if he has committed sins, he *will be forgiven* (James 5:15).

> If we confess our sins, he is faithful and just, and *will forgive* our sins and cleanse us from all unrighteousness (1 John 1:9).

Therefore, forgiveness, like the other aspects of salvation, is both a past event and an ongoing process. And we know this process will not reach its fulfillment until we find mercy from the Lord on the last day, when our sins will be firmly, finally, and forever declared forgiven. Paul mentions this when he expresses his wish concerning Onesiphorus, that "the Lord grant him *to find mercy from the Lord on that Day*" (2 Tim. 1:18).

As a result, there is a sense in which forgiveness (God's mercy in this passage) is something that has yet to be realized.

SANCTIFICATION

Evangelicals often place great emphasis on sanctification as a process Christians undergo. However, many in the Wesleyan tradition (Methodism, Holiness churches, the Church of the Nazarene, and some Pentecostal churches) emphasize sanctification as an event that occurs at a definite point in the life of the believer.

Both groups are correct. Sanctification is both a process and an event in our lives.[2] First, let us look at verses indicating sanctification as a past event in the Christian's life:

But you were washed, you *were sanctified*, you were justified in the name of the Lord Jesus Christ and in the Spirit of our God (1 Cor. 6:11).

[We] *have been sanctified* through the offering of the body of Jesus Christ once for all (Heb. 10:10).

How much worse punishment do you think will be deserved by the man who has spurned the Son of God, and profaned the blood of the covenant by which he *was sanctified*, and outraged the Spirit of grace? (Heb. 10:29).

These verses indicate the occurrence of sanctification as a past event in the life of the believer. But it is also an ongoing process, as the following verses indicate:

[B]rethren, we beseech and exhort in the Lord Jesus, that as you learned from us how you ought to live and to please God, just as you are doing, you do so more and more. . . . For this *is . . . your sanctification*: that you abstain from immorality (1 Thess. 4:1, 3).

Now may the God of peace himself *sanctify you completely*; and may your whole spirit, soul, and body be preserved blameless at the coming of our Lord Jesus Christ (1 Thess. 5:23).

For both he who sanctifies and those who *are being sanctified* are all of one, for which reason he is not ashamed to call them brethren (Heb. 2:11, NKJV).

For by one offering he has perfected forever those who *are being sanctified* (Heb. 10:14, NKJV).[3]

Sanctification is therefore both an ongoing process as well as a past event in the life of the believer. But what about sanctification as a future event in the life of the believer? It is harder to come up with verses illustrating this kind of sanctification, but that such sanctification exists may be easily deduced.

We know from various places in Scripture that we continue to stumble and sin all the way through this life, but we also know that we will not sin after the last day or after our death, whichever comes first. Therefore, we will be made holy in the sense that we no longer sin at all, and since sanctification means being made holy, when this event occurs we will be sanctified. There is thus a future event of sanctification in the life of the believer as well as a past and a present sanctification.

JUSTIFICATION

In future sections, we will examine the nature of justification and how it relates to redemption, forgiveness, and sanctification; but here we should note that it, like the other aspects of salvation, has past, present, and future dimensions.

Justification in the Bible

The following are some verses that show justification as a past event:

Therefore, *having been justified* by faith, let us have peace with God. . . .[4] Through our Lord Jesus Christ, through whom also we have access by faith into this grace in which we stand (Rom. 5:1–2).

Since, therefore, we *are now justified* by his blood, much more shall we be saved by him from the wrath of God (Rom. 5:9).

But you were washed, you were sanctified, you *were justified* in the name of the Lord Jesus Christ and in the Spirit of our God (1 Cor. 6:11).

Justification is therefore clearly a past event in the life of the believer. Unfortunately, many Protestants have concluded that justification is simply a once-for-all event, rather than also an ongoing process.

However attractive the single, once-for-all view of justification may be for some, serious biblical considerations weigh against it. This may be seen by looking at how the New Testament handles the story of Abraham.

One of the classic Old Testament texts on justification is Genesis 15:6. This verse, which figures prominently in Paul's discussion of justification in Romans and Galatians, states that when God gave the promise to Abraham that his descendants would be as numerous as the stars of the sky (Gen. 15:5, cf. Rom. 4:18–22), Abraham "believed God and it was reckoned to him as righteousness" (Rom. 4:3).[5] This passage clearly teaches us that Abraham was justified at the time he believed the promise concerning the number of his descendants.

If justification is a once-for-all event rather than a process, that means that Abraham could not receive justification either *before* or *after* Genesis 15:6. However, Scripture indicates that he did both.

First, the book of Hebrews tells us that "by faith Abraham obeyed when he was called to go out to a place which he was to receive as an inheritance; and he went out, not knowing where he was to go" (Heb. 11:8). Protestants and Catholics agree that the subject of Hebrews 11 is saving faith.

Indeed, Hebrews 11:1–2 tells us, "[F]aith is the assurance of things hoped for, the conviction of things not seen. For by it the men of old received divine approval." One does not get divine approval for one's faith unless it is saving faith. Thus the faith we are told in Hebrews 11:8 that Abraham had must be saving faith.

But *when* did he have this faith? The passage tells us: Abraham had it "*when he was called to go out to the place he would afterward receive as an inheritance.*" The problem for the once-for-all view of justification is that the call of Abraham to leave Haran is recorded in Genesis 12:1–4, three chapters before he is justified in 15:6. We therefore know that Abraham was justified well before (in fact, years before) he was justified in Genesis 15:6.

But if Abraham had saving faith back in Genesis 12, he was justified back in Genesis 12. Yet Paul clearly tells us that he was also justified in Genesis 15. So justification must be more than a once-for-all event. And just as Abraham received justification before Genesis 15:6, he also received it afterward, as we read in the book of James:

> Was not Abraham our father justified by works, when he offered his son Isaac upon the altar? You see that faith was active along with his works, and faith was completed by works, and the scripture was fulfilled which says, "Abraham believed God, and it was reckoned to him as righteousness"; and he was called the friend of God (James 2:21–23).

Abraham offered Isaac upon the altar in Genesis 22. In this instance, the faith Abraham had displayed in the initial promise of descendants was fulfilled in his actions (see also Heb. 11:17–19), thus bringing to fruition the statement of Genesis 15:6 that he believed God and it was reckoned to him as righteousness.

We see, therefore, that Abraham was justified on at least three different occasions:

- in Genesis 12, when he first left Haran and went to the promised land;
- in Genesis 15, when he believed the promise concerning his descendants;
- and in Genesis 22, when he offered his promised son on the altar.

As a result, justification must be seen not as a once-for-all event but as a process that continues throughout the believer's life. In fact, the process extends even *beyond* the believer's life. This is shown by passages in Scripture where Paul indicates that there is a sense in which our justification is still future:

> For it is not the hearers of the law who are righteous before God, but the doers of the law who *will be justified* (Rom. 2:13).

> For no human being *will be justified* in his sight by works of the law, since through the law comes knowledge of sin (Rom. 3:20).

> For through the Spirit, by faith, we *wait for the hope of righteousness* [alternate translation, "we wait for the hope of justification"[6]] (Gal. 5:5).

Commenting on the second of these passages, the famous Protestant exegete James D.G. Dunn points out that Paul's statement alludes to Psalm 142:2 and then remarks:

> The metaphor in the psalm is of a servant being called to account before his master, but in the context here [in Romans] the imagery of final judgment is to the fore. . . . Against the view that Paul sees "justification" simply as an act which marks the beginning of a believer's life, as a believer, here is a further example [in addition to 2:13] of the verb used for a final verdict, not excluding the idea of the final verdict at the end of life.[7]

We could also deduce a future justification on theological grounds apart from these verses. In the Protestant tradition, it is common to emphasize the declarative aspect of justification, or God's *declaring* one righteous. Protestant theologians commonly place special emphasis on the legal/courtroom contexts in which this declaration may occur.

However, the ultimate courtroom declaration does not occur until the believer stands before God, at death in the particular judgment and at the end of the world in the final judgment. So we may infer that the ultimate pronouncement of the believer as righteous does not take place in this life.

Though Catholics do not place as much emphasis on the declarative aspect of justification, they can agree with this. We certainly are declared righteous (as well as made righteous) by God in this life, but the final, consummating declarations of our righteousness will not occur until the particular judgment and the final judgment. As a result, there remains a future justification for all believers.

Justification in Protestant Teaching

While many Protestants conceive of justification exclusively as a once-for-all event, a number of recent Protestant scholars, including Dunn, E.P. Sanders, and Dale Moody, have begun to recognize that it is also a process. In doing so, they are retrieving a concept that was present in the thought of some of the early Reformers.

For example, the Swiss Reformer Martin Bucer (1491–1551) regarded man as receiving a twofold justification. First, he receives the "justification of the impious" (Latin, *iustificatio impii*), in which he is declared righteous before God, and then he receives the "justification of the pious" (Latin, *iustificatio pii*), in which he is actually made to behave righteously.

Though it is not commonly known, Martin Luther conceived of justification the same way. Luther scholar Paul Althaus explains:

Luther uses the terms "to justify" (*justificare*) and "justification" (*justificatio*) in more than one sense. From the beginning [of Luther's writings], justification most often means the judgment of God with which he declares man to be righteous (*justum reputare* or *computare*).

In other places, however, the word stands for the entire event through which a man is essentially made righteous (a usage which Luther also finds in Paul, Romans 5), that is, for both the imputation of righteousness to man as well as man's actually becoming righteous.

Justification in this sense remains incomplete on Earth and is first completed on the last day. Complete righteousness in this sense is an eschatological reality. This twofold use of the word cannot be correlated with Luther's early and later theology; he uses "justification" in both senses at the same time, sometimes shortly after each other in the same text.[8]

In other words, Luther did not shift his view of justification from one to the other over the course of his career. He employed both understandings of justification at once and thus recognized it as having these two different aspects.

Luther wrote, "[W]e perceive that a man who is justified is not yet a righteous man, but is in the very movement or journey toward righteousness,"[9] and "[O]ur justification is not yet complete. . . . It is still under construction. It shall, however, be completed in the resurrection of the dead."[10]

We therefore see a willingness, both on the part of some early Reformers and some contemporary Protestant scholars, to recognize that justification is a process as well as an event.

3

Temporal and
Eternal Salvation

Two Kinds of Atonement

In the introduction to this book, we mentioned that Protestants and Catholics often "talk past each other" because they use terms in different senses. This often happens with the terms *salvation*, *atonement*, and *redemption*.

Protestants tend to use these terms in narrow, specific senses. In particular, Protestants tend to refer these terms specifically to the saving action of Jesus Christ: *He* is the one who saves us, atones for us, and redeems us. Nobody else does.

This is not always the case in Catholic usage, and when Protestants read Catholic documents that use them in broader senses, it can appear to them that Catholics are denying the sufficiency of Christ's cross. For example, many would object to the statement that you can atone for your iniquity by faithfulness and love. This could sound like a direct denial of the sufficiency of Christ's work, and it is easy to imagine a person familiar with Protestant usage responding by asserting that only Christ can make atonement for us.

It's true that only Christ can make atonement for us in one sense (the most important sense). Only he can deliver us from the eternal consequences of our sins. But this is not the only sense in which one can atone for sins.

We can prove this because the statement that love and faithfulness atone for iniquity is found in the Bible:

By love and faithfulness iniquity is atoned for, and by the fear of the LORD a man avoids evil (Prov. 16:6).

Since it is true that only Christ can atone for our sins in the most important sense, we must conclude that Proverbs 16 is speaking of atonement in a *different* sense.

What might that be? For many people today, particularly in the Protestant community, there is only one kind of atonement—the kind that provides eternal salvation. This is often the only kind of atonement that we think about. It can even be tempting to think that it's the only kind of atonement that is worth having.

But there is another kind of atonement in the Bible. In contrast to the *eternal* atonement that Christ provided for us, we may refer to it as *temporal* atonement.

To understand the idea of temporal atonement, we need to set it in its larger biblical context, which includes two parallel concepts: temporal and eternal *salvation*.

Temporal and Eternal Salvation

Christians often begin reading the Bible with the New Testament and only afterward go back to read the Old. This is natural, because the New Testament is more directly relevant to our lives as Christians than is the Old. But it can cause confusion because the New Testament uses some terms differently than the Old Testament does.

This is particularly true when we're talking about *salvation*.

Salvation in the Old Testament

The New Testament focuses primarily on the idea of eternal salvation—salvation from the eternal consequences of sin (i.e., hell). In the New Testament, if you're being saved from something, it is almost always the eternal consequences of sin.

But the Old Testament uses of the term *salvation* is very different. Almost never—*if ever*—does the Old Testament speak of being saved from eternal damnation. Instead, when it speaks of salvation, it overwhelmingly refers to being saved from temporal dangers such as war, famine, disease, oppression, and physical (rather than eternal) death. So great is the focus on temporal salvation that, of the more than two hundred references to salvation in the Old Testament, it is hard to find any that unambiguously refer to eternal salvation.

A few examples will give a taste of how the Old Testament is concerned with salvation from temporal dangers:

I wait for thy salvation, O LORD. Raiders shall raid Gad, but he shall raid at their heels (Gen. 49:18–19).

And Moses said to the people, "Fear not, stand firm, and see the salvation of the LORD, which he will work for you today; for the Egyptians whom you see today, you shall never see again. The LORD will fight for you, and you have only to be still" (Exod. 14:13–14).

Because the LORD your God walks in the midst of your camp, to save you and to give up your enemies before you, therefore your camp must be holy, that he may not see anything indecent among you, and turn away from you (Deut. 23:14).

Now therefore stand still, that I [Samuel] may plead with you before the LORD concerning all the saving deeds of the Lord which he performed for you and for your fathers (1 Sam. 12:7).

The Old Testament sometimes presents such calamities as coming upon the Israelites because of their sins (particularly the sin of idolatry). However, calamities can also come upon people even when they have not sinned, which is the point of the book of Job. In either event, God is present to save his people from these disasters when they turn to him.

This is a major theme in the Old Testament. It is all through the Pentateuch, the historical books, the wisdom literature, and the prophets. It is the dominant understanding of salvation in the Old Testament.

This is, in part, due to the progressive nature of God's revelation. He disclosed his message over the course of centuries, gradually adding to and developing Israel's understanding of various truths. One of the last truths to be fleshed out was the afterlife.

The ancient Israelites had a belief in the afterlife (indeed, God had to warn them against using mediums to summon up the dead (cf. Lev. 19:31, 20:6, 27; Deut. 18:9–13; 1 Sam. 28), but their understanding of it seems to have been rather undeveloped. Over the course of time, it becomes more refined. And so, particularly in the latter books of the Old Testament we begin to see references to resurrection, indicating an awareness that we will not remain disembodied spirits forever (cf. Dan. 12:2–3, 2 Macc. 12:43–45).

With the limited understanding of the afterlife that Israel had early on, it was natural for its focus to be primarily on this life. It thus tended to conceive of God's salvation as deliverance from the dangers of this life, not of the next.

Temporal Salvation in the New Testament

By the time of the New Testament, the afterlife had become a much more important topic, and attention shifted strongly to the question of how to avoid the eternal consequences of our sins, with concern for avoiding the perils of this life receiving less attention.

Though eternal salvation is the major concern in the New Testament, temporal salvation is still discussed. In fact, it is far more common than many would suppose. Let us look at just a few examples:

> And when he [Jesus] got into the boat, his disciples followed him. And behold, there arose a great storm on the sea, so that the boat was being swamped by the waves; but he was asleep. And they went and woke him, saying, "Save us, Lord; we are perishing!" (Matt. 8:23–25).

> And Peter answered him, "Lord, if it is you, bid me come to you on the water." He said, "Come." So Peter got out of the

boat and walked on the water and came to Jesus; but when he saw the wind, he was afraid, and beginning to sink he cried out, "Lord, save me." Jesus immediately reached out his hand and caught him, saying to him, "O man of little faith, why did you doubt?" (Matt. 14:28–31).

And if those days had not been shortened, no human being would be saved; but for the sake of the elect those days will be shortened (Matt. 24:22).

He saved others; he cannot save himself. He is the King of Israel; let him come down now from the cross, and we will believe in him (Matt. 27:42).

Blessed be the Lord God of Israel, for he has visited and redeemed his people, and has raised up a horn of salvation for us in the house of his servant David, as he spoke by the mouth of his holy prophets from of old, that we should be saved from our enemies, and from the hand of all who hate us (Luke 1:68–71).

Here the salvation that is in view is from drowning, death, and one's enemies—all temporal threats.

Mary's Salvation

A particularly interesting passage on salvation is found in the Magnificat:

And Mary said, "My soul magnifies the Lord, and my spirit rejoices in God my Savior, for he has regarded the low estate of his handmaiden—for behold, henceforth all generations will call me blessed; for he who is mighty has done great things for me, and holy is his name.

"And his mercy is on those who fear him from generation to generation. He has shown strength with his arm, he has scattered the proud in the imagination of their hearts, he has put down the mighty from their thrones, and exalted those of low degree; he has filled the hungry with good things, and the rich he has sent empty away.

"He has helped his servant Israel, in remembrance of his mercy, as he spoke to our fathers, to Abraham and to his posterity for ever" (Luke 1:46–55).

This passage is often used by Protestant apologists to argue that Mary was a sinner because she refers to God as her Savior. The inference is that, if God was Mary's Savior, it must have been eternal salvation she is referring to in this passage, and, thus, that God saved her from the eternal consequences of her sins.

Both of these premises are false.

Let's start with the premise that, if God is Mary's Savior, he must be saving her from the eternal consequences of sins she has committed.

Catholic theology *agrees* that God was Mary's Savior, but not from the eternal consequences of sins she had committed. It holds that he saved her in an even more spectacular way than he has saved us. Whereas he allows us to fall into sin and then saves us from the consequences, he saved Mary from falling into sin in the first place.

This makes Mary, as the *Catechism of the Catholic Church* puts it, "the most excellent fruit of redemption" (CCC 508). To put it somewhat informally, Mary is the *most saved* person there is, since by God's grace she was saved from things he let the rest of us fall into.

The other premise—that Mary must have been referring to eternal salvation when she described God as her Savior—is also false. As we've seen, both the Old and the New Testaments refer to temporal salvation. Thus we must ask: How is Mary conceiving of God's salvation in this passage, as temporal or eternal?

When we do this, it seems that the idea of God as Savior from temporal circumstances is at the forefront of her mind. "My spirit rejoices in God my Savior," she declares, "*for* he has regarded the low estate of his handmaiden—for behold, henceforth all generations will call me blessed; for he who is mighty has done great things for me."

As the explanatory connective *for*[11] indicates, the reason Mary rejoices in God as her Savior is that "he has regarded the low estate of his handmaiden" and done marvelous things for her. God has thus saved her from her low estate and given her an exalted estate so that she will be remembered and honored forever: "for behold, henceforth all generations will call me blessed."

That temporal salvation is what Mary has in mind is reinforced as she proceeds to name several kinds of temporal salvation ("He has shown strength with his arm, he has scattered the proud in the imagination of their hearts, he has put down the mighty from their thrones, and exalted those of low degree; he has filled the hungry with good things, and the rich he has sent empty away. He has helped his servant Israel, in remembrance of his mercy, as he spoke to our fathers, to Abraham and to his posterity for ever"). It is also suggested in the parallel canticle in which Zechariah proclaims the praise of God as temporal Savior (Luke 1:68–75; see above).

Temporal and Eternal Saviors

Salvation is provided by a savior, and the fact that salvation can be understood both temporally and eternally leads to the realization that saviors also can be temporal or eternal.

Of course, God is the only one capable of providing eternal salvation. There is no question on this point. As we've seen, the Bible also speaks of God as a Savior from temporal calamities as well.

But what about a man? Is it ever possible to speak of a mere human being as a savior?

Indeed, it is. Not as an eternal savior, of course, but as a temporal one.

We regularly speak of people as providing temporal salvation:

• A sports figure may save his team from defeat.

- A policeman may save a person from being mugged.
- A soldier may save his platoon from being killed.
- A fireman may save someone from a burning building.
- A statesman may save his country from ruin.

And there are many other examples. Anytime anyone saves another from some kind of harm, that individual provides a form of temporal salvation, and that makes him a *temporal* savior.

Because the word *savior* is so closely associated with God, we have a bit of a scruple in contemporary English about describing people as saviors in the temporal sense. But Scripture does not, as the following examples show:

> Then Jehoahaz besought the LORD, and the LORD hearkened to him; for he saw the oppression of Israel, how the king of Syria oppressed them. Therefore the LORD *gave Israel a savior*, so that they escaped from the hand of the Syrians; and the people of Israel dwelt in their homes as formerly (2 Kings 13:4–5).

> Therefore [O, Lord] thou didst give them into the hand of their enemies, who made them suffer; and in the time of their suffering they cried to thee and thou didst hear them from heaven; and according to thy great mercies *thou didst give them saviors who saved them* from the hand of their enemies (Neh. 9:26–27).

> *Saviors shall go up to Mount Zion* to rule Mount Esau; and the kingdom shall be the LORD's (Obad. 21).

In each of these cases, God sends temporal saviors to deliver his people. We therefore have to say that, while God is the only eternal Savior, he uses people as temporal saviors.

FORGIVENESS AND FELLOWSHIP

With this background, we are in a better position to understand the biblical statement that we began this chapter with:

By love and faithfulness iniquity is atoned for, and by the fear of the LORD a man avoids evil (Prov. 16:6).

Given the overwhelming focus in the Old Testament on temporal salvation, it is highly unlikely that this passage concerns the afterlife. The proverb is not saying that we make atonement and are delivered from the eternal consequences of our sins by love and faithfulness. Instead, it has something this-worldly in mind.

While the concept of salvation is focused on a person being delivered or rescued from some form of harm, the concept of atonement is focused on the reconciling of two parties. This is reflected in its word origins in English. It comes from the phrase "at one." To atone is to make two parties "at one" with each other, or to reconcile them. Although the Hebrew word for *atone* (*kapar*) does not share this origin, it does reflect the idea of reconciling two parties.

When Proverbs says that love and faithfulness atone for iniquity, the parties being reconciled are God and an individual man who has committed sins. This is reflected in the second half of the verse, which makes these two parties explicit.

The proverb thus envisions man's sin as creating a barrier in his relationship with God in this life. This barrier could, in the ancient Hebrew understanding, lead to calamities in this life. By reconciling with God, it would be possible to stop or avert these calamities, and so atoning for one's sins could lead to temporal salvation.

Since eternal salvation is rarely in focus in the Old Testament, this is the most likely understanding of the statement in Proverbs 16:6—i.e., that one should do acts of love and faithfulness to repair one's relationship with God so that it may go well for you in this life. In contrast to the eternal atonement that Christ provides, we might refer to this as "temporal atonement."

Although this term is not standard, the underlying concepts have found traction in both Protestant and Catholic circles.

Protestants, especially those who think that it is impossible to lose salvation, often stress the difference between forgiveness and fellowship. They point out, rightly, that even when the eternal consequences of one's sins have been forgiven, one's relationship with God can still be impaired. Thus, even though one is in a state of eternal forgiveness, one may still need to repent in order to be restored to fellowship, or at least full fellowship, with God.

Catholics use different language but share the underlying insight, although, on the Catholic view, only mortal sins cause one to lose eternal salvation. Venial sins merely impair one's relationship with God. The *Catechism of the Catholic Church* states:

> Mortal sin destroys charity in the heart of man by a grave violation of God's law; it turns man away from God, who is his ultimate end and his beatitude, by preferring an inferior good to him. Venial sin allows charity to subsist, even though it offends and wounds it (CCC 1855).

Thus, even when one is not in danger of eternal loss, one's relationship with God—the principle of which is charity, or supernatural love (1 Cor. 13:1–13)—can still be wounded through sin.

This impairment of one's relationship with God is, of course, a temporal rather than an eternal consequence of sin, and by repenting—by being faithful and loving under the impetus of God's grace—one's relationship with God will grow in strength, and one's level of fellowship with God will grow. It is in this sense that love and faithfulness atone for iniquity. The repentant sinner's love and faithfulness show his desire to make up for his former lack of love and faithfulness, and the relationship is restored.

MIDDLE SALVATION

So far, we have discussed temporal and eternal salvation, but Scripture also speaks about salvation in a way that, for the sake of convenience, we will call "middle salvation."

This mode of language refers to one person bringing eternal salvation to someone else. By preaching the gospel, rebuking sinners, administering the sacraments, and so on, one human may, under the providence of God, "save" another human being (bring him eternal salvation).

This language rubs some the wrong way, but it is the language of the New Testament:

> Now I (Paul) am speaking to you Gentiles. Inasmuch then as I am an apostle to the Gentiles, I magnify my ministry in order *to . . . save* some of [my fellow Jews] (Rom. 11:13–14).

> Wife, how do you know whether you *will save* your husband? Husband, how do you know whether you *will save* your wife? (1 Cor. 7:16).

> To the weak I [Paul] became weak, that I might win the weak. I have become all things to all men, that I might by all means *save* some (1 Cor. 9:22).

> Take heed to yourself and to your teaching; hold to that, for by so doing you *will save* both yourself and your hearers (1 Tim. 4:16).

> My brethren, if any one among you wanders from the truth and some one brings him back, let him know that whoever brings back a sinner from the error of his way *will save* his soul from death and will cover a multitude of sins (James 5:19–20).

> [C]onvince some, who doubt; *save* some, by snatching them out of the fire; on some have mercy with fear, hating even the garment spotted by the flesh (Jude 22–23).

As these verses show, the Bible speaks of humans saving other humans, not just with respect to temporal salvation (from physical disasters, illnesses, wars, etc.), but also with respect to eternal salvation. Of course, this does not mean that humans *bestow* eternal salvation on other humans the way Christ does, by earning it for them, but it does mean that humans *serve as agents* of

Christ in bringing his graces to others.

It also should be noted that Scripture speaks of individuals saving themselves (e.g., 1 Tim. 4:16, above). Since we cannot earn eternal salvation ourselves, and since mere temporal salvation does not seem in view in these passages, this language is best understood in terms of the "middle salvation" category. The middle salvation mode of speech thus includes not only one individual helping to bring eternal salvation to another but also one's own pursuit of eternal salvation.

General Salvation

We need to note one final mode of speaking about salvation. Let's call this the "general salvation" mode of speech. In this mode, the term *salvation* is used without differentiation between temporal, middle, and eternal deliverance.

It would be a mistake to assume, merely because Scripture speaks of three kinds of saving, that every use of the word *salvation* must refer to a specific kind. This would be as great a mistake as assuming that because there are two kinds of humans, male and female, every use of the word *human* must have in mind either exclusively males or exclusively females. Just as the term *human* can refer to both male and female without differentiation, *salvation* can refer to temporal, middle, and eternal salvation without specifying any particular one of them.

This general way of speaking about salvation is found in some descriptions of God as Savior. In many passages, like the ones discussed, one particular aspect of his role as Savior may be in the forefront. He may be spoken of as a Savior from temporal distress or as a Savior from eternal agony, or he may be spoken of as a Savior in a general sense without specifying any single type of salvation.

4

Doing Penance

In the previous chapter, we looked at the statement from Proverbs 16:6 that "by loyalty and faithfulness iniquity is atoned for, and by the fear of the LORD a man avoids evil." We noted that this verse appears to envision temporal rather than eternal atonement.

Now we are ready to look at the concept of temporal atonement in more depth. This means doing penance for one's sins. Acts of penance can be formal, such as fasting on a given day, or informal, such as going out of one's way to be nice to someone.

Many in the Protestant community, especially those who claim that it is impossible to lose salvation, stress the difference between forgiveness and fellowship. They point out that even when the eternal consequences of one's sins have been forgiven, one's relationship with God can still be impaired. Thus, even though one is in a state of forgiveness—or what Catholics would call a state of grace—one may still need to repent in order to be restored to full fellowship with God. In this sense, love and faithfulness atone for iniquity.

THE SUFFICIENCY OF CHRIST'S WORK ON THE CROSS

Although penance has been practiced by Jews and Christians since biblical times, the practice has been much less common in Protestant communities. Some have even rejected penance outright, on the grounds that Christ has made atonement for our sins, making it superfluous at best and a denial of the sufficiency of Christ's work at worst.

Christians who do penance are not trying to pay off the eternal debt of their sins. Christ did that, once for all, almost two thousand years ago. No more payment of the eternal debt of our sins is needed. No more payment of the eternal debt of our sins is even possible. And, though it would surprise many Protestants to learn it, this precise point has been stressed vigorously by Catholic theologians throughout history.

For example, the great medieval saint and doctor of the Church, Thomas Aquinas, writes in the *Summa Theologiae* (hereafter ST) that:

> by suffering out of love and obedience, Christ gave more to God than was required to compensate for the offense of the whole human race. First of all, because of the exceeding charity (on account of) which he suffered; secondly, on account of the dignity of his life which he laid down in atonement, for it was the life of one who was God and man; thirdly, on account of the extent of the Passion, and the greatness of the grief endured, as stated above. And therefore Christ's Passion was not only a sufficient but a superabundant atonement for the sins of the human race; according to 1 John 2:2: "He is the propitiation for our sins: and not for ours only, but also for those of the whole world" (ST III:48:2).

Aquinas thus sees Christ's work as not *merely* sufficient but as *superabundant* (more than enough) to atone for the sins of the world.

This understanding has been the understanding of Catholics both before and since Aquinas wrote. As the *Catechism of the Catholic Church* states:

> The Christian tradition sees in this passage (Gen. 3:15) an announcement of the "New Adam" who, because he "became obedient unto death, even death on a cross," makes *amends superabundantly for the disobedience of Adam* (CCC 411).

WHY DO PENANCE?

This still leaves us with the question: If Christ's sufferings were more than sufficient, why should we do penance? This question has three answers.

First, we've already mentioned the distinction that some draw between forgiveness and fellowship. Whether one uses those terms or not, it remains true that even those who are in a state of forgiveness (grace) may have impaired fellowship (communion) with God. Acts that express sorrow over one's sins (penances) are a key way to correct this. This is why, as we will see below, people in both testaments of the Bible did penance in order to restore fellowship with God by mourning their sins.

Second, when God remits the eternal penalty for a sin, he may (and often does) choose to leave a temporal penalty. When he forgave David for his sin concerning Uriah, he still left David the temporal punishments of having his infant son die and having the sword pass through his house (2 Sam. 12:13ff.). Similarly, God forgave Moses for striking the rock a second time (Moses was obviously one of the saved, as his appearance on the Mount of Transfiguration illustrates), but he still suffered the temporal penalty of not being allowed to go into the Promised Land (Num. 20:12).

Why does God leave some temporal penalties in place when he removes the eternal penalties for our sins? Part of this is a mystery, since Christ's sufferings are sufficient to cover even the temporal penalties of our sins. However, one reason is to teach us our lesson. We often learn our lesson far better if we have not just "head knowledge" that what we did was wrong but also experiential knowledge of its wrongness through negative consequences. Thus parents may allow their children to experience the consequences of their bad behavior and tell them, "Look, I love you and I've forgiven you, but you're still grounded." In other words, even when something has been forgiven, we may still experience consequences for our own good, to teach us a lesson.

We find this same thought in the Bible, when we read:

And have you forgotten the exhortation which addresses you as sons?—"My son, do not regard lightly the discipline of the Lord, nor lose courage when you are punished by him. For the Lord disciplines him whom he loves, and chastises every son whom he receives."

It is for discipline that you have to endure. God is treating you as sons; for what son is there whom his father does not discipline? If you are left without discipline, in which all have participated, then you are illegitimate children and not sons.

Besides this, we have had earthly fathers to discipline us and we respected them. Shall we not much more be subject to the Father of spirits and live? For they disciplined us for a short time at their pleasure, but he disciplines us for our good, that we may share his holiness.

For the moment all discipline seems painful rather than pleasant; later it yields the peaceful fruit of righteousness to those who have been trained by it. Therefore lift your drooping hands and strengthen your weak knees, and make straight paths for your feet, so that what is lame may not be put out of joint but rather be healed (Heb. 12:5–13).

God thus leaves us temporal consequences so that this chastisement, on the model of disciplining a child, may have a rehabilitative effect. Penance is one way in which we willingly embrace this discipline in order to learn from it, just as a godly child may embrace his parent's discipline.

Third, we have a need to mourn over tragedies. This inner need must not be short-circuited; and because our sins are tragedies, we have a natural need to mourn over them. We also have an inner need to make a gesture of reparation for our sins when real reparation is impossible.

This process is short-circuited when people are told, "Jesus has forgiven all your sins; now stop mourning them!" This is like telling a man whose wife has just died, "Jesus has taken your wife to heaven; now stop mourning her death!" Jesus wept at the tomb of Lazarus (John 11:35)—even knowing he was about to bring him back to life. If that's the case, the need to grieve is so deep in human nature that trying to prevent it is foolish and can even be harmful.

Of course, there is such a thing as too much grief. As Ecclesiastes says, there is "a time to weep, and a time to laugh; a time to mourn, and a time to dance" (Eccles. 3:4). We must not become morbidly fixated on our sins any more than we should become morbidly fixated on the death of a loved one. At some point, one must move on. But that point is not immediately after the sins have been committed or immediately after a loved one has died. There is a natural process that needs to take place.

Thus, even though Christ's atonement was more than enough to cover both the temporal and the eternal consequences of our sins:

1. We still need to have fellowship restored with God even when we are in a state of forgiveness.
2. After the eternal consequences of them are forgiven, God still often leaves temporal consequences in place (e.g., to teach us our lesson).
3. We still have a need to mourn our sins.

These are the reasons why the discipline of penance exists—and has since biblical times.

The system of penance has been part of the religion of the one, true God since before the time of Christ. It was part of the religion of Christ and his first followers, and it has been part of Christianity ever since. Those in the Protestant community who downplay or deny penance are rejecting a practice with thoroughly biblical roots.

PENANCE IN THE BIBLE: THE OLD TESTAMENT

No one who has read the Old Testament can fail to recognize the role of penance in the spiritual life of ancient Israel. We read passages like:

Then all the people of Israel, the whole army, went up and came to Bethel and *wept*; they sat there before the LORD, and *fasted* that day until evening, and offered burnt offerings and peace offerings before the LORD (Judg. 20:26).

Then Jehoshaphat feared, and set himself to seek the LORD, and *proclaimed a fast* throughout all Judah. And Judah assembled to seek help from the LORD; from all the cities of Judah they came to seek the LORD (2 Chron. 20:3–4).

Then I (Ezra) *proclaimed a fast* there, at the river Ahava, that we might humble ourselves before our God, to seek from him a straight way for ourselves, our children, and all our goods. For I was ashamed to ask the king for a band of soldiers and horsemen to protect us against the enemy on our way; since we had told the king, "The hand of our God is for good upon all that seek him, and the power of his wrath is against all that forsake him." So we *fasted* and besought our God for this, and he listened to our entreaty (Ezra 8:21–23).

Then I (Daniel) turned my face to the Lord God, seeking him by prayer and supplications with *fasting and sackcloth and ashes* (Dan. 9:3).

Especially informative are passages in which God himself, or one of his prophets, commands fasting or another penance. Passages like these show that the practice of penance has God's endorsement:

And when Ahab heard those words, he rent his clothes, and put sackcloth upon his flesh, and *fasted and lay in sackcloth, and went about dejectedly.* And the word of the LORD came to Elijah the Tishbite, saying, "Have you seen how Ahab has humbled himself before me? Because he has humbled himself before me, I will not bring the evil in his days; but in his son's days I will bring the evil upon his house" (1 Kings 21:27–29).

In that day the Lord God of hosts called [you] to weeping and mourning, to baldness and girding with sackcloth; and behold, [instead you engaged in] joy and gladness, slaying oxen and killing sheep, eating flesh and drinking wine (Isa. 22:12–13).

Gird on sackcloth and lament, O priests, wail, O ministers of the altar. Go in, pass the night in sackcloth, O ministers of my God! Because cereal offering and drink offering are withheld from the house of your God. *Sanctify a fast, call a solemn assembly.* Gather the elders and all the inhabitants of the land to the house of the LORD your God; and cry to the LORD (Joel 1:13–14).

"Yet even now," says the LORD, "return to me with all your heart, *with fasting, with weeping, and with mourning. . . .*" Blow the trumpet in Zion; *sanctify a fast; call a solemn assembly* (Joel 2:12, 15).

PENANCE IN THE BIBLE: THE NEW TESTAMENT

The practice of fasting and other acts of penance are also found in the New Testament:

And *when you fast,* do not look dismal, like the hypocrites, for they disfigure their faces that their fasting may be seen by men. Truly, I say to you, they have their reward. But when you fast, anoint your head and wash your face, that your fasting may not be seen by men but by your Father who is in secret; and your Father who sees in secret will reward you (Matt. 6:16–18).

Note that this passage contains an expectation that Jesus' followers *will* fast. He does not say, "if you fast," but "*when* you fast." Fasting is thus part of the Christian life.

The same expectation is found in the Gospel of Mark:

Now John's disciples and the Pharisees were fasting; and people came and said to [Jesus], "Why do John's disciples and the disciples of the Pharisees fast, but your disciples do not fast?" And Jesus said to them, "Can the wedding guests fast while the bridegroom is with them? As long as they have the bridegroom with them, they cannot fast. *The days will come, when the bridegroom is taken away from them, and then they will fast in that day"* (Mark 2:18–20).

You could raise a question here: Are we living in the days when Jesus (the bridegroom) has been taken away from us or not?

On the one hand, he is not ministering on Earth as he was when he made this statement. From that perspective, our age would be an appropriate one in which to fast, with the time of his earthly ministry being an exceptional, nonfasting period.

On the other hand, one could argue that the time he is really speaking of is the time between his Crucifixion and Resurrection. Now that he has risen from the dead, ascended to heaven, and is with us sacramentally in the Eucharist, he is no longer "taken away from" us, making this age inappropriate for fasting.

Which of these perspectives is right? The answer is revealed in the book of Acts, which shows that fasting was deemed appropriate, and part of the Christian life, after the Resurrection and Ascension. We read:

> While they were worshiping the Lord *and fasting,* the Holy Spirit said, "Set apart for me Barnabas and Saul for the work to which I have called them." Then after fasting and praying they laid their hands on them and sent them off (Acts 13:2–3).

Fasting was also a regular part of Christian practice and was done on particularly solemn occasions, such as the appointing of church leaders:

> And when they [Paul and Barnabas] had appointed elders for them in every church, with prayer *and fasting,* they committed them to the Lord in whom they believed (Acts 14:23).

Fasting is not the only form of penance endorsed in the New Testament. The general principle can be expressed in different forms:

Draw near to God and he will draw near to you. Cleanse your hands, you sinners, and purify your hearts, you men of double mind. *Be wretched and mourn and weep. Let your laughter be turned to mourning and your joy to dejection. Humble yourselves before the Lord* and he will exalt you (James 4:8–10).

PENANCE AND THE CHURCH FATHERS

The practice of penance was continued from New Testament times into the age of the Church Fathers.

We can see the bridging of the two ages in documents that were written by Christians in the first century. For example, as we've seen about, A.D. 50 a manual of Christian teaching and discipline known as the *Didache* was written. It tells us:

Before the baptism, let the one baptizing and the one to be baptized fast, as also any others who are able. Command the one who is to be baptized to fast beforehand for one or two days. [After becoming a Christian] do not let your fasts be with the hypocrites. They fast on Monday and Thursday, but you shall fast on Wednesday and Friday (*Didache* 7:1, 8:1).

In early A.D. 70, Pope St. Clement I told the Corinthian rebels:

You, therefore, who laid the foundation of the rebellion [in your church], submit to the presbyters and be chastened to repentance, bending your knees in a spirit of humility (*Letter to the Corinthians* 57).

Around A.D. 110, St. Ignatius of Antioch wrote:

For as many as are of God and of Jesus Christ are also with the bishop. And as many as shall, in the exercise of penance, return into the unity of the Church, these, too, shall belong to God, that they may live according to Jesus Christ (*Letter to the Philadelphians* 3).

About A.D. 203, we find the early Christian writer Tertullian trying to correct the practice of Christians who were interpreting the discipline of fasting so strictly that they would not receive the Eucharist on days of fast. He wrote:

In regard to days of fast, many do not think they should be present at the sacrificial prayers [at the Eucharist], because their fast would be broken if they were to receive the Body of the Lord. Does the Eucharist, then, obviate a work devoted to God, or does it bind it more to God? Will not your fast be more solemn if, in addition, you have stood at God's altar? The Body of the Lord having been received and reserved, each point is secured: both the participation in the sacrifice and the discharge of duty (*Prayer* 19:1–4).

Although in our day the sacrament of reconciliation is administered with private confession and absolution first, followed by a penance, the sequence was somewhat different in the early centuries. Confession was often (though not always) public, and penances were performed *before* absolution rather than after. This is reflected in the writings of St. Cyprian of Carthage. About A.D. 253, he wrote:

Sinners may do penance for a set time, and according to the rules of discipline come to public confession, and by imposition of the hand of the bishop and clergy receive the right of Communion (*Letters* 9:2).

The same sequence—including the doing of penance linked to the sacrament of reconciliation—is also found in the writings of St. Jerome. About A.D. 388, he wrote:

If the serpent, the devil, bites someone secretly, he infects that person with the venom of sin. And if the one who has been bitten keeps silence and does not do penance, and does not want to confess his wound . . . then his brother and his master, who have the word [of absolution] that will cure him, cannot very well assist him (*Commentary on Ecclesiastes* 10:11).

Finally, somewhat before A.D. 395, Augustine instructs his catechumens with these words:

When you shall have been baptized, keep to a good life in the commandments of God so that you may preserve your baptism to the very end. I do not tell you that you will live here without sin, but they are venial sins, which this life is never without. Baptism was instituted for all sins. For light sins, without which we cannot live, prayer was instituted. . . .

But do not commit those sins on account of which you would have to be separated from the body of Christ. Perish the thought! For those whom you see [at the church] doing penance have committed crimes, either adultery or some other enormities. That is why they are doing penance. If their sins were light, daily prayer would suffice to blot them out. . . .

In the Church, therefore, there are three ways in which sins are forgiven: in baptism, in prayer, and in the greater humility of penance (*Sermon to Catechumens on the Creed* 7:15, 8:16).

The practice of penance thus has been part of the true religion since before the time of Christ, during the time of Christ, and after the time of Christ.

5

Indulgences

The subject of indulgences is one of the most misunderstood aspects of Catholic doctrine. Before discussing the biblical basis of it, we should deal with some common myths and misconceptions.

MYTHS ABOUT INDULGENCES

Myth 1: A person can buy his way out of hell with indulgences.

False. Repentance and sacramental confession—not indulgences—are the way to avoid going to hell when one has committed mortal sin. As we will see below, indulgences remit only temporal penalties of sins that have *already* been forgiven, so they cannot stop an unrepentant, unforgiven person from going to hell. Once a person is in hell, no number of indulgences will get him out. The way to avoid hell is by appealing to and accepting God's mercy while still alive. After death, one's eternal fate is set (cf. Heb. 9:27).

Myth 2: A person can buy indulgences for sins not yet committed.

Again, false. The Church has always taught that indulgences do not apply to sins not yet committed. The *Catholic Encyclopedia* notes that an indulgence "is not a permission to commit sin, nor a pardon of future sin; neither could be granted by any power" (1910 ed., s.v. "Indulgences").

Myth 3: A person can buy forgiveness with indulgences.

The definition of indulgences presupposes that forgiveness has already taken place: "An indulgence is a remission before God of the temporal punishment due to sins whose guilt has already been forgiven" (*Indulgentiarum Doctrina*, norm 1). Indulgences in no way forgive sins. They deal only with temporal consequences that may be left after sins have been forgiven.

Myth 4: Indulgences were invented to make money for the Church.

Indulgences developed from reflection on the sacrament of reconciliation. They are a way of encouraging spiritual growth and lessening the temporal consequences that may remain when sins are forgiven. The roots of the practice go back centuries before money-related problems appeared.

Myth 5: An indulgence will shorten one's time in purgatory by a fixed number of days.

The Catholic Church does not teach anything about how long or short purgatory is. Indeed, from a temporal perspective, purgatory may be accomplished instantaneously, "in the twinkling of an eye" (1 Cor. 15:51–52). In such a case, indulgences could affect its intensity but not its temporal duration.

The origin of this myth is the fact that, in the past, a certain number of "days" were attached to many indulgences. These were not days off in purgatory. Instead, they expressed the value of an indulgence by analogizing it to the number of days' penance one would have done *on Earth* under the penitential practices of the early Church.

Moderns had lost touch with the ancient system, which made the reckoning of such "days" confusing. The practice was abolished in 1967 in Pope Paul VI's constitution *Indulgentiarum Doctrina*.

Myth 6: A person formerly could buy indulgences.

One never could buy indulgences. The financial scandal surrounding indulgences involved alms-indulgences, in which the giving of alms to a charitable fund was used as the occasion to grant the indulgence. The practice was the same in principle as modern nonprofit organizations' granting premium gifts in thank-yous for donations. That is not the same as selling.

The purpose of granting indulgences was to encourage people to do good things and to grow spiritually. Only one kind of indulgence involved alms, and giving alms in itself is a good thing. The *Catholic Encyclopedia* notes in its article on indulgences: "Among the good works which might be encouraged by being made the condition of an indulgence, almsgiving would naturally hold a conspicuous place. . . . It is well to observe that in these purposes there is nothing essentially evil. To give money to God or to the poor is a praiseworthy act, and, when it is done from right motives, it will surely not go unrewarded."

The Council of Trent instituted major reforms in the practice of granting indulgences, and because of prior abuses, "in 1567 Pope Pius V canceled all grants of indulgences involving any fees or other financial transactions" (*Catholic Encyclopedia*, loc. cit.). This act proved the Church's seriousness about removing abuses from indulgences.

INDULGENCES TODAY

Many Catholics today feel uncertain about the topic of indulgences. Some even question whether indulgences are part of the Catholic Church's official teaching. The answer is that they are, though not a large part. Of the 2,865 paragraphs in the *Catechism of the Catholic Church*, exactly ten (1471–1479 and 1498) are devoted to the subject of indulgences.

This modest figure reflects the place of indulgences in the hierarchy of truths. While the theological principles underlying indulgences are solid, they are far from being the most important of the Church's teachings.

Despite this, they played a unique role in the history of the Reformation. Martin Luther's famed *Ninety-Five Theses*, which are often used to date the beginning of the Protestant movement, were theses about indulgences and related concepts. The formal title of the work is *Disputation of Doctor Martin Luther on the Power and Efficacy of Indulgences.* They were a set of propositions to be used in theological debate.

Luther and his followers quickly began challenging other, more important aspects of Catholic teaching, but given the early role indulgences had in the controversy, they have played a disproportionately large role in Catholic-Protestant polemics.

While indulgences are not among the most important Catholic teachings, two points regarding them have been infallibly defined. This was done at the Council of Trent, which defined two propositions regarding them: (1) that they are not useless, and (2) that the Church has the ability to grant them.[12]

Let us look at the biblical principles behind the practice of granting indulgences.

THE PRINCIPLES BEHIND INDULGENCES

The principles behind indulgences were employed by the Church for centuries before the controversy over them erupted in the 1500s. Indeed, the principles are found in the Bible itself and are as clear in Scripture as those supporting more familiar and more important doctrines, such as the Trinity.

A good starting point is Pope Paul VI's definition of an indulgence:

> An indulgence is a remission before God of the temporal punishment due to sins whose guilt has already been forgiven, which the faithful Christian who is duly disposed gains under certain defined conditions through the Church's help when, as a minister of redemption, she dispenses and applies with authority the treasury of the satisfactions won by Christ and the saints (*Indulgentiarum Doctrina*, norm 1).

This technical definition can be phrased more simply: An indulgence is the Church's lessening of the temporal penalties to which we may be subject even though our sins have been forgiven.

Are there principles in the Bible that support the idea of the Church's ability to do this?

There are.

Principle 1: Sin results in guilt and punishment.

When a person sins, he acquires certain liabilities: the liability of guilt and the liability of punishment.[13] Scripture speaks of guilt as clinging to our souls, making them discolored and unclean before God: "Come now, let us reason together, says the Lord: Though your sins are like scarlet, they shall be white as snow; though they are red like crimson, they shall become like wool" (Isa. 1:18).

This image of guilt appears in texts that picture forgiveness as a cleansing or washing and the state of our forgiven souls as clean and white: "Wash me thoroughly from my iniquity, and cleanse me from my sin! . . . Purge me with hyssop, and I shall be clean; wash me, and I shall be whiter than snow" (Ps. 51:2, 7).[14]

When we sin, we incur not only guilt but liability for punishment: "I will punish the world for its evil, and the wicked for their iniquity; I will put an end to the pride of the arrogant and lay low the haughtiness of the ruthless" (Isa. 13:11). Judgment pertains even to the smallest sins. In Ecclesiastes, we learn that "God will bring every deed into judgment, with every secret thing, whether good or evil" (Eccles. 12:14).[15]

Principle 2: Punishment is both temporal and eternal.

The Bible indicates that some punishments are eternal, but others last only for a time. Eternal punishment is mentioned in Daniel 12:2: "And many of those who sleep in the dust of the earth shall awake, some to everlasting life and some to shame and everlasting contempt."[16]

We normally focus on the eternal penalties of sin because they are the most important, but Scripture speaks of temporal penalties as well. For example, in Deuteronomy, Moses warns the people:

If you are not careful to do all the words of this law which are written in this book, that you may fear this glorious and awful name, the LORD your God, then the LORD will bring on you and your offspring extraordinary afflictions, afflictions severe and lasting, and sicknesses grievous and lasting. And he will bring upon you again all the diseases of Egypt, which you were afraid of; and they shall cleave to you. Every sickness also, and every affliction which is not recorded in the book of this law, the LORD will bring upon you, until you are destroyed (Deut. 28:58–61).

Scripture is filled with accounts of temporal punishments on account of sin. While it is important to recognize that not all worldly distress we encounter is produced by our own sins (that being the main point of the book of Job), we must recognize the biblical truth that God does allow us to experience temporal calamity on account of our misdeeds.

Principle 3: Temporal penalties may remain when a sin is forgiven.

When someone repents, God removes guilt ("Though your sins are like scarlet, they shall be as white as snow" [Isa. 1:18]) and eternal punishment ("Since . . . we are now justified by his blood, much more shall we be saved by him from the wrath of God" [Rom. 5:9]), but temporal penalties may remain. One passage demonstrating this is 2 Samuel 12, in which Nathan the prophet confronts David about his adultery:

David said to Nathan, "I have sinned against the LORD." And Nathan said to David, "The LORD also has put away your sin; you shall not die. Nevertheless, because by this deed you have utterly scorned the LORD, the child that is born to you shall die" (2 Sam. 12:13–14).

God forgave David to the point of sparing his life, but David still had to suffer the loss of his son as well as other temporal punishments.[17]

In Numbers, Moses speaks to the Lord and says:

"Now if thou dost kill this people as one man, then the nations who have heard thy fame will say, 'Because the LORD was not able to bring this people into the land which he swore to give to them, therefore he has slain them in the wilderness'" (Num. 14:15–16).

God replies:

"I have pardoned, according to your word; but truly, as I live, and as all the earth shall be filled with the glory of the Lord, none of the men who have seen my glory and my signs which I wrought in Egypt and in the wilderness, and yet have put me to the proof these ten times and have not hearkened to my voice, shall see the land which I swore to give to their fathers; and none of those who despised me shall see it" (Num. 14:13–23).

In other words, although he pardoned the people, God would impose a temporal penalty by keeping them from the Promised Land.

Later, Moses is told he will suffer the same temporal penalty:

And the Lord said to Moses and Aaron, "Because you did not believe in me, to sanctify me in the eyes of the people of Israel, therefore you shall not bring this assembly into the land which I have given them" (Num. 20:12, cf. 27:12–14).

Moses died outside the Promised Land, though he was able to see it from a distance (Deut. 32:48–52, 34:1–6).

Some in the Protestant community deny that temporal penalties can remain after forgiveness of sin. But they acknowledge in practice that they do remain—for instance, when they insist that people return things they have stolen. Thieves may obtain forgiveness, but they also must engage in restitution when possible.

Similarly, many Protestants recognize that while Jesus paid

the price for our sins before God, he did not relieve our obligation to repair the harm we have done. They acknowledge that if you steal someone's car, you have to give it back; it isn't enough just to repent of having stolen it. God's forgiveness does not mean that you simply get to keep the stolen car.

Some might object that God gives temporal penalties to teach a sinner a lesson, which would make the penalties discipline rather than punishment; but this is a quibble about terms. Nothing in the above texts draws a distinction between "discipline" and "punishments." The terms are often used synonymously (e.g., "disciplining" a child is synonymous in normal speech with "punishing" a child). And Catholics acknowledge the disciplinary aspect of the temporal penalties.

Pope Paul VI stated:

The punishments with which we are concerned here are imposed by God's judgment, which is just and merciful. The reasons for their imposition are that our souls need to be purified, the holiness of the moral order needs to be strengthened, and God's glory must be restored to its full majesty" (*Indulgentiarum Doctrina* 2).

As we have seen, the Bible makes it clear that temporal penalties may remain after a sin is forgiven. And the Church has been aware of this since its earliest centuries, as illustrated by its penitential discipline.

Principle 4: God blesses some people as a reward to others.

Suppose a father has a seriously ill son and prays, "Dear Lord, if I have pleased you, please heal my son!" The father is asking that his son be healed as a reward for the father having pleased God. Intuitively we recognize this as a valid prayer request, and one that God sometimes answers. But we do not need to stop with our intuitions; Scripture confirms that God sometimes blesses some as a reward to someone else who has pleased him.

After Abraham fought a battle for the Lord, God appeared to him in a vision and said:

"Fear not, Abram [i.e., Abraham], I am your shield; your reward shall be very great."

But Abram said, "O Lord GOD, what wilt thou give me, for I continue childless, and the heir of my house is Eliezer of Damascus?"

And behold, the word of the LORD came to him, "This man shall not be your heir; your own son shall be your heir."

And he brought him outside and said, "Look toward heaven, and number the stars, if you are able to number them." Then he said to him, "So shall your descendants be." And he believed the Lord, and he reckoned it to him as righteousness (Gen. 15:1–2, 4–6).

God promised Abraham a reward—a multitude of descendants who otherwise would not be born. These people received a great gift, the gift of life, because God rewarded Abraham.

God further told Abraham that he would have nations and kings come from him, that God would make a covenant with his descendants, and that they would inherit the Promised Land (Gen. 17:6–8). All these blessings came to Abraham's descendants as God's reward to him.

This principle is also present in the New Testament, as we will see in our discussion of Romans 11:28 in the next section. The principle is also found in passages in which one person approaches Jesus for the healing or exorcism of someone else, such as the story of the Canaanite woman (Matt. 15:22–28).

Principle 5: God remits temporal penalties suffered by some as a reward to others.

When God blesses one person as a reward to someone else, sometimes it is by reducing the temporal penalties to which the first person is subject. For example, Solomon's heart was led astray

from the Lord toward the end of his life, and God promised to
remove the kingdom from him as a result:

> Therefore the LORD said to Solomon: "Since this has been
> your mind and you have not kept my covenant and my statutes
> which I have commanded you, I will surely tear the kingdom
> from you and give it to your servant" (1 Kings 11:11).

But, because David had pleased him, God lessened the temporal punishment Solomon would otherwise have incurred:

> "Yet for the sake of David your father, I will not do it in your
> days, but I will tear it out of the hand of your son. However
> I will not tear away all the kingdom; but I will give one tribe
> to your son for the sake of David my servant and for the sake
> of Jerusalem which I have chosen" (1 Kings 11:12–13).

God lessened Solomon's temporal punishment in two ways:
by deferring the removal of the kingdom until the days of his
son and by leaving one tribe (Benjamin) under Judah.

God was clear about why he did this: It is not for Solomon's
sake, but "for the sake of David your father." If David had not
pleased God, and if God had not promised him certain things
regarding his kingdom, God would have removed the entire
kingdom from Solomon during Solomon's lifetime.

There are other examples. God promised Abraham that if he
could find a small number of righteous men in Sodom, he was
willing not to destroy the entire city for the sake of the righteous
(Gen. 18:16–33).

Also, St. Paul noted that "as regards the gospel they [non-Chris-
tian Jewish people] are enemies of God, for your sake; but as regards election they are beloved for the sake of their forefathers. For
the gifts and the call of God are irrevocable" (Rom. 11:28–29).

Paul indicated that his Jewish contemporaries were treated more gently than they otherwise would have been treated
(God's gift and call were not removed from them) because their

forefathers were beloved by God, who gave them the irrevocable gifts listed in Romans 9:4–5.

Principle 6: God remits temporal punishments through the Church.

Sometimes God uses the Church when he removes temporal penalties. This is a key point in the doctrine of indulgences. The members of the Church became aware of this principle through the sacrament of penance. From the beginning, acts of penance were assigned as part of the sacrament, because the Church recognized that Christians must deal with temporal penalties, such as God's discipline and the need to compensate those injured by our sins.

In the early Church, acts of penance for grave sins such as apostasy, murder, and abortion could stretch over years. But the Church recognized that repentant sinners could shorten their penance by pleasing God through acts that expressed sorrow and a desire to make amends.

The Church also recognized that the duration of temporal punishments could be lessened through the involvement of other persons who had pleased God (Principle 5). Sometimes a confessor[18] or someone soon to be martyred would intervene and ask the competent authority to lessen the penance another person was performing. Thus the Church recognized its role of administrating temporal penalties.

This role is part of the ministry of forgiveness that God has given the Church. Scripture tells us that God gave the authority to forgive sins "to men" (Matt. 9:8) and to Christ's ministers in particular. Jesus told them, "As the Father has sent me, even so I send you. . . . Receive the Holy Spirit. If you forgive the sins of any, they are forgiven; if you retain the sins of any, they are retained" (John 20:21–23).

If Christ gave his ministers the ability to forgive the eternal penalty of sin, how much more would they be able to remit the temporal penalties of sin![19]

Christ also promised his Church the power to bind and loose on earth:

"Truly, I say to you, whatever you bind on earth shall be bound in heaven, and whatever you loose on earth shall be loosed in heaven" (Matt. 18:18).

As the context makes clear, binding and loosing cover Church discipline, and Church discipline involves administering and removing temporal penalties (such as barring from and readmitting to the sacraments). Therefore, the power of binding and loosing includes the administration of temporal penalties.

Principle 7: God blesses the departed as a reward to the living.

From the beginning, the Church recognized the validity of praying for the dead to ease their transition into heaven. This meant praying for the lessening or removal of temporal penalties that might be holding them back from the full glory of heaven.

This is a natural thing to do. A widower might pray to God and ask that, if he has pleased God, his wife's transition to heaven be swift and easy. For this reason the Church teaches that "indulgences can always be applied to the dead by way of prayer."[20]

A parallel is found in 2 Maccabees, when Judah Maccabee finds the bodies of soldiers who died wearing superstitious amulets during one of the Lord's battles. Judah and his men "turned to prayer, beseeching that the sin which had been committed might be wholly blotted out" (2 Macc. 12:42).

The phrase "wholly blotted out" refers to the sin's temporal penalties. The author of 2 Maccabees tells us in verse 45 that, for these men, Judah "was looking to the splendid reward that is laid up for those who fall asleep in godliness." Judah believed that these men fell asleep in godliness, which would not have been the case if they were in mortal sin. If they were not in mortal sin, they would not have eternal penalties to suffer, and thus the complete blotting out of their sin must refer to temporal penalties for their superstitious actions.

Judah did more than pray:

He also took up a collection, man by man, to the amount of two thousand drachmas of silver, and sent it to Jerusalem to provide for a sin offering. In doing this he acted very well and honorably, taking account of the resurrection.

Therefore, he made atonement for the dead, that they might be delivered from their sin (2 Macc. 12:43, 45).

Judah not only prayed for the dead but performed what was then the appropriate action for lessening temporal penalties: a sin offering.[21] The modern equivalents of this are obtaining an indulgence and having Mass offered for the departed. In both of these cases, the Church intervenes by way of prayer to assist the departed.

The qualification "by way of prayer" is significant. Christians in the hereafter are no longer under the earthly Church's jurisdiction. They no longer can receive sacraments, including penance, and the Church does not have authority to release their temporal penalties. All it can do is look to God and pray that he will lessen them. This is a valid form of prayer, as 2 Maccabees indicates, and we may have confidence that God will apply indulgences to the dead in some way. But the precise manner and degree of application are unknown.[22]

QUESTIONS ABOUT INDULGENCES

These seven biblical principles are the underpinnings of the doctrine of indulgences, but answering a few common questions may clarify matters further.

1. Who are the parties involved in an indulgence?

There are four parties: The first pleases God and moves him to grant a reward, providing the basis for the indulgence; the second requests the indulgence and obtains it by performing the act prescribed for it; the third issues the indulgence (this is God working through the Church); and the fourth receives the benefit of the indulgence by having his temporal penalties lessened.[23]

2. How many of one's temporal penalties can be remitted?

Potentially, all of them. The Church recognizes that Christ and the saints are interested in helping penitents deal with the aftermath of their sins, as indicated by the fact that they pray for us (Heb. 7:25, Rev. 5:8). Fulfilling its role in the administration of temporal penalties, the Church draws upon the rewards God chose to bestow on the saints, who pleased him, and on his Son, who pleased him most perfectly.[24]

The rewards on which the Church draws are infinite—because Christ is God, the rewards he accrued are infinite and can never be exhausted. His rewards alone, apart from the saints', could remove all temporal penalties from everyone everywhere. The rewards of the saints are added to Christ's, not because anything is lacking in his but because God has chosen to associate man with the application of salvation, as we saw in chapters 2 and 3.

Thus the Church acknowledges that "a conversion which proceeds from a fervent charity can attain the complete purification of the sinner in such a way that no punishment would remain" (CCC 1472).

3. If the Church has the resources to wipe out everyone's temporal penalties, why doesn't it do so?

First, because God doesn't want it to. God himself instituted the pattern of temporal penalties being left after forgiveness. They fulfill valid functions, one of them disciplinary. If a child were never disciplined, he would never learn obedience. God disciplines us as his children: "For the Lord disciplines him whom he loves, and chastises every son whom he receives" (Heb. 12:6).

Second, the Church *cannot* wipe out everyone's temporal punishments, because their remission depends on the dispositions of the persons who suffer those temporal punishments. Just as repentance and faith are needed for the remission of eternal penalties, so they are needed for the remission of temporal penalties. As Pope Paul VI explained, "Indulgences cannot be gained without a sincere conversion of outlook and unity with

God."[25] We might say that the degree of remission depends on how well the penitent has learned his lesson.

4. How does one determine by what amount penalties have been lessened?

Today, indulgences are classified as either plenary or partial.

In the case of a plenary indulgence, all of the temporal penalties are removed. This is the type the *Catechism* speaks of when it says that "a conversion which proceeds from a fervent charity can attain the complete purification of the sinner in such a way that no punishment would remain" (CCC 1472).

In the case of a partial indulgence:

> The faithful who at least with a contrite heart perform an action to which a partial indulgence is attached obtain, in addition to the remission of temporal punishment acquired by the action itself, an equal remission of punishment through the intervention of the Church (*Indulgentiarum Doctrina,* norm 5).

In other words, when a person contritely performs any pious action to which an indulgence is attached, the performance of the act itself pleases God (because it is a good action) and thus of itself removes a portion of the temporal penalties to which the person was subject. Because an indulgence is attached to the act, the Church intervenes, using its power of the keys to remove an additional, equal amount of the temporal penalties.

There is no mechanical way of calculating the precise values. Only God knows exactly how efficacious any particular partial indulgence is or whether a plenary indulgence was received when there was the opportunity for one.

5. Don't indulgences duplicate or even negate the work of Christ?

Despite the biblical underpinnings of indulgences, some charge that the doctrine supplants the work of Christ and turns us into our own saviors. This objection involves a misapprehension of the nature of indulgences and of how Christ's work is applied to us.

As we have seen, indulgences apply only to temporal penalties, not eternal ones. The Bible indicates that these penalties may remain after a sin has been forgiven and that God lessens these penalties as a reward to those who please him. Since the Bible indicates this, Christ's work cannot be said to have been supplanted by indulgences. The Church merely acts as Christ's servant in the application of what he has done for us, and we know from Scripture that Christ's work is applied to us over time and not all at once (see Phil. 2:12, 1 Pet. 1:9).

6. What about the merits of the saints—by the doctrine of indulgences are the saints made co-saviors with Christ?

They're not eternal saviors, but it is not wrong to describe them as saviors in the temporal sense we discussed in chapter 2—i.e., as those who help deliver from temporal difficulties. Being a savior in this way is something any human may do for another without blaspheming Christ.[26]

Further, this role the saints play is based on God's grace. The saints have the ability to please God because the love of God has been put in their hearts (Rom. 5:5), but it is only because of God's grace that this is so. His grace produces all their good actions, and his grace is given to them because of what Christ did. The good actions of the saints therefore are produced by Christ's working through them, which means Christ is the ultimate cause of even this temporal salvation.

This objection may be simply met by pointing out, as was done in chapter 2, that Scripture uses the word *savior* to talk about ordinary humans as temporal saviors. This in no way undercuts the unique role of Christ as eternal Savior.

7. Should we be talking along these lines? Isn't it better to put all of the emphasis on Christ alone?

No. If we ignore the principles underlying indulgences, we neglect what Christ does through us, and we fail to recognize the value of what he has done in us. Paul used this very sort of language: "Now I rejoice in my sufferings for your sake, and in my flesh I complete what is lacking in Christ's afflictions for the sake of his body, that is, the Church" (Col. 1:24).

Even though Christ's sufferings were far more than needed to pay for everything, Paul spoke of completing what was "lacking" in Christ's sufferings. If this mode of speech was permissible for Paul, it is permissible for us to acknowledge what Christ does through us.

8. Catholics sometimes talk about "expiating" sin in connection with indulgences. Isn't expiation something only Christ can do?

Protestant Scripture scholar Leon Morris notes that most people "don't understand 'expiation' very well" and explains its meaning in simple terms: "expiation is . . . the making amends for a wrong."[27]

The *Wycliff Bible Encyclopedia* gives a similar definition: "The basic idea of expiation has to do with reparation for a wrong, the satisfaction of the demands of justice through paying a penalty."[28] It also notes that the term has somewhat impersonal connotations.[29]

The terms used in these definitions—*expiation, amends, satisfaction, reparation*—refer basically to the same thing. To make expiation or satisfaction for a sin is to make amends or reparation for it. When someone makes reparations, he tries to repair the situation caused by his sin.

Certainly when it comes to the eternal effects of our sins, only Christ can make amends or reparation. Only he was able to pay the infinite price necessary for our sins. We are unable to do so, not only because we are finite creatures incapable of making an infinite satisfaction but also because everything we have is given to us by God.

This does not mean we cannot make amends or reparation for the temporal effects of our sins. If someone steals an item, he can return it. If someone damages another's reputation, he can publicly correct the slander. When someone destroys a piece of property, he can compensate the owner for its loss. All these are ways one can make at least partial amends (expiation) for harm done.

Illustrations of this principle are given in Leviticus 6:1–7 and Numbers 5:5–8, which tell us that in the Old Testament a penitent had to pay an extra twenty percent in addition to the value of the thing he took or damaged. (This applied to a penitent who voluntarily made compensation; a captured thief had to pay back double the value of the item taken (Exod. 22:7–9).) One of the most significant passages dealing with this issue is one we have quoted before—Proverbs 16:6: "By loving-kindness and faithfulness iniquity is atoned for." Here we are told that a person makes temporal atonement for his sins through acts of loving-kindness and faithfulness.

In any event, since expiation is the same thing as making amends, and since those in the Protestant community agree that one who has sinned should make amends as best he can, there should be no objection to the principle of making temporal expiation for one's sins. To dispute this would be to quarrel about the term being used but not the teaching in question.

9. For what kind of acts are indulgences granted?

The Church's official collection of indulgences is found in a book known as the *Enchiridion of Indulgences* (or *Handbook of Indulgences*). At the beginning of the *Enchiridion* there are three "general grants" of indulgences:

> A partial indulgence is granted to the faithful who, in the performance of their duties and in bearing the trials of life, raise their mind with humble confidence to God, adding— even if only mentally—some pious invocation.
>
> A partial indulgence is granted to the faithful who, in a spirit of faith and mercy, give of themselves or of their goods to serve their brothers in need.

A partial indulgence is granted to the faithful who, in a spirit of penance, voluntarily deprive themselves of what is licit and pleasing to them.

In short, indulgences may be granted for praying with faith, assisting those in need, and practicing voluntary self-denial.
There are other indulgenced acts, including:

- adoring the Blessed Sacrament
- reading Scripture
- making the Way of the Cross
- saying the rosary
- visiting a cemetery to pray for those buried there
- making an act of spiritual Communion
- teaching or learning Christian doctrine
- performing spiritual exercises on a retreat
- devoutly using a blessed religious object (e.g., a cross, crucifix, rosary, or medal)
- listening to the preaching of God's word
- making the sign of the cross
- visiting a church
- renewing one's baptismal promises
- and saying various particular prayers.

For the details of indulgences and how they are obtained, see the *Enchiridion of Indulgences*.

6

Faith, Works, and Boasting

The New Testament uses several terms in connection with salvation that have been hotly debated: *works, good works, works of the Law, faith,* and *boasting*. Especially controversial are the ways several of these terms are used by St. Paul and St. James and how their differing modes of expression can be harmonized.

"NOT BY WORKS OF THE LAW"

St. Paul is clear that we do not achieve salvation through "works of the Law." For example, he writes:

> For we hold that a man is justified by faith apart from works of law (Rom. 3:28).

And in Galatians, he is even more emphatic:

> [We] know that a man is not justified by works of the law but through faith in Jesus Christ, even we have believed in Christ Jesus, in order to be justified by faith in Christ, and not by works of the law, because by works of the law shall no one be justified (Gal. 2:16).

From the time of the Reformation, passages like these have received a great deal of attention in Protestant preaching. Justification *sola fide* (Latin, "by faith alone") became a defining mark of the Protestant movement, and these passages were used to support the Protestant view of justification by faith alone in contrast to the Catholic view of justification "by works of the law."

What is Paul talking about when he refers to "works of the law"? This phrase has been interpreted in various ways. Popular

Evangelical preacher John MacArthur explained Romans 3:28 in this way: "Men do not become right with God by something they do" (*Justification by Faith*, 33).

This would seem to equate "works of the law" with "something you do"—and this is a popular theme in much Evangelical preaching, the idea that you don't have to "do anything" to be saved.

Later, again commenting on Romans 3:28, MacArthur elaborates a bit: "You can't earn your way into the kingdom. A works salvation system blasts the glory of God. Man becomes a usurper who boasts that he has earned his way to God" (op. cit., 80).

Here MacArthur introduces another theme that is popular in Evangelical preaching: the idea that salvation by "works of the law" would involve "earn[ing] your way into the kingdom," allowing you to "boast" that you have "earned your way to God."

What kind of works might allow you to earn your place before God? Certainly works (actions) of an evil nature would not do that. God is infinitely holy, and Scripture makes it clear that sin separates us from God. Therefore, any works that would allow us to earn a place before God would have to be morally good works. Many Protestant preachers and theologians have concluded precisely this—that in saying we are not saved by "works of the law," St. Paul is saying that we are not saved by doing good works.

Most are quick to point out that this does not mean that good works are not an important part of the Christian life. In fact, they will note, St. Paul says that we are "created in Christ Jesus for good works, which God prepared beforehand, that we should walk in them" (Eph. 2:10). Therefore, we most definitely should do good works, but they come *from* the grace God gives us when we are saved. We do not do good works in order to earn our place before God and become saved.

With variations, this is the basic Protestant theory of what St. Paul is saying in epistles like Romans and Galatians.

How accurate is it?

A New Perspective on Paul

Despite how common this view is, in recent years some Protestant scholars have begun to question it. This has led to the development of what is often called "the new perspective on Paul." Prominent scholars such as E.P. Sanders, James D.G. Dunn, and N.T. Wright have concluded that the common account is based on a mistake that was made at the beginning of the Protestant Reformation.

That mistake involved reading the controversy in St. Paul's letters as a direct reflection of the controversy between Protestants and Catholics. The Reformers identified their own "faith alone" position with what they perceived St. Paul to be saying, and they identified the position of St. Paul's opponents, who were teaching salvation "by works of the law," with that of the Catholics that they opposed.

This, according to the New Perspective scholars, fundamentally misread St. Paul, and it has had a distorting effect on Protestant biblical scholarship ever since. Dunn explains:

> Since Paul's teaching on justification by faith seems to speak so directly to Luther's subjective wrestlings, it was a natural corollary to see Paul's opponents in terms of the unreformed Catholicism which opposed Luther, with first-century Judaism read through the 'grid' of the early sixteenth-century Catholic system of merit. To a remarkable and indeed alarming degree, throughout this [twentieth] century the standard depiction of the Judaism which Paul rejected has been the reflex of Lutheran hermeneutic. . . . And the most recent full-scale treatment of this area of Pauline theology, on Paul and the law, still continues to work with the picture of Paul as one who rejected the perverted attempt to use the law as a means of earning righteousness by good works (*Jesus, Paul, and the Law*, 185).

What do New Perspective scholars propose as an alternative to this? They vary among themselves. The "New Perspective"

is not actually a single perspective, and different authors make
different proposals on particular points. There are, however,
certain common themes.

In general, New Perspective authors do not see Paul's opponents as claiming that one needs to earn one's place before God
by good works. Instead, Paul's opponents recognized that salvation was a gift of God's grace. The point at issue between Paul
and his opponents was whether this gift was given exclusively
to the Jewish people. This was what was under discussion at the
council of Acts 15, and it is what Paul is discussing in Romans
and Galatians.

According to Paul's opponents, the Jewish people were chosen by God in such a way that, in order to experience forgiveness and salvation, one must become a Jew. For men, that would
mean accepting circumcision, and for both men and women it
would mean adopting a Jewish identity and embracing the Law
of Moses as a way of life—in other words, practicing "works of
the Law."

How, precisely, should the phrase "works of the Law" be understood according to New Perspective authors? This is one of
the points on which they differ, but a common understanding
of it is those acts required by the Mosaic Law that set Jews apart
from Gentiles and thus served as Jewish identity markers. These
would not be things like refraining from committing murder,
theft, or adultery, because the Gentiles acknowledged the sinfulness of these things and the need to avoid them. Instead, they
would be things like circumcision, keeping the Jewish food
laws, and observing the Jewish feast days.

Dunn explains:

> "Works of law," [or] "Works of the law" are nowhere
> understood here, either by his Jewish interlocutors or by Paul
> himself, as works which *earn* God's favor, as merit-amassing
> observances. They are rather seen as *badges*: they are simply
> what membership of the covenant people involves, what
> mark out the Jews as God's people; given by God for precisely

that reason, they serve to demonstrate covenant status. They are the proper response to God's covenant grace, the minimal commitment for members of God's people (op. cit., 194).

How much justice does the New Perspective do Paul's thought and writings? Let us look into the question.

Understanding "Works of the Law"

"Works of the Law" is a literal translation of the Greek phrase *erga nomou*. The first word in this phrase—*erga*—means *works, actions,* or *deeds*. The second word—*nomou*—means "of law" or "of *a* law" or "of *the* law" (from *nomos* = "law").

Without further context or qualification, *nomos* could refer to any of a number of laws. It could refer to the natural law that God has put in every human heart. It could refer to the Mosaic Law. It could refer to the various civil laws established by human rulers. It could refer to a body of laws or a single, specific law. It could even refer to a habitual practice or custom.

Given this, some have sought to retain this broad, general meaning in St. Paul's phrase. Thus the twentieth-century Catholic scholar A. Theissen translated Romans 3:28 to refer to justification by faith "without *works of a law*" and wrote:

> Christian justification is obtained by faith; no one can earn it by works according to this or that system of law, whatever the name or character of that law may be: be it the law of Israel, or the law of the Gentiles; be it natural, moral, or ceremonial law (*A Catholic Commentary on Holy Scripture*, at Rom. 3:28).

This is a tempting interpretation that would sidestep a lot of thorny questions about Paul's meaning. It also true that no one can *earn* his place before God through any system of law.

However, it isn't clear that this is what St. Paul means. An initial reason for caution is that Paul does speak of Christians as being under and obligated to fulfill "the Law of Christ":

> Bear one another's burdens, and so fulfill the law of Christ (Gal. 6:2).

> To those outside the law [of Moses] I became as one outside the law—not being without law toward God but under the law of Christ—that I might win those outside the law (1 Cor. 9:21).

Paul thus described himself as being under the Law of Christ and told others what they needed to do to fulfill it, indicating that there is an expectation that they do so. This "Law of Christ" is an evident alternative to the Law of Moses, and it is part of the Christian life.

This seems to have an impact on the theory that Paul says we are justified apart from *any* law. Would Paul really say that we are justified by faith apart from the Law *of Christ*? He would presumably balk at the idea of pitting faith in Christ against the Law of Christ and prefer seeing both as in harmony with each other. Indeed, he states that one of the key goals of his ministry is "to bring about the obedience of faith for the sake of his name among all the nations" (Rom. 1:5). We also know that the obedience of faith requires certain things, such as repentance from sin and baptism (cf. Acts 2:38, Rom. 2:4, 6:3–4, Gal. 3:27).

There is thus an interesting parallel between Paul and his opponents. Paul believes that to be justified one must have faith in Christ, repent of sin, and be baptized. These may be regarded as core elements of what Paul elsewhere refers to as "the Law of Christ." His opponents—who are Judaizing Christians—believe the same things but add the requirement of becoming Jewish by embracing the Law of Moses.

This raises the possibility that Paul may have been thinking *specifically* of the Law of Moses when he rejected the idea of justification by works of the Law.

"THE LAW"

In Jewish circles, the first five books of the Bible are commonly called the *Torah*. This is a Hebrew word that does not quite mean *law* (some have suggested *instruction* or *teaching* as better translations).

In the centuries just before the time of Christ, the language that most Jews spoke became Aramaic. After the conquests of Alexander the Great, Greek became a prominent international language, and many Jews—particularly those living in Gentile lands such as Egypt—became Greek speakers.

Without the ability to speak Hebrew, many Jews needed translations of their sacred scriptures, and in particular the Torah. In the 200s B.C., a Greek translation was prepared. It is known as the Septuagint, because of a legend that seventy scholars had done the translating (Latin, *septuaginta* = "seventy").

The translators of the Septuagint picked the Greek word *nomos* to represent the Hebrew word *Torah*, and so it became common for Greek-speaking Jews to refer to the Torah as the Nomos, or "Law" of Moses.

Sometimes the linkage with Moses is made explicit, as in New Testament passages like these:

And when the time came for their purification according to the law of Moses, they brought him up to Jerusalem to present him to the Lord (Luke 2:22).

"If on the sabbath a man receives circumcision, so that the law of Moses may not be broken, are you angry with me because on the sabbath I made a man's whole body well?" (John 7:23).

But some believers who belonged to the party of the Pharisees rose up, and said, "It is necessary to circumcise them, and to charge them to keep the law of Moses" (Acts 15:5).

More often, however, Moses is not mentioned, and we find passages like these:

So whatever you wish that men would do to you, do so to them; for this is the law and the prophets (Matt. 7:12).

And when they had performed everything according to the law of the Lord, they returned into Galilee, to their own city, Nazareth (Luke 2:39).

[A]nd [they] set up false witnesses who said, "This man never ceases to speak words against this holy place and the law" (Acts 6:13).

Because it was so foundational, so all-embracing for a Jew, speaking of "the law" without further qualification would instantly call to mind the Law of Moses.

WORKS OF TORAH

Since the Law of Moses doesn't play a large role in the minds of Christians, when they read St. Paul's statements about "works of the Law," they can miss the fact that he is most likely talking about the Law of Moses. To combat this tendency, we're going to use a variant of the phrase that more clearly brings out its Jewish connections. Instead of speaking of "works of the Law," we will speak of "works of Torah."

This phrase was not unique to Paul. It also appears in the Dead Sea Scrolls, Jewish writings found in the mid-twentieth century in caves on the shore of the Dead Sea. They were deposited there in the second half of the first century, and the most popular view among scholars is that they were written by a Jewish sect known as the Essenes. This sect is not mentioned in the New Testament, but it is known from other historical sources. It has points of contact with the early Christian movement, sharing some similarities but having clear differences.

What is significant for us is that many of the Dead Sea Scrolls are written in Hebrew, and it is in some of these that the phrase "works of Torah" appears. Indeed, it appears in one of the most important of all the Dead Sea Scrolls. Multiple copies were found among the scrolls, and it may have served as the Essenes' foundational manifesto.

Today this work goes by several different names. Sometimes it is called the *Halakhic Letter*; sometimes it is called the *Sectarian Manifesto*. Often it goes by the scholarly code 4QMMT. The "MMT" in refers to a Hebrew phrase that appears in the document itself: *Miqsat Ma'ase ha-Torah*, and this phrase translates into English as "some works of the Law."

Note that the phrase includes the Hebrew word *Torah*, and 4QMMT deals extensively with the correct observance of the Mosaic Law. This provides further reason to see the law in St. Paul's "works of the law" not as an abstract principle but as the Torah.

In any event, it is likely that Paul uses the phrase "works of Torah" *precisely because* his Judaizing opponents used the same phrase in telling people what they needed do to in order to be justified.

"WORKS" IN PAUL

To explore how well the view that "works of the Law" should be understood as "works of Torah" in Paul, let us take a look at the occurrences of the relevant phrase. As we do so, we will frequently use the word *Torah* in place of *Law* to see whether the result makes sense in context.

The first occurrence of "works of Torah" in Paul is in Romans 3:20. Before this point in the epistle, the term *ergon* ("work" or "deed") and its cognates were found only in Romans 2:6, 7, and 15. In none of these places does the term indicate what Paul has in mind in 3:20.

In 2:6, Paul states that God will judge every man according to his works. Obviously he does not mean works of Torah because the judgment of Gentiles was in view as well as the judgment of Jews (cf. Rom. 2:9–10).

In 2:7 Paul says that God will reward those who persevered "in well-doing" (literally, "good work") by giving them eternal life, or immortality (as well as glory and honor). But this is precisely what Paul says works of Torah will *not* get one, because Torah does not give the power to deal with sin. Thus there is a distinction in Paul's mind between "good work(s)" and "works of Torah."

In 2:15 Paul states that when Gentiles do by nature what Torah requires, they show that "what the Torah requires" (literally,
"the work [singular] of Torah") is written on their hearts. This is
the core of Torah—the important part, which God has written
on the hearts even of Gentiles. It is the same thing Paul has in
mind in 8:4 when he says that God has done what Torah could
not do by sending his Son "in order that the just [righteous]
requirement of the Torah might be fulfilled in us." "The work
of Torah" in 2:15 is the same as "the righteous requirement of
the Torah" in 8:4. It is this—and not all the Torah's commands
about diet and festival and ceremony—that is written on the
hearts of Gentiles, and it is what Paul says in 8:4 that God sent
his Son to empower us to accomplish.

Thus when in Romans 3:20 Paul introduces the term "works
[plural] of Torah," it is a new theme. It is not the general "works"
(actions, whether good or bad) according to which men will be
judged nor the "good work" that God will reward with eternal
life nor the "work [singular] of the Law" that is written on the
hearts of Gentiles.

Unfortunately, 3:20 itself doesn't give us much of a clue to
what Paul means by this phrase, but the concept becomes clear
as we proceed. Once the term "works of Law" has been introduced, evidence accumulates rapidly concerning what Law Paul
has in mind: the Torah.

The next verse, 3:21, states: "But now the righteousness of
God has been manifested apart from the Law, although the Law
and the Prophets bear witness to it." This points to the Torah
as the Law in question, since "the Law and the Prophets" was
a standard first-century way of referring to the Torah and the
other books of the Old Testament.

In 3:28, Paul reiterates his thesis that "a man is justified by
faith apart from works of Torah."[30] To support this, he asks rhe-
torically, "Or is God the God of Jews only? Is he not the God
of Gentiles also? Yes, of Gentiles also" (Rom. 3:29). "Works
of Torah" must therefore be characteristic of Jews rather than
Gentiles. This supports the identification of the Law that Paul is

talking about as the Torah, since this was the only law characteristic of Jews and not of Gentiles.

It is in chapter 4 that we have the first *concrete* example of what
Paul means by "works of Torah," and the example, confirming
what we have just read, is circumcision (Rom. 4:9–12). Paul
emphasizes with great force that circumcision is not necessary
for justification. In fact, the whole purpose of his discussion, in
chapter 4, of Abraham as the father of the faithful is to show that
circumcision is not necessary for being right with God.

Paul was concerned with circumcision in particular because it
was the Jewish rite of initiation, just as baptism is for Christians.
By being baptized one becomes part of the New Covenant and
a member of the Christian people; by being circumcised one became part of the Mosaic Covenant and a member of the Jewish
people. Many at the time thought that one could not be saved
without becoming a Jew, and it is this idea that Paul is addressing.

Because circumcision was the Jewish rite of initiation and
made one part of the Mosaic Covenant, Paul views circumcision
as the work of Torah par excellence—a view expressed earlier in
the epistle when he discussed the irrelevance of circumcision to
salvation (Rom. 2:25–3:1), and when, after he asserted in 3:27
that works of Torah are not necessary, he said God "will justify
the circumcised on the ground of their faith and the uncircumcised through their faith" (Rom. 3:30). The identification of
"works of Law" with "works of Torah" is thus confirmed by the
discussion of circumcision in Romans.

It is further confirmed by the discussion of circumcision in
Galatians. There, Paul greatly stresses the fact that Titus was not
compelled to be circumcised at Jerusalem (Gal. 2:3). Paul char-
acterizes the agitators who prompted Peter to behave hypocriti-
cally as "the circumcision party" (Gal. 2:12). He emphasizes
that "if you receive circumcision, Christ will profit you nothing" (Gal. 5:2).

His statement that "every man who receives circumcision . . .
is bound to keep the whole Torah" (Gal. 5:3) indicates that circumcision was the sign of embracing Torah as a whole. And he

states that "in Christ Jesus neither circumcision nor uncircumcision is of any avail" (Gal. 5:6).

Paul emphasizes the difference between his preaching and the preaching of circumcision by asking, "But if I . . . still preach circumcision, why am I still persecuted?" (Gal. 5:11). He does wish the circumcisers "would go the whole way and emasculate themselves!" (Gal. 5:12, NIV). He warns his readers that those "that would compel you to be circumcised . . . [do so] only in order that they may not be persecuted" (Gal. 6:12). "Even those who receive circumcision," he adds, "do not themselves keep the Torah, but they desire to have you circumcised that they may glory in your flesh" (Gal. 6:13). Finally, he reminds his readers again that "neither circumcision counts for anything, nor uncircumcision, but a new creation" (Gal. 6:15).

While circumcision is the work of Torah par excellence, Paul also has in mind that there are other works of Torah, as indicated by the text of Galatians. When Paul reminds Peter in Galatians 2:16 that they both "know that a man is not justified by works of Torah," it is in a context in which Peter and the other Jewish Christians had separated themselves from eating with the Gentile Christians of Antioch (Gal. 2:12–13). Because Gentiles and their food were regarded as unclean (cf. Acts 10:9–16 with 11:3–12), eating with them was a breach of the separation between clean and unclean people (stressed in the Torah) and a partaking of unclean food (forbidden in the Torah). Thus the laws of separation between clean and unclean are in view when Paul discusses "works of Torah."

Paul also laments that the Galatians "observe [Jewish ceremonial] days, and months, and seasons, and years!" (Gal. 4:10). This indicates that, in addition to circumcision, separation laws, and food laws, Jewish festival laws are also subsumed under what Paul has in mind when he speaks of "works of Torah."

Ceremonial Works of Law?

Scholars have grouped the requirements of the Mosaic Law into different categories.

In Jewish circles, for example, it has been common to divide them into positive commandments and negative commandments. The first are requirements to do something (e.g., honor your father and mother) and the second are requirements not to do something (e.g., you shall not murder). According to a popular way of classifying them, there are 248 positive commandments and 365 negative commandments, for a total of 613 commandments in total. Jewish scholars do not agree universally about precisely how the material in the Torah is to be grouped to achieve these numbers, which suggests that the scheme is somewhat artificial.

In Christian circles, it has been common to divide the requirements of the Mosaic Law into three large divisions, consisting of moral, ceremonial, and judicial (or civil) precepts. This division has been used for a number of centuries, and it dates back at least to the time of Thomas Aquinas (cf. *Summa Theologiae* I–II:99).

The moral precepts consist of items that belong to God's natural moral law, which applies to all people in all times and cultures. Both "Honor your father and mother" and "You shall not murder" belong in this category.

The ceremonial precepts were given by God to Israel to regulate its religious life. This category includes things such as regulations about sacrifices, dietary laws, feast days, and circumcision.

The judicial (or civil) precepts deal with the regulation of Jewish social life: the penalties assigned to various crimes (e.g., which carry the death penalty and which do not), rules of evidence (e.g., no one is to be put to death on the testimony of just one witness), and various other matters that regulated nonreligious aspects of life in ancient Israel (e.g., build rails around the edge of your roof so people don't fall off when you socialize there, have cities of refuge to which people accused of capital crimes may flee, allow daughters to inherit property when there are no sons, etc.).

In some modern-day circles, it has become customary to speak as if the Mosaic Law could be divided into three sublaws—a moral law, a ceremonial law, and a civil law. However, this way of speaking is of recent invention and would not have occurred

to the ancients. But to first-century Jews, the Torah represented
a single code of law. Even after the two- and threefold divisions
became common much later, there was still a recognition of
the Torah as one Law. Thus, if you read Jewish divisions of the
precepts, they don't talk about a positive Torah and a negative
Torah, and if you read Aquinas's treatment in the *Summa Theologiae*, you'll see that he speaks of a single law (which he calls "the
Old Law"), that has moral, ceremonial, and judicial precepts.

Many have noted that when Paul speaks of works of Torah,
the examples he gives pertain to the ceremonial precepts of the
Mosaic Law—e.g., circumcision, food laws, and days and seasons on the Jewish liturgical calendar. This raises the question of
whether Paul has *only* the ceremonial requirements in mind. Are
"works of the Law" for him simply obedience to the ceremonial
precepts of the Torah?

Some New Perspective authors seem to suggest this, pointing
out that it was adherence to these requirements that maintained
one's identity as a Jew, specifically. They served as identity markers, and their observance guaranteed one's place in the covenant
that God had made with the Jewish people. On this view, Paul is
saying that you don't have to maintain a Jewish identity in order
to be saved. It is membership in the New Covenant established
by Christ, not the Old Covenant, that is important.

Other authors, including critics of the New Perspective, have
resisted this narrowing of "works of Torah" to ceremonial works
only. For Paul and other Jews, the Torah was a single work, and
if one were obligated to perform its ceremonial requirements,
one was required to perform its moral and judicial requirements
also. The plain meaning of the phrase "works of Torah" would
refer to the actions required by the Torah. Period. Not some
subdivision of those actions.

One could argue that the phrase had acquired a technical meaning that did restrict the range of actions it included, but this would
have to be argued. It is not the obvious meaning of the phrase.

The fact that Paul gives examples from the ceremonial precepts is not itself a sufficient argument to say that these were all

he meant by "works of Torah." This is because the ceremonial precepts would be the natural flash points for the audience to whom he was writing. The judicial precepts tended to deal with matters in Israel and at a time when it was self-governed. These would be less relevant to Paul's international audience. Similarly, the moral precepts applied to people in all nations, they were written on the hearts of the Gentiles by God, and Paul expected people in every land to act morally. That left the ceremonial precepts of the law to serve as flash points for whether an international audience "kept Torah" or not.

One *can* and, in the absence of a compelling argument to the contrary, *should* recognize that the ceremonial precepts would be prominent in the debate, but that this did not restrict "works of Torah" to *just* those precepts. The phrase itself suggests *anything* done in order to obey the Torah.

ANOTHER MISTAKEN INFERENCE

One might try arguing like this: Since St. Paul says that works of Torah are not relevant to our salvation, and since "works of Torah" is most naturally taken as a reference to actions done in obedience to the Mosaic Law, therefore not only are obeying its ceremonial precepts irrelevant to our salvation, but obeying its moral precepts are also irrelevant. Therefore, you don't have to do "good works" to be saved. Your moral conduct is not relevant to your salvation.

This line of reasoning might be appealing to some (though by no means all) in the Protestant community, but it is flawed.

One of its most fundamental flaws is that it commits what is known as the fallacy of division. In the fallacy of division, a property that can be attributed to something as a whole is improperly applied to each of its parts. For example, one cannot reason that just because a brick building weighs many tons that each of the bricks that compose it weighs many tons. The property of weighing many tons applies to the whole structure, not its individual parts.

In the same way, just because keeping Torah is not necessary for salvation does not mean that everything the Torah discusses is irrelevant for salvation. To use an analogy that is a little closer to the situation at hand than the brick building analogy, a dietician might tell us that drinking Diet Coke is not necessary to good health, but we would not be permitted to draw the inference from this that drinking water (the principal ingredient of Diet Coke) is not necessary to good health. In the same way, we cannot infer from the fact that Torah is not necessary to salvation that none of the things in the Torah are necessary to salvation. The property "not necessary for salvation" applies to the keeping of Torah as a whole, not to individual things required by the Torah.

For example, one of the things required by the Torah is belief in God, which on anyone's account *is* necessary for salvation.[31]

In the same way, we have very clear indications from St. Paul that he does consider moral behavior relevant to salvation, as when he states:

> Do you not know that the unrighteous will not inherit the kingdom of God? Do not be deceived; neither the immoral, nor idolaters, nor adulterers, nor homosexuals, nor thieves, nor the greedy, nor drunkards, nor revilers, nor robbers will inherit the kingdom of God (1 Cor. 6:9–10).

For St. Paul, keeping Torah may not be required for salvation, but avoiding grave sin is.

A QUESTION OF MOTIVE

We've seen that "works of Torah" appear to mean any acts that are undertaken to fulfill the requirements of the Law of Moses—whether moral, ceremonial, or judicial. In other words, if someone is doing things because they are prescribed in Torah, then that person is doing works of Torah.

This leaves open the question of *why* a person is doing works of Torah. Is it because he wishes to live as a Jew and does it as a

matter of Jewish custom only? Is it because he is a Jewish Christian who feels that—as a Jew—he is obligated to do it, even
though Gentile Christians are not? Or is it because he feels that
salvation itself hinges on willingness to live under Torah?

Let's consider the first of these options. What would Paul
say about someone who does works of Torah for cultural rather
than theological reasons? Paul is not opposed to people who
were born Jewish continuing their ancestral customs, at least for
the time being.[32] He is not concerned with and never condemns
people for doing works of Torah because they are Jews and are
simply observing Jewish custom. At least in the transitional era
in which he lived, Paul doesn't think that Christian Jews have to
cease attending the synagogue or the Temple or similar things.
This is his point when he wrote:

> Was any one at the time of his call (to Christ) already circum-
> cised? Let him not seek to remove the marks of circumcision.
> Was any one at the time of his call uncircumcised? Let him
> not seek circumcision (1 Cor. 7:18).

Paul even was not opposed to administering circumcision to
individuals as long as it was understood that this was not being
done to obtain salvation. We read in Acts 16:

> Paul wanted Timothy to accompany him; and he took him
> and circumcised him because of the Jews that were in those
> places, for they all knew that his father was a Greek. As they
> went on their way through the cities, they delivered to them
> for observance the decisions which had been reached by the
> apostles and elders who were at Jerusalem (Acts 16:3–4).

Here, while on his second missionary journey, Paul circumcises Timothy, whose mother was Jewish, to enable him to
minister better to the Jewish people he would encounter on the
missionary journey they were pursuing. Timothy thus accepted
circumcision by Paul as an act of adherence to Jewish *culture*, not

for salvation. We know that it was already very clear in Paul's mind that circumcision was not needed for salvation because this is *after* the Acts 15 council decreed that Gentiles did not need to be circumcised.

That had been a great victory for Paul, who had been preaching that circumcision was not necessary for a long time, and it was these very "decisions which had been reached by the apostles and elders who were at Jerusalem" that he was anxious to deliver to the churches in the cities on their journey. Yet in the midst of his "circumcision is unnecessary" triumph, Paul circumcises Timothy. The irony is marked: Acts 16:3 indicates that Paul circumcised Timothy, while Acts 16:4 indicates that Paul was delivering to the churches confirmation from Jerusalem that circumcision was not necessary! We can only conclude from this, and from his exhortation to Jews not to seek to be uncircumcised, that Paul does not object to circumcision (and, by extension, other works of Torah) as long as they are being done as matters of custom and not as paths to salvation.

What of the second option we mentioned—the case of a Jewish Christian performing works of Torah because he believes that he is obligated as a Jew to do them, though Gentile Christians are not? Ultimately, Paul would say that Jewish Christians are not bound to do works of Torah, for he tells us that Christ "abolish[ed] in his flesh the Torah of commandments and ordinances" (Eph. 2:15) and that he himself was not under Torah (1 Cor. 9:20).

However, for the sake of ecclesiastical peace and for the sake of individuals' consciences, he seems content to allow Jewish Christians to continue to act on the premise that they are still obligated by Torah. Thus he acknowledges that all foods are lawful and that one is not bound to observe Jewish holy days, but he allows a conscience exception for those who think differently (Rom. 14). He only objects to people doing works of Torah when they cause harm—such as making Gentile Christians feel like second-class citizens (as was the case in Antioch; Gal. 2:11–16)—or when they are used as a repudiation of the Christian faith (as the author of

Hebrews is concerned with) or when people have the idea that salvation is tied to them.

This leads us to the third reason someone might be doing works of Torah. Paul is very concerned when individuals begin saying—as happened at Antioch, Rome, and in Galatia—that "unless you are circumcised according to the custom of Moses, you cannot be saved" (Acts 15:1). That presents the Mosaic Law, rather than Jesus Christ, as the basis of salvation, and that constitutes a false gospel (Gal. 1:8–9). It is at this point that customs such as circumcision and keeping kosher become a problem. As long as they are not done to achieve salvation, they are permissible for Paul. But when they are done as requirements for salvation, a false gospel is being pursued.

To understand Paul's thought on this subject better, we need to consider another aspect of what he teaches. At the same time that Paul is emphatic that works of Torah are not necessary, he also *exhorts* people to do good works—including many good works taught in the Torah itself, such as love of God and love of neighbor, the two great commandments of the Torah (Matt. 22:36–40, 2 Thess. 3:5, cf. Rom. 13:9). He thus excoriates reliance on works of Torah for salvation, but he commands certain things Torah enumerates—things (such as faith) that *are* required for salvation. How are we to understand this paradox?

Part of the explanation is that Paul is free to exhort people to do good things—have faith, love God, love one's neighbor—as long as the individual doesn't get the idea that he must obey the Torah generally to be saved. The real question is: If we're not obliged to obey the Torah in general, why are these particular things required of us?

WHAT REQUIRES US TO DO GOOD?

The answer is: There is something other than the Torah that requires them of us. They may be mentioned in the Torah, but that isn't what obligates us to do them. The reason we must do these things is that they are commanded by a higher law that is reflected both in the Torah and in the hearts of men (Rom. 2:15), and in a law that unambiguously applies to Christians: the Law of Christ (1 Cor. 9:21, Gal. 6:2). To understand this, one needs to understand the relationships among the different forms of divine law.

The most fundamental law is known in theology as the eternal law. It consists of God's plan for the universe by which all creation is directed.

One subset of the eternal law is the natural law. In the sciences this term has a different meaning, but in theology the natural law is understood to be rational creatures' participation in the eternal law—namely, those things that reason tells us about God's plan and how we as rational creatures ought to behave (e.g., that murder, lying, and stealing are wrong). It is this law Paul tells us God has written in the hearts of men (Rom. 2:15), whether Jew or Gentile. Unfortunately, due to the effects of sin, our perception of this law is often faulty (Rom. 1:19–28); therefore, to keep us from rationalizing sin, it helps to have an explicit statement of what God requires.

This need has led God to give two bodies of what is called positive law. Positive law consists of law that is communicated to man overtly, by divine revelation.[33]

The two bodies of positive law God has given are the Old Law and the New Law. They are known in the Bible as the Law of Moses (i.e., the Torah) and the Law of Christ. These bodies of law contain material found in the natural law (and thus in the eternal law), such as that one should love God and love one's neighbor.

They also both contain particular positive precepts (i.e., explicitly stated precepts) that apply only to the ages in which the laws are in operation (and thus are not part of eternal law, which is immutable). For example, the Law of Moses commands circumcision, the observance of the Sabbath, and the creation of cities of refuge within Israel (Exod. 20:8–11, Num. 35:2). The Law of Christ commands baptism, the reception of the Eucharist, and the observance of the Lord's Day (Matt. 28:19, John 6:53–54, 1 Cor. 16:2, Rev. 1:10).

The reason Christians are obligated to obey the Ten Commandments is not that they are commanded by the Law of Moses. Christians are not obligated to obey the Law of Moses. In
fact, the only people who were *ever* bound to obey the Law of
Moses were the Jewish people prior to the time of Christ (ST
I–II:98:5). Christians are, however, bound to obey the natural
law that God has written in their hearts and the Law of Christ (1
Cor. 9:21). This is explained in the section on the Third Commandment in the *Roman Catechism*:[34]

> [T]he other commandments of the Decalogue (besides the Sab-
> bath commandment (are precepts of the natural and perpetual
> law, under all circumstances unalterable, whence, notwith-
> standing the abrogation of the law of Moses, all the command-
> ments contained in the two tables are observed by the Christian
> people, not because Moses so commanded, but because they
> agree with the law of nature, by the dictates of which men are
> impelled to their observance (*Roman Catechism* III:IV:IV).

This understanding of why Christians must keep the moral
precepts found in the Law of Moses—because they are *also* found
in the natural law (Rom. 1:19–20, 2:14) or in the Law of Christ
(Gal. 6:2)—resolves the paradox in Paul's writings of praising
good works, including ones named in the Law of Moses, but
condemning reliance on works of Torah (Gal. 3:10).

It also explains why he insists that Christians do certain things
named in the Torah (i.e., have faith, love God, love neighbor),
but that other things (circumcision, kosher diet, Jewish feasts) are
irrelevant to salvation (Gal. 5:6) or even harmful to it (Gal. 5:2).

The rule is: The commands of Torah that are ceremonial or
judicial in nature are not binding on us except insofar as they
contain a moral element. If ceremonial or judicial works of Torah
are done as a matter of ethnic custom (as with Timothy), they are
harmless for Paul, in his own day. But if they are done to achieve
salvation, they are harmful—indeed, deadly—because they are
being observed in pursuit of a false gospel.

Fundamental in Paul's mind is a separation between two different systems of salvation: one in which a person seeks to be put right with God through the Torah and one in which a person seeks to be put right with God through Jesus Christ. This contrast between salvation by Torah and salvation by Christ is the key to understanding one aspect of the letter to the Romans that is otherwise very difficult to grasp: Paul's discussion of Jewish and Christian boasting.

JEWISH BOASTING IN ROMANS

A theme in Romans that deserves special mention is boasting of one's relationship to God. Paul speaks of both Jews and Christians doing this. He speaks of Jews boasting a number of times:

> You call yourself a Jew and rely upon the Torah and boast of your relation to God (Rom. 2:17, literally, "in God").
> You who boast in Torah, do you dishonor God by breaking Torah? (Rom. 2:23).
> Then what becomes of our boasting? It is excluded. On what principle? On the principle of works? No, but on the principle of faith (Rom. 3:27).
> For if Abraham was justified by works, he has something to boast about, but not before God (Rom. 4:2).

Many Protestants argue that these passages describe self-righteousness and an attempt to earn one's place before God by one's own efforts. They claim that in these passages the people in question were boasting about their own righteous deeds. As we will see, this is not correct.

While in contemporary English the idea of "boasting" connotes arrogance, this is not always the case in Greek. The word used by Paul—*kauchaomai*—means not just to boast but also to glory, to rejoice, or to exult. The point is: It's not automatically negative, the way the word *boast* is in English. Indeed, we will see later that Paul *recommends* "boasting" about certain things. So one must not assume that he's criticizing people for "boasting" in the English sense. One should take the term as neutral until there is evidence that it is to be taken otherwise.[35]

Now, let's look at what Paul says the Jewish person is boasting in. Is it his own moral deeds? No. In Romans 2:17 Paul says the Jewish person is boasting "in God," talking about how great God is. He is, as Jeremiah put it, "glorying in the Lord" (Jer. 9:24). Here the object of the Jew's boast is God—Yahweh—not his own self-righteous works. He is boasting to the Gentile, saying, "*My* God is greater than *your* god," not boasting in front of the Lord saying, "Look how righteous *I* am, God."

Similarly, in Romans 2:23 we see that the object of the Jew's boasting is the Torah. Paul addresses those "who boast in Torah." The Torah is an object of boasting in front of Gentiles because it is seen as a divine gift. The Jew thus reasons in front of his Gentile neighbor: "How glorious is Torah! It is the wisdom of God and his gift to his people!" This attitude reflects one illustrated in Deuteronomy itself, where Moses says that when the Gentiles hear of the precepts of the Torah, they will say:

"Surely this great nation is a wise and understanding people." For what great nation is there that has a god so near to it as the Lord our God is to us, whenever we call upon him? And what great nation is there, that has statutes and ordinances so righteous as all this Law which I set before you this day? (Deut. 4:6–8).

That the Jew is not boasting about his own moral accomplishments in the passage from St. Paul is evident because, immediately after acknowledging the Jewish person's boast in the Torah, Paul asks, "Do you dishonor God by breaking Torah? For, as it is written, 'The name of God is blasphemed among the Gentiles because of you'" (Rom. 2:23–24). Paul pricks his reader's conscience by pointing out that the Jewish person himself has broken Torah. He says, in effect, "Okay, so you glorify God's Torah in front of Gentiles. But do you dishonor God in front of Gentiles by breaking his Torah?"

Of course, Paul does not deny that the greatness of the first five books of the Bible should be celebrated. He is concerned about the fact that many Jewish people in the first century held that the Torah was the exclusive way to salvation. The Gentiles do not keep Torah, it was reasoned, so they are not united to God. For Jews who had this idea, their boasting in God and in the Torah was problematic.

Nowhere in the Torah or anywhere else in the Old Testament did God say that one has to become a Jew to be saved. As the revelation of the Christian age made clear, this idea was false. But at the time, many Jewish Christians were preaching it. They boasted before Gentiles of the greatness of God and the greatness of the Torah as necessary for being united to God, so that only Jews could be saved. This is not boasting of self-righteous accomplishments. The focus is still on the Torah and the Mosaic Covenant as a *gift* from God, as a *grace* given to his chosen people.

Jewish people recognized that their relationship with God was one of grace and loving-kindness, as many contemporary Protestant commentators have noted (including E.P. Sanders and James D.G. Dunn). Paul knows this, and he is not criticizing his opponents because he thinks they are trying to earn their position before God. What he has a problem with is their claim that to be saved one must become a Jew.

This form of boasting is not without an element of pride— pride not in one's own moral accomplishments but in one's favored position with God. We see this in Romans 2:17–21:

> But if you call yourself a Jew and rely upon Torah and boast [in God] and know his will and approve what is excellent, because you are instructed in Torah, and if you are sure that you are a guide to the blind, a light to those who are in darkness, a corrector of the foolish, a teacher of children, having in Torah the embodiment of knowledge and truth—you then who teach others, will you not teach yourself?

Some readers may wonder about the difference between prideful boasting about one's accomplishments and prideful boasting about one's relationship to God, so an analogy may be helpful. Imagine two boys bickering, one adopting a superior attitude and saying, "Well, *my* dad is better than *your* dad." In this case, the child is boasting about his father and his relationship with his father, not about anything he has done himself. This is not unlike a Jew saying before a Gentile, "*My* God is better than *your* god. I have the living God, and you have only dead idols."

Now, let's change the analogy a little to bring out the favored relationship aspect. Suppose there are two children in a family, one born to the mother and father, the other adopted. The natural child may say to the adopted child, "Well *I* was born to Mom and Dad, *not* adopted; I'm their *real* child." In this case he is boasting of having a relationship to the parents that is superior to that of the other child. The argument is that because the one child lacks a certain quality (being a biological child), he must therefore lack the favored relationship of the first child. A child may even boast that he is more favored by the parents on the basis of having greater knowledge. Thus an older child may tell a younger child, "Mom and Dad like me better because *I* am in first grade, while *you* aren't even in kindergarten yet."

This is similar to the boast that Paul's opponents were making to Gentiles: "*We* are God's children by the *covenant* he made through Moses, and that Law of Moses gives us perfect knowledge of his will. If *you* want to be right with the living God, *you* must become part of the covenant, too, by being circumcised and living under Torah."

Living under Torah, of course, did not mean living sinlessly. Dealing with sin was the purpose of many of the rituals and sacrifices that Torah itself prescribed. Jewish people—especially in an age when the Temple was still in operation—were fully aware of this, and Paul does not imagine that his opponents believed that they had to live sinlessly in order to be acceptable to God. Indeed, no Jew would believe such a thing. It was enough, when one sinned, to repent and take the course of action prescribed by Torah for the kind of sin one had committed. *That* was life under the Covenant. Otherwise, what could the Torah mean by all of its prescriptions for dealing with sin?

Thus Paul is not faulting his opponents because he thinks that they are trying to earn their place before God by good works. His problem is not that they are failing to take into account the role of grace. His problem is that they think that living under Torah—including its sacrifices for sin—is necessary and sufficient for being put right with God. In fact, it is neither. It is not necessary, so Gentiles do not need to become Jews. And it is not sufficient, for, as the letter to the Hebrews points out, the sacrifices and rituals authorized for dealing with sin are incapable of dealing with sin's eternal consequences (Heb. 10:4). What *is* both necessary and sufficient for being put right with God is a proper relationship with Christ. *He* is the one who saves, not Torah.

Paul thus rebukes those who, as Romans 2:17 puts it, "rely upon Torah" and on that basis "boast in God." Jews do not have a saving relationship with God either on the basis of being children of Abraham (Rom. 4:11–12, 9:7; cf. Matt. 3:9) or on the basis of living under Torah. To correct this attitude, Paul stresses that "no human being will be justified in his [God's] sight by works of Torah" (Rom. 3:20) and that, instead, God "justifies him who has faith in Jesus" (Rom. 3:26). In the very next verse he says, "Then what becomes of our boasting? It is excluded. On what principle? Of works? No, but on the principle of faith. For we hold that a man is justified by faith apart from works of Torah" (Rom. 3:27).

Just prior to this, Paul stated that Jews are also under the power of sin and that the Gentiles *can* be justified by faith in Jesus Christ (Rom. 3:19–26). So how must contemporary Jewish boasting before Gentiles be evaluated? It is excluded because, according to "the principle of faith" in Christ, those who have faith in Jesus are put right with God,[36] and so Jewish boasting about having an exclusive, saving relationship with God through Torah is ruled out.

Notice that Paul says the principle of works *does not* exclude boasting. This has implications for the kind of boasting being considered. If it were boasting about righteousness based on

one's own efforts, then Paul would say that the principle of
works *does* exclude such boasting: "for even those who receive
circumcision do not themselves keep the Torah" (Gal. 6:13) and
Jewish people "are under the power of sin" (Rom. 3:9). If it were
boasting about one's own moral purity, then Paul would say that
the principle of *works* excludes boasting. But since he says the
opposite, we must conclude that the boasting he is talking about
is not boasting in self-accomplishment. Instead, it is boasting
about the Jews' privileged relationship with God.

Finally, the reference to boasting in Romans 4:2 further confirms that this kind of boasting is under discussion: "What then
shall we say about Abraham, our forefather according to the flesh?
For if Abraham was justified by works, he has something to boast
about, but not before God. For what does the Scripture say? 'Abraham believed God, and it was reckoned to him as righteousness.'"

Paul argues that Abraham was justified by faith without
works. He does this by offering a common-ground principle,
with which he expects his Jewish audience to agree, that "if
Abraham was justified by works, he has something to boast
about" (Rom. 4:2). This common-ground principle would hold
true regardless of how works are interpreted. If the works are
acts of personal accomplishment, a person who has been justified by works would have grounds for boasting. "Look what I
have done!" such a person would have a right to cry. "See, God,
I have justified myself before you!"

Similarly, if the works are, as we maintain, acts done to live in
accord with Torah (including its prescriptions for dealing with
sin), a person justified by those acts would also have grounds to
boast. He could say to a Gentile: "See: I am right with God. I
have obtained his favor by living in accord with Torah."

But Paul does not stop at this point. His next comment tells
us what kind of works and what kind of boasting are being
discussed, for he says that a person justified by works would
have grounds to boast, *"but not before God"* (Rom. 4:2). If the
works and boasting Paul was talking about were of personal
moral accomplishment, then this last statement would make no

sense. A person justified by his moral accomplishments *would* have grounds to boast in front of God. He could look to God and say, "See, Lord, all of the wonderful things I have done that have earned me my place before you." Therefore Paul is not talking about that kind of boasting or works.

On the other hand, if Abraham was justified by keeping Torah, he could boast of this before Gentiles, yet this would give him no grounds for boasting before God, since Torah, with its prescriptions for dealing with sin, is itself a gift from God.

This reading not only makes the statement intelligible, it suits the common-ground argument Paul is making. Any Jewish person hearing Paul's argument could be expected to say at this point, "Yes. That's obvious. Just because Abraham might have had grounds to boast in front of Gentiles does not mean he had grounds to boast in front of God."

A Jewish person would know that he, like any person, must adopt an attitude of humility, not boasting, before God. As the prophet says, "the LORD requires you . . . to walk humbly with your God" (Mic. 6:8). This would strike a pious Jewish individual as obvious.

By contrast, Paul's opponents thought they were put right with God by Torah, and in this they were mistaken. Their boasting was thus misplaced.

This suffices for an analysis of Paul's remarks on Jewish boasting. As we see in Romans 5:1–11, however, Paul has something quite different to say about Christian boasting: He recommends it.

CHRISTIAN BOASTING IN ROMANS

While a discussion of Jewish boasting in front of unbelievers occupied Paul in Romans 2 through 4, in Romans 5 he takes up the parallel subject of Christian boasting in front of unbelievers:

Therefore, since we are justified by faith, let us have peace with God[37] through our Lord Jesus Christ. Through him we have obtained access to this grace in which we stand, and *let us boast in our hope of sharing the glory of God* (Rom. 5:1–2).

Paul rejected Jewish boasting in God as improper because it was based on Torah (Rom. 2:23). Now he discusses Christian boasting in God, which is proper because it is based on Christ (Rom. 5:11). The goal of Christian boasting in God is to win people to the Christian faith (cf. Rom. 11:13). In chapter 5 of Romans, Paul tells us to boast in three things: our hope (v. 2), our sufferings (v. 3), and God himself through Christ (v. 11).

In Romans 5:2, the term that is translated in many Bibles as "rejoice" should be "boast." It is the same word (*kauchaomai*) that has already been used in the book and consistently translated as "boast." Translating the term consistently makes explicit the contrast between the Jewish boasting that Paul has discussed and Christian boasting.

The first thing Paul says we should boast about as Christians is our hope of sharing the glory of God. Contemporary preaching needs to pay attention to this statement. As part of evangelism, we should speak of our Christian hope as a way of making Christianity attractive to those who do not have this hope.

In 5:3 Paul goes beyond this and says, "More than that, let us boast in our sufferings" (literal translation). Human nature does not normally boast of or exult in sufferings, so we need to be encouraged to do so. Paul explains why in vv. 3–5: Suffering triggers a chain of events that will end up fulfilling our hope (of sharing in the glory of God; v. 2). We will not be disappointed in this hope because God's love has been poured (infused) into our hearts through the Holy Spirit (v. 5).

To illustrate the depth of God's love for us, Paul points out that Christ was willing to die for us when we were still sinners (that is, before we became Christians; vv. 6, 8). This goes beyond what one person will naturally do for another (v. 7), showing the supernatural character of God's love. Because of Christ's blood and death, we have been justified (v. 9) and reconciled (v. 10), so—Paul reasons—how much more will we be saved through Christ's risen life from God's wrath on the last day! Thus we should not be afraid to boast of our sufferings as Christians. But we should especially boast about our relationship with God through Christ. In 5:11, Paul tells us that "we also rejoice [literally, "boast"] in God through our Lord Jesus Christ, through whom we have now received our reconciliation." This is the apex of Christian boasting.

For St. Paul, the Judaizers' boasting in God was misplaced, because it claimed one was justified through the Torah; but true Christian boasting in God is appropriate because it recognizes that it is through Christ that we have received reconciliation. Both forms of "boasting" in front of unbelievers are boasts "in God" rather than of one's own accomplishments. Of course, we must never be arrogant when we speak of our Faith, but we should make the Faith attractive to others by humbly showing how great the grace is that God has given us.

The Effectiveness of Christian versus Jewish Boasting

The final reference to Christian boasting in Romans is in 15:17, where Paul tells us, "I have reason to boast in Christ Jesus in the things which pertain to God" (literal translation). The context makes clear what he is talking about:

> I have written more boldly to you on some points, as remind-ing you, because of the grace given to me by God, that I might be a minister of Jesus Christ to the Gentiles, minister-ing the gospel of God, that the offering of the Gentiles might be acceptable, sanctified by the Holy Spirit. Therefore I have reason to glory [literally, "boast"] in Christ Jesus in the things which pertain to God. For I will not dare to speak of any of those things which Christ has not accomplished through me, in word and deed, to make the Gentiles obedient—in mighty signs and wonders, by the power of the Spirit of God, so that from Jerusalem and round about to Illyricum I have fully preached the gospel of Christ (Rom. 15:15–19, NKJV).

Paul is explicit that he is not boasting of his own accomplishments: "I will not dare to speak of any of those things which Christ has not accomplished through me." So his only boasting of his work is boasting "in Christ Jesus in the things which pertain to God." Rather than boasting of his righteousness in front of God, he is boasting of Christ's accomplishments through him—"in mighty signs and wonders, by the power of the Spirit of God." Accomplished why? "To make the Gentiles obedient" to the Faith—there is an evangelistic purpose to the boasting.

Earlier in Romans, Paul told us he does this kind of boasting a lot: "Inasmuch then as I am an apostle to the Gentiles, I magnify my ministry in order to make my fellow Jews jealous, and thus save some of them" (Rom. 11:13–14). In front of his Jewish brothers, Paul thus boasts of how many converts he has won to Christ in an attempt to make them desirous ("jealous") of having what Paul has—the Christian faith—so that they also may be saved.

The issue of the conversion of the Gentiles was important to Jews of the first century. The conversion of the Gentiles to God had been prophesied in the Old Testament, and many first-century Jews were striving to fulfill this prophecy by preaching about ("boasting in") God in front of Gentiles. Jesus himself notes their zeal in doing this. "Woe to you, scribes and Pharisees, hypocrites!" he says. "You traverse sea and land to make a single proselyte, and when he becomes a proselyte, you make him twice as much a child of hell as yourselves!" (Matt. 23:15).

Yet despite the effort, Jewish evangelism never took off the way Christian evangelism did. It was through Jesus that the Old Testament prophecy of the conversion of the Gentiles to the God of the Jews was fulfilled.

One reason that Jewish evangelism never took off the way Christian evangelism did had to do with the kind of boasting in God the two groups were doing. Jews were boasting of having a relationship with God through the Torah, making one's adherence to the Mosaic Law the condition for conversion to God. Christians were boasting of having a relationship with God through Christ, making adherence to Christ the condition for conversion

THE DRAMA OF SALVATION

to God. Needless to say, professing faith in Christ and being baptized was a much easier way for Gentiles to come to God than being circumcised and submitting to all the regulations of the Torah (written and oral) that governed Jewish life after conversion.

A large group of people in the first century known as "God-fearers," though intellectually convinced of the folly of paganism and the truth of the Jewish religion, could not bring themselves to convert by accepting circumcision and the regulations of the Torah. Thus the very thing that many Jews held out as the basis for uniting with God became the barrier to effective Jewish evangelism. When Christians began proclaiming the sufficiency of Christ as the basis for union with God, they made numerous converts, and in just 350 years the Roman Empire, the enemy of Jews and Christians alike, embraced worship of the true God.

While this still lay in the future, Paul could (and did) go to his Jewish brethren and boast of how Christ had won many converts to God through him. Christ, not Torah, was the reality that drew people to the God of the Jews (cf. John 12:32), and, thus, the reality through whom the long-prophesied conversion of the Gentiles was happening. Paul's Jewish brothers had better get on board, he might claim, if they want to be part of God's program for the ages and not be left behind, clinging to the Torah as a way of union with God when it was never intended to be that (Rom. 4:14).

Paul's discussion of his own boasting thus provides confirmation that the boasting he speaks of in Romans, both Jewish and Christian, is not boasting about one's own righteousness. Every passage in which Paul discusses boasting is about boasting in the greatness of God and how human beings can have union with him.

"Not Because of Works, Lest Any Man Should Boast"

One passage often cited as a prooftext against the Catholic view of salvation is Ephesians 2:8–9: "For by grace you have been saved through faith; and this is not your own doing, it is the gift of God—not because of works, lest any man should boast."

Typically, those who use this verse assume that the works Paul is speaking of are good works. If that were true, it would not conflict with Catholic theology. Note that the passage speaks of salvation as a past event—"you *have been* saved." In Greek this is the perfect tense, which denotes a past, completed action that has continuing effects in the present. The passage thus refers back to the salvation one received at the beginning of the Christian life, the effects of which are still with one through the possession of sanctifying grace.

We know from other passages in Paul that salvation also has present and future aspects (see chapter 2), so the kind of salvation Paul is discussing in Ephesians 2:8–9 is *initial* salvation. It is the kind we received when we first came to God and were justified, not the kind of salvation we are now receiving (see 1 Pet. 1:8–9, Phil. 2:12) or the kind we will one day receive (see Rom. 13:11, 1 Cor. 3:15, 5:5).

Ephesians 2:8–9 is not a successful prooftext against Catholic theology, even on the assumption that the "works" Paul mentions are good works, because the Catholic Church does not teach that we receive initial justification by good works. We do not have to do good works in order to come to God and be justified. According to the Council of Trent, "we are said to be justified by grace because nothing that precedes justification, whether faith or works, merits the grace of justification. For 'if it is by grace, it is no longer by works; otherwise,' as the apostle says, 'grace is no more grace' (Rom. 11:6)" (*Decree on Justification* 8).

However, Paul probably does not mean "good works" in this passage. Normally when he says "works" he means "works of Torah"—those done out of obedience to the Law of Moses. His point is to stress that we are saved by faith in Jesus Christ and not by the Mosaic Law. Jews cannot boast in front of Gentiles of having a privileged relationship with God because of the Mosaic Law and its requirement of circumcision (see Rom. 2:6–11, 17–21, 25–29, 3:21–22, 27–30).

These same elements—works, boasting, circumcision, and the Jew-Gentile distinction—are present in Ephesians 2. Paul discusses how God has shown mercy to us in Christ, and before turning to the subject of circumcision and membership in Christ, he mentions works in connection with boasting (Eph. 2:9), stating:

> Therefore remember that at one time you Gentiles in the flesh, called the uncircumcision by what is called the circumcision, which is made in the flesh by hands—remember that you were at that time separated from Christ, alienated from the commonwealth of Israel, and strangers to the covenants of promise, having no hope and without God in the world.
>
> But now in Christ Jesus you who once were far off have been brought near in the blood of Christ. For he is our peace, who has made us both one, and has broken down the dividing wall of hostility, by abolishing in his flesh the Law (Torah) of commandments and ordinances, that he might create in himself one new man in place of the two, so making peace, and might reconcile us both to God in one body, through the cross, thereby bringing the hostility to an end.
>
> And he came and preached peace to you who were far off and peace to those who were near; for through him we both have access in one Spirit to the Father. So then you are no longer strangers and sojourners, but you are fellow citizens with the saints and members of the household of God (Eph. 2:11–19).

Because of the common themes in both passages, Paul is probably using *works* and *boasting* here in the same senses he does in Romans—that is, of Jews boasting before Gentiles of having privilege with God because of their observing the Mosaic Law. Paul says we are saved not in that manner but by faith—meaning faith in Christ. So in terms of salvation, no one, neither Jew nor Gentile, can boast of having a more privileged position with God. All people are saved on the same basis: through Christ.

After rejecting works of the Mosaic Law, the apostle turns our attention to the kind of works a Christian *should* be interested in—good works: "For we are his workmanship, created in Christ Jesus for good works, which God prepared beforehand, that we should walk in them" (Eph. 2:10).

The sense of what Paul is saying is that God himself has raised us up, Jews and Gentiles, to sit in the heavenly places because of Christ Jesus, for we received initial salvation as a gift. We obtained it by faith in Christ—which was expressed in baptism (Rom. 6:3–11)—not by works of obedience to the Mosaic Law. All of this is a grace, so neither Jewish nor Gentile Christians can boast over the other of having a superior relationship with God.

Instead, to paraphrase Ephesians 2:8–10, we Christians are the result of God's work, for he created us anew in the body of Christ so that we might do *good* works, the kind of works we *should be* concerned about, for God intended ahead of time for us to do them.

"Justified by Works and Not by Faith Alone"

As we've noted, the phrase "by faith alone" (Greek, *ek pisteos monon*) does appear once in the Bible—in James 2:24—where it is rejected: "You see that a man is justified by works and not by faith alone."

At first glance, this appears to contradict what St. Paul says about justification and works, but in actuality, it doesn't. The inspiration of Sacred Scripture guarantees that.

The question is: *Why* doesn't it contradict Paul?

Because Paul and James are using terms differently. Either *faith, works,* or *justify* must be being used in different senses. But which one or ones—and how?

A common proposal among some Protestants is that the term *faith* is being used differently in James. Specifically, it is sometimes proposed that he is referring to "dead faith." They treat James' statement that "faith apart from works is dead" (v. 26; see also v. 17) as referring to a specific kind of faith—"dead faith." James is thus taken as saying that if faith does not produce works it is "dead faith," and "dead faith" won't save us.

But reading the context shows that James is not using the phrase in this way. He is not defining the term *dead faith*—a term that does not even appear in the text. By saying that "faith apart from works is dead," he is stating a fact, not offering a definition.

The problem with the interpretation is demonstrated when we test it by substituting "dead faith" wherever the text mentions "faith." Here is the text itself:

James 2:14–26

14 What does it profit, my brethren, if a man says he has faith but has not works? Can his faith save him?

15 If a brother or sister is ill-clad and in lack of daily food,

16 and one of you says to them, "Go in peace, be warmed and filled," without giving them the things needed for the body, what does it profit?

17 So faith by itself, if it has no works, is dead.

18 But some one will say, "You have faith and I have works." Show me your faith apart from your works, and I by my works will show you my faith.

19 You believe that God is one; you do well. Even the demons believe—and shudder.

20 Do you want to be shown, you shallow man, that faith apart from works is barren?

21 Was not Abraham our father justified by works, when he offered his son Isaac upon the altar?

22 You see that faith was active along with his works, and faith was completed by works,

23 and the Scripture was fulfilled which says, "Abraham believed God, and it was reckoned to him as righteousness"; and he was called the friend of God.

24 You see that a man is justified by works and not by faith alone.

25 And in the same way was not also Rahab the harlot justified by works when she received the messengers and sent them out another way?

26 For as the body apart from the spirit is dead, so faith apart
    from works is dead.

On the reading that James means "dead faith" when he refers
to faith, people would be *boasting* of having dead faith (v. 14).
James would make the redundant statement that dead faith apart
from works is dead (vv. 17, 26) and offering to prove that dead
faith is barren (v. 20). He would be offering to show people his
dead faith by his works (v. 18) and commending people ("you
do well") for having dead faith (v. 19). Finally, he would be telling us that Abraham's dead faith was active with his works (v.
22) and that Abraham believed God with dead faith and it was
reckoned to him as righteousness (v. 23).

This interpretation is clearly in error.

Another interpretation holds that the faith in this passage is
mere intellectual faith. Supporters of this may appeal to James's
statement, "Even the demons believe—and shudder" (v. 19).
What kind of faith do demons have? *Mere intellectual assent.* They
intellectually assent to the truths of theology, but this is as far as
their faith goes.

This understanding is closer to the truth, but it still creates
problems—in fact, many of the same problems. People would be
boasting of having mere intellectual assent (v. 14). James would
be offering to show others his mere intellectual assent by his
works (v. 18). He would be commending people for having mere
intellectual assent (v. 19) and saying that Abraham's mere intellectual assent was active along with his works (v. 22), in which
case it wouldn't be *mere* any more. Finally, he would be saying
that Abraham's mere intellectual assent was reckoned to him as
righteousness, contradicting verse 23, which tells us that mere
intellectual assent is barren.

The "mere intellectual assent" solution thus also fails. So does
any solution that conceives of the faith James is talking about as bad
or inferior faith. This can be seen by going through the passage
and substituting "bad faith" and "inferior faith" wherever faith is
mentioned (the reader can do that for himself). Such solutions fail

because James *does not see anything wrong* with the faith he is talking about. The *faith* isn't the problem; its being *alone* is the problem.

To understand what kind of faith James has in mind, one must avoid the temptation to read something bad into it. This is where the "mere intellectual assent" solution errs. Its advocates correctly identify verse 19 as the key to understanding the faith being discussed, which *is* intellectual assent. The problems are created by adding the pejorative term *mere*.

Leave off *mere*, and the problems vanish. Someone can go around boasting that he intellectually assents to God's truth (v. 14), prompting James's need to show that intellectual assent without works is dead and barren (vv. 17, 20, 26). James could offer to show his intellectual assent by his works (v. 18). And he could commend a person for having intellectual assent (v. 19), while saying that even though the demons have it they still shudder at the prospect of God's wrath (v. 19). Finally, he can speak of how Abraham's intellectual assent was active with and completed by his works (v. 22), concluding that man is not justified by intellectual assent alone (v. 24).

James views intellectual assent as a good thing ("you do well," v. 19), but not as a thing that will save us by itself (vv. 14, 17, 20, 24, 26).

Having identified what James means by *faith*, we need to ask what he thinks needed to be added to it for justification. That will let us determine whether he contradicts Paul.

If he were of the view that one needs to do works of Torah in order to be justified, then he would contradict Paul—if they meant the same thing by justification. But it does not appear that this is what James has in mind by "works." He does not give examples of things, such as circumcision, that might be done in obedience to the Law of Moses, specifically. We also know from Acts that James *supported* the idea that Gentiles do not need to be circumcised in order to be saved (cf. Acts 15:13–19) so the idea that James means "works of Torah" is implausible.

Unfortunately, what James *does* mean by "works" is somewhat elusive. One possibility is that he means good works, such as acts of charity toward the needy. He writes:

What does it profit, my brethren, if a man says he has faith but
has not works? Can his faith save him? If a brother or sister is
ill-clad and in lack of daily food, and one of you says to them,
"Go in peace, be warmed and filled," without giving them
the things needed for the body, what does it profit? So faith
by itself, if it has no works, is dead (2:14–17).

This might make it look like he's talking about good works,
and he may be, but it isn't clear, because the analogy he's using
doesn't directly parallel saying "Go in peace, be warmed and
filled" with faith. Wishing someone well and having faith are
not the same thing, and so we must be open to the possibility
that the passage should be read like this: Just like having intellectual assent without acting on it is useless, so is wishing someone
well without doing anything to help him.

In other words: He may have picked the example of giving
food or clothing to the needy simply as a way of showing that
thought without action is of no practical value. He may not have
meant to provide an example of what he meant by "works." On
this view, he could have picked a different example, such as, "It
doesn't matter if you have a guaranteed money-making plan if
you never put it into action."

Further indication that he may not be thinking about standard good works, such as acts of charity, may be found in the
examples he goes on to name:

Do you want to be shown, you foolish fellow, that faith apart
from works is barren? Was not Abraham our father justified
by works, when he offered his son Isaac upon the altar? You
see that faith was active along with his works, and faith was
completed by works (2:20–22).

And in the same way was not also Rahab the harlot justified by works when she received the messengers and sent
them out another way? (2:25).

Here we have two clear examples of what James means by

works: Abraham offering Isaac on the altar and Rahab helping the spies escape (see Genesis 22, Joshua 2). Neither of these is a "good work" in the traditional sense. But they are both actions that flow from faith in God. Abraham was willing to do what God wanted because he believed in God, and Rahab helped the spies because she recognized that God was with the Hebrews, and she wanted herself and her family to survive.

James may mean no more than this when he refers to "works": acting in the appropriate ways based on one's belief in God.

A final hint that James may be thinking in this generic sense of "works" may be found in his final statement on the subject:

> For as the body apart from the spirit is dead, so faith apart from works is dead (2:26).

This is an analogy in which the body corresponds to faith and the spirit corresponds to works. It's always tricky trying to use an analogy to determine matters like this (as we saw when he discussed feeding and clothing the needy), but this analogy may be instructive for our purposes.

It is the spirit that makes the body alive and enables it to take action. Given what we've already seen, this may be the reason that he analogizes the body and the spirit to faith and works. If he is conceiving of "works" as generic actions that flow from one's faith, then the fact that the spirit enables a body to take action may be the point of contact between the two realms. The body is brought to completion—and life—by the spirit that gives it motion, just as faith is brought to completion—resulting in spiritual life—by the actions that flow from it.

If James means merely "actions appropriate to faith" by "works," then it is clear that he does not contradict Paul.

However, the text indicates that there is also another reason that he is not in contradiction to Paul: James is talking about a different kind of justification than Paul normally does.

James is discussing ongoing justification, or growth in righteousness. This is illustrated by his citing the example of

Abraham being justified when he offered Isaac on the altar (2:21). That was *years* after Abraham had been initially justified and, since Abraham was not repenting of a sin at the time, we know that it is a progressive, ongoing justification that is being discussed. Some call this sanctification, and sanctification does indeed involve the performance of good works and not intellectual assent alone.

It should be noted that this is also the understanding of the passage that the Council of Trent held. The *only time* the Council of Trent's *Decree on Justification* quotes James's statement that "a man is justified by works and not by faith alone" (2:24) is in reference to ongoing growth in righteousness.

The reference occurs in chapter 10 of the decree, "The Increase of the Justification Received." It reads:

> Having, therefore, *been thus justified* [i.e., having received initial justification] and made the friends and domestics of God, advancing from virtue to virtue, they are renewed, as the Apostle says, day by day, that is, mortifying the members of their flesh, and presenting them as instruments of justice unto sanctification, they, through the observance of the commandments of God and of the Church, faith cooperating with good works, *increase in that justice received through the grace of Christ and are further justified* [i.e., experience ongoing justification], as it is written: "He that is just, let him be justified still" (Rev. 22:11); and, "Be not afraid to be justified even to death" (Sir. 18:22); and again, "Do you see that by works a man is justified, and not by faith only?" (James 2:24).
>
> This increase of justice holy Church asks for when she prays: "Give unto us, O Lord, an increase of faith, hope and charity" (DJ 10).

The Council of Trent thus did not apply the statement that man is "justified by works and not by faith alone" to initial justification but to the ongoing growth in righteousness that occurs after initial justification, through cooperation with God's grace.

Indeed, this passage could not apply to initial justification, because Catholic theology holds that it is impossible for man to do anything meritorious prior to justification. The Council Fathers at Trent stated:

> [W]e are therefore said to be justified gratuitously, because none of those things that precede justification, whether faith or works, merit the grace of justification.
>
> "For, if by grace, it is not now by works, otherwise," as the Apostle says, "grace is no more grace" (Rom. 11:6) (DJ 8).

7

Justification in Catholic Teaching

A key document explaining the Church's teaching on justification was issued at the sixth session of the Council of Trent
(1545–1564). Known as the *Decree on Justification*, this document
consists of a set of sixteen short chapters followed by a series of
canons excommunicating the teachers of various false views.

The Council first deals with fallen man's need for justification and the provision that God has made for fulfilling this need
(chapters 1–2). Then there is a group of chapters that deals with
the initial justification that the believer receives when he first
becomes a Christian (chapters 3–9). The Council then deals
with the ongoing process of justification, (chapter 10). It turns
to the possibility of failing to persevere in God's grace, of losing one's justification, and of subsequently regaining it (chapters
11–15). And finally, it takes up the issue of how good works will
be rewarded in the next life (chapter 16).

As we've discussed previously, justification can be divided
into a number of stages: first, there is an *initial justification* that
occurs at conversion; second, there is a *progressive justification* that
occurs as a person grows in righteousness; and lastly there is a
final justification that occurs on the last day. There is also the possibility of a loss of justification and a subsequent *re-justification*,
which occurs when a believer returns to the Faith. We will now
look at what Trent teaches concerning each of these.

Before Justification

Original Sin

The first chapter of the *Decree on Justification* deals with the doctrine of original sin, stating that "all men had lost innocence in

the prevarication of Adam, having become unclean, and, as the Apostle says, by nature children of wrath [Eph. 2:3]." It notes that "they were so far the servants of sin and under the power of the devil and of death, that not only the Gentiles by the force of nature, but not even the Jews by the very letter of the law of Moses, were able to be liberated or to rise therefrom, though free will, weakened as it was in its powers and downward bent, was by no means extinguished in them."

Original sin is a term that has different meanings in different theological circles. In Catholic circles, it refers to the deprivation of righteousness in which we are born. In Protestant circles, it normally refers to more than this (e.g., to both the deprivation of righteousness and to the disordered desires that are caused by our damaged nature).

Both groups agree that we are born with a lack of righteousness and a tangled mess of sinful inclinations; they simply label these differently. Protestants lump them both together under the term *original sin*, while Catholics call the lack of guilt original sin itself, and the sinful inclinations they call the *stain* of original sin.

This is not something the two groups need to fight over. The term *original sin* is a theological term, not a biblical one. It does not appear in the Bible and so gains its meaning from what theologians give it. If different theologians use it differently, that is not cause for strife. It simply means that we need to be aware of how other Christians use it. This is thus a case where St. Paul's warnings against getting in fights about words apply (cf. 2 Tim. 2:14, 1 Tim. 6:4).

The Coming of Christ

Because of mankind's fallen condition, we could not rescue ourselves, and God himself intervened. Chapter 2 of the *Decree* thus deals with the coming of Christ, "who had both before the law and during the time of the law been announced and promised to many of the holy fathers, that he might redeem the Jews who were under the Law, and that the Gentiles who followed not after justice [righteousness] might attain to justice [righteousness], and that all men might receive the adoption of sons."

The Council notes that Christ died "for our sins, and not for our sins only, but also for those of the whole world (1 John 2:2)." He thus made it possible for us to be justified.

RECEIVING RIGHTEOUSNESS: INITIAL JUSTIFICATION

Being Justified

Chapter 3 of the *Decree on Justification* notes that, although Christ's death made salvation possible for all men, not all men receive the benefit of his death. All men inherited original sin by being born in the line of Adam, and, if they are to be justified, they must be born anew into the line of the second Adam, Jesus Christ.

The Council explains, "[I]f they were not born again in Christ, they would never be justified, since in that new birth there is bestowed upon them, through the merit of His passion, the grace by which they are made just."

Chapter 4 of the decree explains the nature of justification, defining it as "a translation from that state in which man is born a child of the first Adam, to the state of grace and of the adoption of the sons of God through the second Adam, Jesus Christ, our Savior."

The Council states:

This translation however cannot, since promulgation of the Gospel, be effected except through the laver of regeneration [i.e., baptism] or its desire, as it is written: "Unless a man be born again of water and the Holy Ghost, he cannot enter into the kingdom of God" (John 3:5).

Note that the Council acknowledges that justification can be received through the desire of baptism (see chapter 9 for more on this subject).

Chapter 5 of the decree notes that, in the case of adults who
become Christians and are baptized, God must first do a work of
grace in their hearts. The Council thus rejects the Pelagian and
Semi-Pelagian heresies, which held that men could turn to God
initially without needing God's grace. Salvation was thus seen as
a matter of man's initiative rather than God's.

By contrast, the Council teaches:

> The beginning of that justification must proceed from the
> predisposing grace of God through Jesus Christ, that is, from
> His vocation, whereby, without any merits on their part, they
> are called; that they who by sin had been cut off from God,
> may be disposed through His quickening and helping grace
> to convert themselves to their own justification by freely as-
> senting to and cooperating with that grace; so that, while
> God touches the heart of man through the illumination of
> the Holy Ghost, man himself neither does absolutely nothing
> while receiving that inspiration, since he can also reject it, nor
> yet is he able by his own free will and without the grace of
> God to move himself to justice in His sight.

The sixth chapter describes the manner in which adults are
converted and prepared for justification:

> They are disposed to that justice when, aroused and aided by
> divine grace, receiving faith by hearing, they are moved free-
> ly toward God, believing to be true what has been divinely
> revealed and promised, especially that the sinner is justified
> by God by his grace, through the redemption that is in Christ
> Jesus; and when, understanding themselves to be sinners,
> they, by turning themselves from the fear of divine justice, by
> which they are salutarily (i.e., beneficially) aroused, to con-
> sider the mercy of God, are raised to hope, trusting that God
> will be propitious to them for Christ's sake; and they begin
> to love Him as the fountain of all justice, and on that account
> are moved against sin by a certain hatred and detestation, that

is, by that repentance that must be performed before baptism; finally, when they resolve to receive baptism, to begin a new life and to keep the commandments of God.

They are thus, by God's grace, led to repentance from sin, faith in God and in Christ, and the sacrament of baptism.

The Nature of Justification

Chapter 7 of the decree fleshes out the definition of justification and provides an explanation of its causes.

Previously, the Council had defined justification in terms of being a translation from the state of being a child of Adam to "the state of grace and of the adoption of the sons of God through the second Adam, Jesus Christ." Now the Council expands on this, explaining that justification "is not only a remission of sins but also the sanctification and renewal of the inward man through the voluntary reception of the grace and gifts whereby an unjust man becomes just and from being an enemy becomes a friend, that he may be an heir according to hope of life everlasting."

This is different from the way many Protestants conceive of justification. They often understand it as God bestowing on us a legal righteousness in a way that results in him forgiving our sins but that does not involve a sanctification or "making holy" of the individual. It is common in Protestant circles for sanctification to be conceived of as strictly separate from and subsequent to justification.

Both groups acknowledge that God both forgives sins and makes us holy, but the way the term *justification* is used in Catholic circles it includes "not only a remission of sins but also the sanctification and renewal of the inward man"—what St. Paul refers to as becoming a "new creation" (2 Cor. 5:17, Gal. 6:15).

Some Protestants accuse Catholics of "confusing" justification and sanctification by grouping the two together in this fashion.

While it is true that the terms *justify* and *sanctify* convey different notions (being made righteous and being made holy, respectively), we have already seen that there is a great deal of flexibility in how the biblical authors use terms connected to salvation (see chapters 2 and 3).

In fact, as we will see, the Bible does not draw a rigid line between the concepts of justification and sanctification. Consider the following passage from Romans:

> What shall we say then? Are we to continue in sin that grace may abound? By no means! How can we who died to sin still live in it? Do you not know that all of us who have been baptized into Christ Jesus were baptized into his death? We were buried therefore with him by baptism into death, so that as Christ was raised from the dead by the glory of the Father, we too might walk in newness of life.
>
> For if we have been united with him in a death like his, we shall certainly be united with him in a resurrection like his. We know that our old self was crucified with him so that the sinful body might be destroyed, and we might no longer be enslaved to sin. For he who has died is freed from sin (Rom. 6:1–7).

At the end of this passage, Paul states that he who has died has been "freed" from sin, and the context is obviously one of sanctification. Paul is discussing why we must not "continue in sin," how we have "died to sin," and how we must not "still live in it." He explains that "our old self was crucified with him" so that "the sinful body might be destroyed" and we might "no longer be enslaved to sin." It is on this basis that Paul says, "he who has died is freed from sin." The context here is so obviously one of sanctification that every modern translation renders the last sentence of the passage as saying that one who has died through baptism into Christ's death has been "freed" from sin.

But that is not what the passage says in Greek. Instead of the word *freed*, the Greek text says that he "has been justified" (*dedikaiotai*; a perfect passive form of *dikaioo*, "justify"). What Paul actually wrote was, "He who has died has been *justified* from sin." Yet, because of the context of sanctification, modern translators render this "freed."

The rationale for this translation is strengthened when one realizes that there is a parallel later in the same chapter where Paul does actually use the Greek word for "free" (*eleutheroo*). After having noted in Romans 6:6–7 that we should "no longer be enslaved to sin. For he who has died *has been justified* from sin," he states in 6:17–18 that, although "you who were once slaves of sin have become obedient from the heart . . . and, *having been set free* [*eleutherothentes*] from sin, have become slaves of righteousness."

We therefore see that, in Paul's thought, being *justified* from sin can include being *freed* from sin through sanctification. For Paul, there is not the rigid division between justification and sanctification that many suppose.

There are passages where Paul uses the terms *justify* and *sanctify* in different senses, but the point is that for him these terms are fluid. We have already seen that they apply to many different events and periods in the believer's life—to things past, present, and future—and they also overlap. "To be made righteous" and "to be made holy" can be the same thing, as in Romans 6:7.

As we saw in chapter 2, a growing number of Protestant Bible scholars recognize that justification is a process and thus that it is linked to the sanctification that occurs over the course of the Christian life. Contemporary scholars who hold this position include James D.G. Dunn, E.P. Sanders, and Dale Moody. A number of the early Reformers also recognized this, including even Martin Luther himself.

The Causes of Justification

In chapter 7 of the *Decree on Justification*, the Council also offers a discussion of various causes of justification. The ones it treats are the *final* cause, the *efficient* cause, the *meritorious* cause, the *instrumental* cause, and the *formal* cause.

This way of classifying different types of causes has often been used by philosophers to consider different aspects of something that happens. In this case, the Council is considering different aspects of how justification comes about.

The final cause is the ultimate purpose or goal of the event. Here, the Council identifies "the glory of God and of Christ and life everlasting" as the final cause of our justification. This means that we are justified so that God and Christ are glorified and so that we may have eternal life.

The efficient cause is the thing that brings about the event. The Council identifies the efficient cause of justification as "the merciful God who washes and sanctifies gratuitously, signing and anointing with the Holy Spirit of promise, who is the pledge of our inheritance." This means that we do not bring about our own justification. We are not capable of doing so. Instead, God gratuitously washes and sanctifies us, as well as sealing and anointing us with the Holy Spirit.

The meritorious cause (a category not typically used in philosophy, but relevant here theologically) is the basis on which the efficient cause acts—the thing that merits the action. The Council identifies the meritorious cause of justification as "His most beloved only begotten, our Lord Jesus Christ, who, when we were enemies, for the exceeding charity wherewith he loved us, merited for us justification by His most holy Passion on the wood of the cross and made satisfaction for us to God the Father." This means that we do not merit our own justification. In fact, prior to justification, we have no merits at all. Instead, Jesus Christ merited justification on our behalf by his death on the cross and the satisfaction this made for our sins before God.

The instrumental cause is the instrument that the efficient cause uses to bring about the event. The Council identifies the instrumental cause of justification as "the sacrament of baptism, which is the sacrament of faith, without which no man was ever justified finally." This means that God uses baptism to bring about our justification. The Council also notes that baptism is "the sacrament of faith," for it requires faith in the case of adults. It also stresses the necessity of baptism, though it has already noted that justification can be achieved through the desire for baptism, as in the case of catechumens.

Finally, the formal cause is the nature of the thing itself. In this case of justification, this means that *nature* of the justice or righteousness that one receives in justification. On this subject, the Council states that "the single formal cause is the justice of God."

This requires a bit of unpacking. The fact that the Council refers to "the *single* formal cause" means that it is rejecting a theory that had been floated that there might be *two* formal causes of justification. According to this theory of "dual justification," *one* formal cause of justification was God imputing to us Christ's own righteousness, resulting in the forgiveness of our sins, and *another* formal cause of justification was a gift of righteousness that inhered in our souls, accomplishing sanctification.

The Council rejected this view, indicating that our justification has only a single formal cause, which accomplishes *both* of the effects in question—i.e., both the forgiveness of sins and inward sanctification.

The Council identified this cause as "the justice of God." It explained that this is not the righteousness "by which He Himself is just, but that by which He makes us just."

This can be a bit confusing. The righteousness that God has is infinite. Since God possesses all possible perfections in the highest degree, it could not be otherwise. Yet we are finite beings, and any righteousness we could have must be finite. Therefore, we need to distinguish between the kind of righteousness that God has and the kind that he gives us as a gift. By his grace, we are able to share in some of his attributes (2 Peter 1:4), such as power, knowledge, and holiness, but only to a finite degree. We will never become omnipotent, omniscient, or infinitely holy.

Related to this is a view often advocated in Protestant circles, according to which we receive Christ's own personal righteousness when we are justified. In this view, when we are justified God treats us "just like Christ." It is even sometimes said that God looks at us and "sees Christ instead."

This view does not fit the biblical data.

First, if God simply saw us as Christ, if he gave us Christ's own personal righteousness, then we would all be rewarded equally in heaven. We would all have the exact same level of righteous as each other (i.e., Christ's level of righteousness). Since Scripture clearly teaches that there will be different degrees of reward in heaven (1 Cor. 3:12–15), we must conclude that we will have different degrees of righteousness. We will be free of any unrighteousness—by virtue of our sins having been taken away—but we will not all share the same degree of positive righteousness before God.

Second, if we all received Christ's own personal righteousness, then we would all be rewarded equally with Christ. We would all have exactly the same level of glory as our Savior. But Scripture indicates that we will not. For example, Scripture teaches that because of Jesus' work on the cross, God gave him "the name above every name" (Phil. 2:8–9, Eph. 1:20–21). But logic dictates that we can't *all* have "the name above every name." That is Christ's alone.

Similarly, Scripture states that Christ has the preeminence in all things (Col. 1:18). But if we all received a level of glory equal to him, then he would no longer be preeminent in all things.

Finally, there are simply no verses in Scripture that state that we receive Christ's own personal level of righteousness. This can be surprising to some in the Protestant community, because they have so often heard the theory that we are given Christ's own personal righteousness that they assume Scripture teaches it. But there are no passages anywhere in the New Testament that state we are given Christ's own personal level righteousness.

There are passages (such as Rom. 5:17–19) that state we are given the gift of righteousness and made righteous on account of Christ, but these do not say that we receive Christ's personal level of righteousness. This means that the proposition does not meet the *sola scriptura* or "by Scripture alone" test that is used in Protestant theology.

Even apart from this, the idea that we are made just as righteous as God or as Christ in justification does not fit the biblical data. We may be given a righteousness that is just as *pure* as that of God and of Christ, in the sense that all of our sins are removed, but we do not have the same infinite *degree* of righteousness that they do.

The righteousness that we receive in justification is thus a gift to us that is distinct from their own, personal righteousness.

Three Kinds of Righteousness

The basic meaning of the term *justify* (Latin, *iustificare*, Greek, *dikaioo*) is "to make righteous" or "to make just."

We have noted in passing that Protestants often conceive of the righteousness we receive in justification as *legal* righteousness (sometimes called "forensic" righteousness), relying on a courtroom metaphor in which God declares a sinner innocent or righteous in the eyes of the court.

We have also seen that, in Catholic circles, the term is used to refer to something more than this. Thus the Council of Trent defined the concept of justification as including a sanctification and renewal of the inner man.

This is a point that can be easily misunderstood since, in Protestant circles, the term *sanctification* is often used to refer to the process by which God purifies our behavior over the course of the Christian life. In other words, sanctification is understood in terms of how we behave—a *behavioral* righteousness.

This is not how the term is used in Trent's *Decree on Justification*. Instead, Trent is referring to an objectively real holiness that God gives us at the time of justification. This may be referred to as a *metaphysical* or *ontological* holiness. Metaphysics (sometimes called ontology) is the study of what is ultimately real, and the idea here is that when we sin, it changes the condition of our souls in an objective, real way by depriving them of holiness. This is reflected in the biblical images depicting sin as dirty, unclean, or defiling.

But when God justifies us, he changes this and gives us the objective holiness that we had been deprived of due to our sins. This inward transformation is reflected in passages like the famous line in Isaiah, "though your sins are like scarlet, they shall be as white as snow; though they are red like crimson, they shall become like wool" (Isa. 1:18)—what was previously defiled is now clean and pure.

Catholic theologian Michael Schmaus explains:

Rightly understood, the Tridentine doctrine that the justice of God alone, through which he makes us just, is the formal cause of justification contains nothing which would contradict the statement that God by his creative word takes away sin, in the deepest metaphysical sense of sin as a guilt interiorly clinging to man, so that he transforms man interiorly—again in a deep metaphysical sense. This transformation consists in a resemblance to God which is produced in man. Thus the sinner becomes a "saint" (or "holy") not in the sense that he is no longer the one who has committed the sin or is no longer tempted to sin, but rather in the sense that he reflects in his inner being the holiness of God (*Dogma 6: Justification and the Last Things*, 71).

Understanding that Trent is referring to a different type of sanctification here can help clear away some difficulties.

For example, it is obvious to all that, when a person is justified, he still remains tempted and prone to sin. He is not completely *behaviorally* sanctified. But that is not what is being claimed. In justification, God takes away "the whole of that which belongs to the essence of sin" (Trent, *Decree on Original Sin* 5)—all that belongs to the *objective, metaphysical* change that occurred in us due to sin—and replaces it with an objectively real holiness or righteousness that comes from him and that reflects his own holiness and righteousness.

Similarly, understanding this resolves a difficulty that would otherwise be encountered in chapter 10 of the decree, which deals with growth in justification. If justification is understood simply as a bestowal of legal righteousness, so that a sinner is declared innocent, how could one grow in righteousness? Understood that way, justification would seem to be an all-or-nothing thing, for a person may be declared either innocent or guilty. If the former has occurred, it can seem that there is no room for further growth in righteousness.

But when one recognizes that a different type of righteousness is being discussed, the matter becomes clear. It is true that God forgives our sins and declares us innocent, so we are legally righteous before him as a result of justification. But he also gives us a gift of objective holiness—commonly identified in Catholic theology as sanctifying grace, the grace that makes us holy before him—and this gift can vary in quantity. We will never have the infinite, objective holiness that God does, but we can receive a gift of objective, metaphysical holiness from him that can grow over time.

In other words, righteousness is not simply a matter of quality; it is a matter of quantity as well. It operates on more than one axis. In justification, we are given a righteousness that is pure, because it comes from God, but the quantity we have of that righteousness can grow over time.

This is what Trent means when it says that in justification we receive righteousness from God with which we "are renewed in the spirit of our mind, and not only are we reputed but we are truly called and are just, receiving justice within us, each one according to his own measure, which the Holy Ghost distributes to everyone as He wills, and according to each one's disposition and cooperation."

Imputed versus Infused Righteousness

Sometimes a distinction is drawn between the common Protestant understanding that justification involves righteousness being "imputed" to us and the common Catholic understanding that it is "infused" into us. Neither "impute" nor "infuse" are common terms today, and so a word about their meaning is in order:

- Imputation is an act by which something is *attributed* to someone, and in the legal/courtroom understanding of justification, the idea is that God attributes to us a legal righteousness.
- Infusion, by contrast, conveys the idea of pouring. The idea, in this context, is that God pours righteousness into us rather than merely attributing it to us.

These two images do not need to be understood as in opposition to each other.

The image of infusion is drawn from the symbolism of baptism and passages in which the Holy Spirit (Acts 2:17, 18, 33, 10:45, Titus 3:5–6) and God's love (Rom. 5:5) are said to be poured out upon us or into our hearts. The essential content of the image is the fact that God communicates his invisible graces to us. While Scripture uses the image of pouring for this, the graces themselves are intangible and are not literally poured through space like liquid.

While the degree to which the New Testament understands justification in terms of a courtroom metaphor can be questioned, it does at times use court imagery (notably for the final judgment), and one can envision justification as occurring in a courtroom setting.

The problem, from a Catholic perspective, would be if one were to stop there and hold that God gives one *only* legal righteousness without *also* making the person actually, metaphysically righteous. The result would be a legal fiction, in which God treats a person as righteous who is actually still wicked.

There is another way of looking at the matter, however. God's word has creative power. It is the means by which he formed the world (Gen. 1:3, Ps. 33:6, Isa. 55:11, John 1:1–3). It is thus possible to understand God as imputing righteousness to a person and, by the creative power of his word, thereby *making* the person actually, metaphysically righteous.

Or one may look at it the other way around: By his grace God *makes* the person actually, metaphysically righteous and then declares the person legally righteous.

Either way, the two images do not need to be understood in opposition to each other.

The Virtues

Chapter 7 of the *Decree on Justification* also notes the connection between the act of justification and the reception of the three theological virtues of faith, hope, and charity:

In that justification of the sinner, when, by the merit of the most holy passion, the charity of God is poured forth by the Holy Ghost in the hearts (Rom. 5:5) of those who are justified and inheres in them; whence man through Jesus Christ, in whom he is ingrafted, receives in that justification, together with the remission of sins, all these infused at the same time, namely, faith, hope and charity.

For faith, unless hope and charity be added to it, neither unites man perfectly with Christ nor makes him a living member of His body.

For which reason it is most truly said that faith without works is dead (James 2:17, 20) and of no profit, and in Christ Jesus neither circumcision avails anything nor uncircumcision, but faith that works by charity (Gal. 5:6, 6:15).

Trent thus makes the point that, in justification, one receives the three theological virtues, which are necessary for salvation.

Justified by Faith and Freely

In chapter 8 of the decree, the Council adds to notes about the sense in which we are justified by faith (Rom. 5:1) and freely or "as a gift" (Rom. 3:24).

Concerning the first, it says that:

We are therefore said to be justified by faith, because faith is the beginning of human salvation, the foundation and root of all justification, without which it is impossible to please God (Heb. 11:6) and to come to the fellowship of His sons.

Here the Council again stresses the importance of faith for justification. It also contains an implicit warning against false understandings of the role of faith, which would imply that charity and hope are not also necessary, as it stated in the previous chapter.

Concerning the gratuity of justification, the Council states:

We are therefore said to be justified gratuitously, because none of those things that precede justification, whether faith or works, merit the grace of justification. "For, if by grace, it is not now by works, otherwise," as the Apostle says, "grace is no more grace" (Rom. 11:6).

Here the Council warns against a common misunderstanding of Catholic theology: the idea that we must do things like good works to merit entrance into the state of justification. This is not the case for, as the Council says, "none of those things which precede justification, whether faith or works" merit it.

It is, in fact, intrinsically impossible (as we shall see later in our discussion of Trent's chapter 16) for an unjustified person to merit justification. This makes explicit what was taught in chapter 7: Christ, not us, is the meritorious cause of our justification.

False Confidence of Justification

In chapter 9 of the decree, the Council responds to certain themes that were common in Protestant preaching of the day and that can still be found in our own day.

These have to do with the confidence that we have received God's grace of justification. According to some, the fact that our sins are remitted gratuitously for the sake of Christ meant that all we had to do was be confident of this fact and this alone would save us. The Council indicates that this is not the case:

> But though it is necessary to believe that sins neither are remitted nor ever have been remitted except gratuitously by divine mercy for Christ's sake, yet it must not be said that sins are forgiven or have been forgiven to anyone who boasts of his confidence and certainty of the remission of his sins, resting on that alone.

Worse yet, some claimed that unless you were convinced, without any doubt, that you were justified, you weren't. Further, it was claimed that unless you had this certainty, you were insulting God by casting doubt on his promises and on the work of Christ. This kind of preaching could, and did, cause people to panic, for they felt that if they had the slightest, momentary doubt of their salvation, they were in fact damned. Thus the Council stated:

> Moreover, it must not be maintained, that they who are truly justified must needs, without any doubt whatever, convince themselves that they are justified, and that no one is absolved from sins and justified except he that believes with certainty that he is absolved and justified, and that absolution and justification are effected by this faith alone, as if he who does not believe this, doubts the promises of God and the efficacy of the death and resurrection of Christ.

Finally, the Council taught a balanced view that, while we may be confident of God's mercy and promises, we also can have reason for doubting ourselves:

> For as no pious person ought to doubt the mercy of God, the merit of Christ and the virtue and efficacy of the sacraments, so each one, when he considers himself and his own weakness and indisposition, may have fear and apprehension concerning his own grace, since no one can know with the certainty of faith, which cannot be subject to error, that he has obtained the grace of God.

Sometimes this has been misrepresented as saying that Catholics can have *no* assurance of salvation, but this is not what the text says. The Council merely said that one cannot have "the certainty of faith, which cannot be subject to error." One may, indeed, have assurance that God is working in one's life and that one has received the grace of justification (1 John 3:19–24). Assurance is one thing, but infallible certitude is something that the limitations of human knowledge and the possibility of self-deception prevent us from having in this life (Jer. 17:9).

Growing in Righteousness: Progressive Justification

Chapter 10 of the decree deals with the ongoing growth in justification to which we referred above (cf. "Three Kinds of Righteousness"). The Council states:

> Having, therefore, been thus justified and made the friends and domestics of God (Eph. 2:9), advancing from virtue to virtue (Ps. 84:7), they are renewed, as the Apostle says, day by day (2 Cor. 4:16), that is, mortifying the members (Col. 3:5) of their flesh, and presenting them as instruments of justice unto sanctification (Rom. 6:13, 19), they, through the observance of the commandments of God and of the Church, faith cooperating with good works, increase in that justice received through the grace of Christ and are further justified.

The fact that this justification occurs after initial justification is indicated both by the word "further" and by the fact that the Council speaks of the believer already "having . . . been thus justified."

Here we are again talking about a growth in objective, metaphysical righteousness (not behavioral righteousness), as in chapter 7 of the decree.

The means by which this growth in righteousness is accomplished are "faith cooperating with good works" through "the observance of the commandments of God and the Church." The latter represent authoritative rules for conduct made by the authority that Christ gave his Church in the power of the keys and the authority to bind and loose (cf. Matt. 16:19, 18:18).

While this language might make some Protestants uncomfortable, this should be due to it being an unfamiliar way of putting things rather than a disagreement in substance.

The New Testament does expect us to cooperate with God's grace after initial justification and do good works. In fact, St. Paul specifically says that we are "created in Christ Jesus for good works, which God prepared beforehand, that we should walk in them" (Eph. 2:10). We are similarly expected to obey

God's commandments (1 John 2:3–4), including those lawfully given by Church leaders (Heb. 13:17). As a result of behaving righteously, in cooperation with God's grace, we may be said to grow in righteousness—or, to translate the key term the other way, to grow in justification and be "further justified."

It is instructive to note that it is in connection with this ongoing form of justification that Trent quotes James 2:24—"Do you see that by works a man is justified, and not by faith only?" Trent does not quote this text with respect to initial justification for, as it has said, nothing that precedes justification, "whether faith or works," is capable of meriting it. However, it makes sense to quote the text in regard to progressive justification because, in its original context, James applies the saying to Abraham's sacrifice of Isaac, which occurred in Genesis 22, long after Abraham began to walk with God in faith in Genesis 12 (cf. Heb. 11:1–2, 8). Abraham's willingness to sacrifice his son thus represented his subsequent growth in righteousness, not his initial justification.

Finally in this chapter, the Council states: "This increase of justice holy Church asks for when she prays: 'Give unto us, O Lord, an increase of faith, hope, and charity.'" Faith, hope, and charity are divine gifts that can be received in greater degrees as we cooperate with God's grace, and so is righteousness or justification.

LOSING AND REGAINING RIGHTEOUSNESS: RE-JUSTIFICATION

Observing the Commandments

Chapter 11 of the decree deals with the ongoing requirement to keep the commandments of God. This chapter responds to several of the more extreme claims being made at the time (and subsequently) in some Protestant preaching.

One claim that was sometimes made was that the justified man does not need to keep the commandments. Sometimes this was claimed on the grounds that it is impossible to do so. The Council rejects these claims:

But no one, however much justified, should consider himself exempt from the observance of the commandments; no one should use that rash statement, once forbidden by the Fathers under anathema, that the observance of the commandments of God is impossible for one that is justified.

The graces that God gives us in justification are such that we *can* avoid mortal sin, and to illustrate this the Council notes several passages of Scripture:

His commandments are not heavy (1 John 5:3), and his yoke is sweet and burden light (Matt. 11:30). For they who are the sons of God love Christ, but they who love Him, keep His commandments, as He Himself testifies (John 14:23); which, indeed, with the divine help they can do.

Avoiding mortal sin does not mean living in sinless perfection, however. The Council notes:

For though during this mortal life, men, however holy and just, fall at times into at least light and daily sins, which are also called venial, they do not on that account cease to be just, for that petition of the just, "forgive us our trespasses" (Matt. 6:12), is both humble and true; for which reason the just ought to feel themselves the more obliged to walk in the way of justice, for being now freed from sin and made servants of God (Rom. 6:18, 22), they are able, living soberly, justly, and godly (Titus 2:12), to proceed onward through Jesus Christ, by whom they have access unto this grace (Rom. 5:1–2).

Trent indicates that God will give those who are justified the graces needed to avoid mortal sin unless they deliberately turn their backs on him:

For God does not forsake those who have been once justified by His grace, unless He be first forsaken by them.

Some in the Protestant community argued that it was impossible, even after justification, to avoid mortal sin and that this showed that avoiding mortal sin was unnecessary for salvation. Only faith was required. Since it has rejected the premise that God will not give the graces needed to avoid mortal sin to the believer, the Council rejects the conclusion of the argument:

> Wherefore, no one ought to flatter himself with faith alone, thinking that by faith alone he is made an heir and will obtain the inheritance, even though he suffer not with Christ, that he may be also glorified with him (Rom. 8:17).

To commit mortal sin is to reject repentance and to cast charity from one's soul. This endangers one's soul because, as we have seen, repentance is a requirement to come to God and be justified, and it is faith "working by charity" (Gal. 5:6) that unites us to God.

Although Trent does not quote this passage, we also know of the possibility of substantively keeping the commandments, because the apostle Paul tells us:

> No temptation has overtaken you that is not common to man. God is faithful, and he will not let you be tempted beyond your strength, but with the temptation will also provide the way of escape, that you may be able to endure it (1 Cor. 10:13).

The Council does, however, quote from the previous chapter of the letter, where St. Paul tells his readers (who are Christian and thus who have been justified):

> Do you not know that in a race all the runners compete, but only one receives the prize? So run that you may obtain it.
> I do not run aimlessly, I do not box as one beating the air; but I pommel my body and subdue it, lest after preaching to others I myself should be disqualified (1 Cor. 9:24, 26–27).

The Council also rejects several other claims being made in Protestant circles—namely, that every good work involves at least venial sin, that it merits eternal punishment, and that it is sinful to obey God with a view to obtaining an eternal reward:

> [I]t is clear that they are opposed to the orthodox teaching of religion who maintain that the just man sins, venially at least, in every good work; or, what is more intolerable, that he merits eternal punishment; and they also who assert that the just sin in all works, if, in order to arouse their sloth and to encourage themselves to run the race, they, in addition to this, that above all God may be glorified, have in view also the eternal reward.

As to all actions of the righteous man involving at least venial sins, there are no biblical verses that say this. When proposals are read in their original context, it invariably turns out that they are talking about "the wicked" in contrast to "the righteous" or they are being misread. The proposal thus, even from a Protestant perspective, should be ruled out on grounds of *sola scriptura*.

We have already looked at passages that illustrate the possibility of avoiding mortal sin, which indicate that not every action involves a sin meriting eternal punishment.

Further, there are multiple passages that indicate that our actions in response to God's grace are actually pleasing to him. Paul tells the Philippians that the gifts they sent are "a fragrant offering, a sacrifice acceptable and pleasing to God" (Phil. 4:18). Similarly, the author of Hebrews states, "Do not neglect to do good and to share what you have, for such sacrifices are pleasing to God," and that God will "equip you with everything good that you may do his will, working in you that which is pleasing in his sight, through Jesus Christ" (Heb. 13:16, 21).

Finally, it is clear from Scripture that one does not sin when one obeys God in hope of an eternal reward. One text indicating this, which the Council cites, is Hebrews 11:26, which states that Moses "considered abuse suffered for the Christ greater wealth than the treasures of Egypt, for he looked to the reward." There are, however, many other texts indicating the same thing (cf. Rom. 2:6–10, 2 Cor. 9:6–10, Gal. 6:6–10). Among the most notable is Jesus' cautionary statement, "For what does it profit a man, to gain the whole world and forfeit his life?" (Mark 8:36), where "life" is understood as eternal life (cf. Mark 8:35).

Predestination and Perseverance

In chapter 12 of the decree, the Council takes the subject of mortal sin and rejects two errors that were being proposed in conjunction with the doctrine of predestination. According to some in the Protestant community, Christians could have certainty (note the extreme claim: it's not a relative or human certainty but an absolute one) that they are among the predestined—that is, that they are among those who will certainly be in heaven.

If this were possible, given the reality of mortal sin, one of two things would follow: People who knew themselves to be among the predestined either would not be able to commit mortal sin or, if they did commit it, they would be assured of the fact that they would repent and be reconciled before they die.

The Council rejects both of these as being beyond our ability to know, though it does acknowledge that God could reveal to a person by way of private revelation that he will make it to heaven, as in the case of some saints.

The Council states:

> No one, moreover, so long as he lives this mortal life, ought in regard to the sacred mystery of divine predestination, so far presume as to state with absolute certainty that he is among the number of the predestined, as if it were true that the one justified either cannot sin any more, or, if he does sin, that he ought to promise himself an assured repentance.
>
> For except by special revelation, it cannot be known whom God has chosen to Himself.

Chapter 13 of the decree deals with the gift of perseverance, a concept related to predestination. According to various Scripture passages, it is necessary to persevere to the end in order to be saved (cf. Matt. 10:22, 24:13). Since our salvation is a product of God's grace, this perseverance is recognized as a gift of God.

In view of later magisterial statements about God offering the possibility of salvation to all men (see chapter 9), one might conclude that God at least offers the grace needed for final perseverance to all men, though whether or not they accept this gift is a matter determined by their free will.

However, because our free will is involved, and because we cannot know our future free will actions with certainty, the Council holds that no one should promise himself the gift of final perseverance "with an absolute certainty, though all ought to place and repose the firmest hope in God's help. For God, unless men themselves fail in His grace, as he has begun a good work, so will he perfect it, working to will and to accomplish" (Phil. 1:6, 2:13).

Note, again, a claim of "absolute certainty" is to be avoided, not a claim of merely being confident. Indeed, the Council stresses that one can have confidence that God will bring the work of salvation in us to completion unless we refuse his grace.

Chapter 14 of the decree deals with what happens if we do fall into mortal sin. The Council states:

> Those who through sin have forfeited and received grace of justification, can again be justified when, moved by God, they exert themselves to obtain through the sacrament of penance the recovery, by the merits of Christ, of the grace lost.
>
> For this manner of justification is restoration for those fallen, which the holy Fathers have aptly called a second plank after the shipwreck of grace lost.

Having lost the state of justification, it is possible to regain it, to be re-justified, and Christ himself has provided the means through the sacrament of confession. The Council notes:

For on behalf of those who fall into sins after baptism, Christ Jesus instituted the sacrament of penance when He said: "Receive ye the Holy Ghost, whose sins you shall forgive, they are forgiven them, and whose sins you shall retain, they are retained" (John 20:22–23).

As with baptism, the sacramental reception of confession is not an absolute, and the Council notes that sacramental confession is required "at least in desire," indicating the possibility of reconciliation through perfect contrition when the sacrament is not available (cf. CCC 1451–1453). The Council states that the eternal punishment of sin is "together with the guilt, remitted either by the sacrament or by the desire of the sacrament."

It also notes, however, that the temporal punishment of sin is not always wholly remitted (see chapter 5) and notes the role of penance in the Christian life (see chapter 4).

In chapter 15 of the decree, the Council rejects the view of Luther that the only sin that would cost one salvation is the loss of faith itself (here called infidelity). It also rejects a related view that all mortal sins involve a loss of faith. They don't; they involve a loss of charity (CCC 1855), but faith can remain. In that case, it is not "faith working by charity" (Gal. 5:6) but the kind of intellectual assent that does not provide salvation (James 2:19). The Council states:

It must be maintained that the grace of justification once received is lost not only by infidelity, whereby also faith itself is lost, but also by every other mortal sin, though in this case faith is not lost; thus defending the teaching of the divine law which excludes from the kingdom of God not only unbelievers, but also the faithful (who are) fornicators, adulterers, effeminate, liars with mankind, thieves, covetous, drunkards, railers, extortioners (see 1 Cor. 6:9–10, 1 Tim. 1:9–10), and all others who commit deadly sins, from which with the help of divine grace they can refrain, and on account of which they are cut off from the grace of Christ.

FINISHING IN RIGHTEOUSNESS: FINAL JUSTIFICATION

The final chapter of the *Decree on Justification*, chapter 16, deals with the subject of merit and rewards, which implicitly deals with the subject of our final justification on the Last Day.

This is a challenging subject to discuss with those in the Protestant community, for their theological tradition has rejected the use of the term *merit* in connection with our actions before God, and they understand it to mean something very different than what the Church does. It is commonly thought, for example, that the Catholic Church holds that, by good works, the Christian is able to put God in his debt so as to earn his salvation the way a workman earns his wages. As we will see, this is not true.

Before we look at what the Council of Trent had to say, it may be helpful to take a look at the origin and development of the term *merit*. This word is taken from the Latin word *meritum*, which means "recompense" or "reward." The *Catechism of the Catholic Church* explains:

> The term "merit" refers in general to the recompense owed by a community or a society for the action of one of its members, experienced either as beneficial or harmful, deserving reward or punishment (CCC 2006).

Because of this meaning, the term was a natural one to use when discussing the biblical doctrine of rewards. Scripture discusses on numerous occasions how God will reward believers, without implying that the believers "earn" the things that God rewards them with. Thus the *Catechism* states:

> With regard to God, there is no strict right to any merit on the part of man. Between God and us there is an immeasurable inequality, for we have received everything from him, our Creator (CCC 2007).

All of the rewards are things promised by God out of his grace, and the actions that he rewards are themselves done at the prompting of and with the power supplied by his grace. These concepts are taken over into the doctrine of merit, which is itself a way of expressing the biblical doctrine of rewards. The Council states:

> To those who work well unto the end (Matt. 10:22) and trust in God, eternal life is to be offered, both as a grace mercifully promised to the sons of God through Christ Jesus, and as a reward promised by God himself, to be faithfully given to their good works and merits (Rom. 6:22).

In Romans 6:22, St. Paul states:

> But now that you have been set free from sin and have become slaves of God, the return you get is sanctification and its end, eternal life.

This does present the final obtaining of eternal life as a consequence of the sanctification that occurs during the Christian life.

A passage that similarly speaks of eternal life as a reward is found earlier in Romans, where St. Paul writes:

> For he [God] will render to every man according to his works: to those who by patience in well-doing seek for glory and honor and immortality, he will give eternal life (Rom. 2:6–7).

Similarly, in Galatians, he states:

> Do not be deceived; God is not mocked, for whatever a man sows, that he will also reap. For he who sows to his own flesh will from the flesh reap corruption; but he who sows to the Spirit will from the Spirit reap eternal life. And let us not grow weary in well-doing, for in due season we shall reap, if we do not lose heart. So then, as we have opportunity, let us do good to all men, and especially to those who are of the household of faith (Gal. 6:6–10).

Here Paul identifies "do(ing) good to all men" as the sowing to the Spirit that will result in "eternal life."

In these passages, eternal life is spoken of as being obtained as a result of doing good. This is not to be understood as good works done apart from God's grace, for there is no such thing. But we must be prepared to acknowledge that Scripture speaks of eternal life *both* as a gift (Romans 6:23) *and* as something obtained through the good works the Christian does in cooperation with God's grace.

The Council notes:

> For this [eternal life] is the crown of justice which after his fight and course the Apostle [Paul] declared was laid up for him, to be rendered to him by the just judge, and not only to him, but also to all that love his coming (see 2 Tim. 4:8).

The phrase "the crown of justice" or "the crown of righteousness" (Greek, *ho stephanos tes dikaosunes*) is significant, because it indicates the final stage of justification (see chapter 2).

The Council is also concerned that people do not understand merit as a matter of our own doing, apart from God's grace:

> Christ Jesus Himself, as the head into the members and the vine into the branches (John 15:1–2), continually infuses strength into those justified, which strength always precedes, accompanies, and follows their good works, and without which they could not in any manner be pleasing and meritorious before God.

Similarly, the Council issues the warning:

> Far be it that a Christian should either trust or glory in himself and not in the Lord (see 1 Cor. 1:31, 2 Cor. 10:17), whose bounty toward all men is so great that He wishes the things that are His gifts to be their merits.

And since in many things we all offend (James 3:2), each one ought to have before his eyes not only the mercy and goodness but also the severity and judgment (of God); neither ought anyone to judge himself, even though he be not conscious to himself of anything (see 1 Cor. 4:3–4) because the whole life of man is to be examined and judged not by the judgment of man but of God, who will bring to light the hidden things of darkness, and will make manifest the counsels of the hearts, and then shall every man have praise from God (1 Cor. 4:5) who, as it is written, will render to every man according to his works (Matt. 16:27, Rom. 2:6, Rev. 22:12).

THE CANONS ON JUSTIFICATION

The *Decree on Justification* was followed by a set of canons rejecting particular errors on the topic. These canons used the conventional formula, "If anyone says X, let him be *anathema*," where X is a rejected proposition.

This formula dates back to the first ecumenical council, the First Council of Nicaea, held in A.D. 325. It does not, contrary to some reports, mean that a person is damned by God, nor does it apply automatically to individuals who teach the condemned proposition, much less does it apply to large groups of people (e.g., Protestants).

At this time, the term *anathema* referred to a kind of excommunication that was accomplished by a particular ceremony performed by the local bishop. The purpose of this was to wake a person up to the fact that he had done something that endangered him and others spiritually so that he might repent and be restored to fellowship with the Church (cf. 1 Cor. 5:1–13, 2 Cor. 2:5–11). There was thus a parallel ceremony that the bishop performed to lift the excommunication and restore the person to full fellowship.

Canons like those attached to the *Decree on Justification* thus did not take effect automatically. They proscribed an ecclesiastical penalty that was to be applied to people who denied points of Catholic doctrine that had been defined. In practice, such penalties were only applied to people who made a pretense of remaining within the Catholic community. There would have been no point in performing innumerable anathema ceremonies on those who no longer claimed to be Catholic.

Historically, the *anathema* ceremony came to be so little used that it was abolished with the release of the 1983 *Code of Canon Law*. As a result, the penalty no longer exists today. Excommunication still does, but it also does not apply to those who have never been members of the Catholic Church.

The text of the canons can be found in the Bonus Materials at the back of this book. They serve as an authoritative summary of the *Decree on Justification*, selecting particular erroneous propositions that have already been rejected in the decree and then assigning the penalty of anathema to them.

Although this penalty no longer exists in canon law, the canons retain their doctrinal force, which actually makes them even more authoritative than the decree itself. It is commonly recognized among Catholic scholars that, while the decrees of ecumenical councils, such as the *Decree on Justification*, are generally not infallible, the canons dealing with matters of faith and morals are.

This means that the canons must be read with great care, with attention being paid both to what they *do* and what they *do not* say, for "No doctrine is understood as defined infallibly unless this is manifestly evident" (*Code of Canon Law* 749 §3).

Over time, Catholic scholars have concluded that, although the condemnations contained in the canons are valid and identify points that genuinely contradict the Catholic Faith, they do not apply in as many situations as previously thought.

That is the subject of the next chapter.

Justification and
Ecumenism

On October 31, 1999, the Catholic Church and the Lutheran World Federation (LWF) signed a historic document known as the *Joint Declaration on the Doctrine of Justification* (JD). This document, the fruit of almost thirty years of ecumenical dialogue, was widely misinterpreted and misrepresented by many in both the secular and the religious press.

The present chapter is intended to help readers understand the most important things that the document does *and does not* say.

How We Got Where We Are

The Reformation was a time of great tension between Protestants and Catholics, and for many years afterward individuals on one side frequently portrayed the other side in the least favorable light. Too often, they were not interested in giving the other side a sympathetic hearing nor in "getting inside the heads" of the other group to understand what their writings meant. To the extent they read the works of the other party at all, they did so only to look for ammunition for theological controversy.

Today, scholars on both sides show a growing willingness to give a more nuanced reading to the theology of the other group. The resulting openness has borne fruit—good and bad—in the current ecumenical movement. Among the good fruit is the progress that has been made with Lutherans on the subject of justification. The Lutheran view of justification has always been closer to the Catholic view than that of many other Protestants. For example, Luther taught the necessity of baptism for justification, the practice of infant baptism, and the possibility of losing one's salvation—things hotly denied by others in the Protestant community.

As Lutheran and Catholic scholars read each other's writings, it became clear that the two sides were not as far apart on justification as had been supposed. A number of apparent disagreements could be cleared up by translating Lutheran language into Catholic language and vice versa. Also, some disputes were due to differences of emphasis rather than fundamental disagreement.

Since 1972, many Catholic-Lutheran ecumenical statements on justification have been written and released by local ecumenical groups, and the extent of agreement was such that the Holy See and the Lutheran World Federation decided to explore the possibility of issuing a joint declaration on the subject. Beginning in 1994, representatives appointed by the Holy See and the Lutheran World Federation drafted and circulated a proposed text for such a joint declaration. The text was finalized in 1997, and the Lutheran World Federation approved it unanimously on June 16, 1998. It was expected that the Holy See would approve it also, and it could then be issued.

But the process was suddenly derailed.

The Holy See announced that it would be releasing a document titled *The Response of the Catholic Church to the Joint Declaration of the Catholic Church and the Lutheran World Federation on the Doctrine of Justification* (Response). When the document was released a few days later, on June 25, the Holy See did not endorse the Joint Declaration as it stood but expressed a number of reservations and indicated that certain points needed to be clarified.

This was extremely embarrassing. The drafting of the Joint Declaration had been a years-long process, and the text had already been finalized. From the Lutherans' perspective, the concerns that were announced on June 25 should have been brought up and corresponding clarifications given *before* the text was finalized and the Lutherans committed themselves by voting on and approving it.

Journalist John Allen commented:

Outsiders fairly wondered what sense it made for the Vatican to issue a "response" to a document for which it was supposedly one of the authors. If Vatican officials had problems with the text, they asked, why sign in the first place? Alternatively, if the Vatican was going to back away from its own agreements before the ink was even dry, why invest time and treasure producing them?[38]

The apparent explanation for this series of events was a lack of proper communication between two departments, or dicasteries, at the Vatican. One—the Pontifical Council for Promoting Christian Unity (PCPCU)—developed the Joint Declaration with the Lutheran World Federation. But another— the Congregation for the Doctrine of the Faith (CDF)—had final responsibility for making sure it was theologically sound. Apparently, the two did not communicate in a timely manner, and the CDF—then headed by Cardinal Joseph Ratzinger (later Pope Benedict XVI)—felt it had no choice but to slam the breaks on the process due to potential problems with the final document. Allen noted:

> Many Lutherans were furious. One claimed that the Holy See had betrayed both the Lutheran and the Roman Catholic theologians who worked on the document, and that it would take decades to reestablish trust.
>
> In the German press, Ratzinger quickly emerged as the villain of the story, which brought a rare flash of personal pique. On July 14, 1998, he published a letter in the *Frankfurter Allgemeine* calling reports that he had torpedoed the agreement a "smooth lie," insisting that to scuttle dialogue with Lutherans would be to "deny myself."
>
> Perhaps stung by the backlash, Ratzinger stepped in to put the dialogue back on track. On November 3, 1998, he quietly invited a small working group to assemble in Regensburg, Germany, in the home he shared with his brother Georg. In addition to Ratzinger, the group consisted of Lutheran

Bishop Johannes Hanselmann, Catholic theologian Heinz
Schuette, and Lutheran theologian Joachim Track.[39]

Cardinal Ratzinger's key role in bringing the Joint Declaration to fruition was noted by others.

Bishop George Anderson of the Evangelical Lutheran Church
of America, who was not present in Regensburg but who was
briefed by the Lutheran participants, said Ratzinger's role was
critical: "It was Ratzinger who untied the knots . . . Without
him we might not have an agreement."
. . . [T]he Joint Declaration on the Doctrine of Justification
remains the ecumenical agreement in which Pope Benedict
XVI was most intimately involved, first as a critic and then
as its savior.[40]

It was saved by Cardinal Ratzinger's working group
producing a new joint document that clarified the first one. This
document became known as the *Annex to the Joint Declaration*
(Annex), and the two parties released it the following year
on June 11. They also announced that the formal signing of
the Joint Declaration would take place October 31, 1999, in
Augsburg, Germany.

The history of the Joint Declaration and its Annex reveals
something significant. As the process of ecumenical discussion
has unfolded over the last few decades, there have been repeated
concerns expressed that ecumenists were papering over actual
differences between different groups of Christians. This form
of false ecumenism portrays a greater unity than actually exists.

The fact that, in the case of the Joint Declaration, the Holy See
was willing to pursue a course of action so painful to both sides,
at the last minute, and not proceed until clarifications were made,
shows that the Holy See was determined that this not happen with
the document. The involvement of Cardinal Ratzinger in crafting
the clarifications of the Annex ensured that the two documents,
taken together, do not misrepresent Catholic teaching.

Important Cautions

The text of the Joint Declaration contains a number of important cautions to prevent the meaning and significance of the document from being misunderstood:

1. *Neither side retracted its position, went back on its history, or "caved in"*: "[T]his Joint Declaration rests on the conviction that . . . the churches neither take the condemnations (of the sixteenth century) lightly nor do they disavow their own past" (JD 7).
2. *The document does not cover all of the doctrine of justification*: "The present Joint Declaration . . . does not cover all that either church teaches about justification; it does encompass a consensus on basic truths of the doctrine of justification and shows that the remaining differences in its explication are no longer the occasion for doctrinal condemnations" (JD 5).
3. *The condemnations of the reformation era were not wrong*: "Nothing is . . . taken away from the seriousness of the condemnations related to the doctrine of justification. . . . They remain for us 'salutary warnings' to which we must attend in our teaching and practice" (JD 42).
4. *The document does not cover all disagreements between Catholics and Lutherans*: "[T]here are still questions of varying importance which need further clarification. These include, among other topics, the relationship between the Word of God and church doctrine, as well as ecclesiology, authority in the church, ministry, the sacraments, and the relation between justification and social ethics" (JD 43).
5. *Due to the remaining differences, the two sides still cannot unite*: "Doctrinal condemnations were put forward both in the Lutheran Confessions and by the Roman Catholic Church's Council of Trent. These condemnations are still valid today and thus have a church-dividing effect" (JD 1).

One final caution:

6. *This declaration applies only to the signatories*: This is obvious enough that the document does not point it out explicitly. The initial signers were the Catholic Church and the Lutheran World Federation.

Later, in 2006, the World Methodist Council adopted the statement as well, and a new signing ceremony was held on July 23 of that year in Seoul, Korea, where representatives of the Catholic Church, the Lutheran World Federation, and the World Methodist Council issued a common statement enduring the Joint Declaration.

But this does not mean that the statement speaks for all Protestants. Many Protestant denominations have not accepted it. In fact, the Lutheran World Federation does not speak for all Lutherans, and the World Methodist Council does not speak for all Methodists.

THE BIG PICTURE

The Joint Declaration expresses its general conclusion a number of times, but perhaps most clearly in the following statement:

> The understanding of the doctrine of justification set forth in this Declaration shows that a consensus in basic truths of the doctrine of justification exists between Lutherans and Catholics. In light of this consensus the remaining differences of language, theological elaboration, and emphasis in the understanding of justification described in paras. 18 to 39 are acceptable. Therefore the Lutheran and the Catholic explications of justification are in their difference open to one another and do not destroy the consensus regarding basic truths (JD 40).

It is important to note that, though the Joint Declaration above speaks of a consensus on the basic truths regarding justification, there remain "differences of language, theological elaboration, and emphasis." In other words, the parties at times use different language, have different ways of elaborating the basic truths both agree upon, or they emphasize different concepts.

The differences do not amount to a contradiction on any of the basic truths. This is what the text means when it says that the two parties' "explications of justification are in their difference open to one another." That's a fancy way of saying that, though there may be differences of language, elaboration, and emphasis, they don't fundamentally contradict each other and so "destroy the consensus regarding basic truths."

"Thus," says the document, "the doctrinal condemnations of the sixteenth century, insofar as they relate to the doctrine of justification, appear in a new light: The teaching of the Lutheran churches presented in this Declaration does not fall under the condemnations from the Council of Trent. The condemnations in the Lutheran Confessions do not apply to the teaching of the Roman Catholic Church presented in this Declaration" (JD 41).

Note that the above passage states only that the condemnations of the Council of Trent do not apply to "the teaching of the Lutheran churches *presented in this Declaration*." Teachings of the Lutheran churches not presented in the Joint Declaration can and do fall under Trent's condemnations.

Ideas of other Protestant groups on justification are also rejected by Trent. There was no single Protestant view of justification in the 1500s, any more than there is today. The Council of Trent was faced with an array of mutually contradictory Protestant ideas on justification. It therefore condemned the gravest errors, regardless of which individuals or groups were advocating them. As a result, one has to consider which condemnations issued by Trent apply to which groups.

In recent decades, a dialogue developed between Catholics and Lutherans in which the two groups reassessed the degree to which the mutual condemnations of the 1500s applied to each other. One of the dialogues that laid the groundwork for the Joint Declaration was a 1986 study done by representatives of the German conference of bishops and the parallel German Lutheran body. Cardinal Ratzinger served as the Catholic chairman of the Joint

Ecumenical Commission responsible for the document, which was published in English as *The Condemnations of the Reformation Era: Do They Still Divide?*[41] This study concluded that the condemnations found in a number of the canons[42] of Trent's *Decree on Justification* (DJ) did not apply to modern German Lutherans.

Seven Topics

One of the most important sections in the Joint Declaration, "Explicating the Common Understanding of Justification," clarifies seven contentious issues: (1) Human Powerlessness and Sin in Relation to Justification, (2) Justification as Forgiveness of Sins and Making Righteous, (3) Justification by Faith and Through Grace, (4) The Justified as Sinner, (5) Law and Gospel, (6) Assurance of Salvation, and (7) The Good Works of the Justified.

1. Human Powerlessness and Sin in Relation to Justification

Lutherans often use language suggesting that humans are powerless to seek justification without God's grace. This is something with which Catholics agree. God's grace is required for us to seek him. But Lutherans also have used language that suggests humans are unable to cooperate in any way with God's grace and must receive justification in a merely passive manner. When Catholics balk at this language, Lutherans have seen it as a denial of man's inability to seek justification without God's grace. The Joint Declaration seeks to resolve this misunderstanding:

> We confess together that all persons depend completely on the saving grace of God for their salvation . . . for as sinners they stand under God's judgment and are incapable of turning by themselves to God to seek deliverance, of meriting their justification before God, or of attaining salvation by their own abilities. Justification takes place solely by God's grace. . . . When Catholics say that persons "cooperate" in preparing for and accepting justification . . . they see such personal consent

as itself an effect of grace, not as an action arising from innate human abilities (JD 19–20).

Unfortunately, this section of the Joint Declaration went on to use the Lutheran description of man as "merely passive" with respect to justification (n. 21) without fully explaining it. The Response of the Holy See stressed that this needed to be clarified further. Consequently, the *Annex to the Joint Declaration* made the following affirmation:

The working of God's grace does not exclude human action: God effects everything, the willing and the achievement, therefore we are called to strive (cf. Phil. 2:12ff.). "As soon as the Holy Spirit has initiated his work of regeneration and renewal in us through the Word and the holy sacraments, it is certain that we can and must cooperate by the power of the Holy Spirit . . ." (*The Formula of Concord*, FC SD II, 64f. [Annex 2C]).

2. *Justification as Forgiveness of Sins and Making Righteous*

Another perennial subject of disagreement has been the nature of justification. Frequently, Lutherans have characterized it as only a forgiveness (or nonimputation) of sins, whereas the Church insists that it is more than this and involves a renewal of life. The Joint Declaration makes this statement:

We confess together that God forgives sin by grace and at the same time frees human beings from sin's enslaving power and imparts the gift of new life in Christ. When persons come by faith to share in Christ, God no longer imputes to them their sin and through the Holy Spirit effects in them an active love. These two aspects of God's gracious action are not to be separated.

When Lutherans emphasize that the righteousness of Christ is our righteousness, their intention is above all to insist that the sinner is granted righteousness before God in Christ through

the declaration of forgiveness and that only in union with
Christ is one's life renewed. When they stress that God's grace
is forgiving love ("the favor of God"), they do not thereby deny
the renewal of the Christian's life (JD 22–23).

This description of justification as both forgiveness of sins
and inward renewal reflects Trent's statement that justification
"is not only a remission of sins but also the sanctification and
renewal of the inward man" (DJ 7).

Some Catholics have been concerned that this section of the
Joint Declaration does not explicitly mention what Trent called
the "formal cause" of justification, which refers to the *kind* of
righteousness one receives in justification. According to Trent
(DJ 7, can. 11), there is a single formal cause of justification:
sanctifying grace (see L. Ott, *Fundamentals of Catholic Dogma*,
251–52). The nature of sanctifying grace has not been finally determined. According to the common view, that of the Thomists,
sanctifying grace is a quality that God gives the soul that always
accompanies but is distinct from the virtue of charity. According
to the less common view, that of the Scotists, sanctifying grace
and charity are the same thing.

The Joint Declaration does not raise this discussion, perhaps
because it involves what is still an open question among Catholics, perhaps also from unwillingness to delve into scholastic terminology not used by the partner in ecumenical dialogue. The
document is content to simply say that in justification God no
longer imputes sin (that is, he forgives or remits it) and that he
creates charity in the believer.[43]

3. Justification by Faith and Through Grace

Two key Protestant affirmations are "justification by grace
alone" and "justification by faith alone." At first glance, these
two might seem to contradict each other, but they are speaking
on different levels. The point of the first affirmation is that justification comes to us by God's grace, without our earning our

place before God. The point of the second affirmation is that justification comes to us when we respond in faith, not because of "works" (however those are understood).

It is often thought that Catholics must reject both of these affirmations.

This is certainly not true in the case of the first. Catholics have no trouble attributing our justification to God's grace in an exclusive and unique sense. While the Church does, in keeping with the language of Scripture, use the terminology of merit and reward, these are understood themselves as the product of God's grace and not as something we have or could offer to God apart from grace.

Consequently, the Joint Declaration states:

> Together we (Lutherans and Catholics) confess: *By grace alone,* in faith in Christ's saving work and not because of any merit on our part, we are accepted by God and receive the Holy Spirit, who renews our hearts while equipping and calling us to good works (JD 15).

What about the other affirmation—"by faith alone"? The situation here is more complex.

The Council of Trent

There is a particular passage in the Council of Trent's *Decree on Justification* that is often presented as a blanket condemnation of the formula "by faith alone." However, the matter is not this simple. Canon 9 of the *Decree on Justification* states:

> If anyone says that the sinner is justified by faith alone, so that thus he understands[44] nothing else is required to cooperate in order to obtain the grace of justification, and that it is not in any way necessary that he be prepared and disposed by the action of his own will, let him be anathema.[45]

In writing this, the Council used the term *faith* as it was commonly used at the time—a reference to the theological virtue of faith, which conceives of faith "primarily as assent to revealed doctrine."[46] Understood in this way, to say that one is saved "by faith alone" would mean that one is justified merely by assenting to revealed doctrine, so that "nothing else is required to cooperate in order to obtain the grace of justification, and that it is not in any way necessary that he be prepared and disposed by the action of his own will."

While some in the Protestant community may take such an extreme position, many do not. Indeed, many of the original Protestant Reformers, as well as their modern counterparts, reject the idea of justification "by intellectual assent alone." They would point to many of the same passages that Catholics would to show the insufficiency of a purely intellectual faith, such as the famous passage in which St. James notes that "Even the demons believe—and shudder" (James 2:19). Merely knowing the truths of theology does not save them.

What Trent rejects is not every possible use of the formula "by faith alone" but a particular use that even many Protestants would reject. This leaves us with the question: "What about other uses of the formula?"

"Faith Alone" before Luther?

One reason the Council of Trent phrased itself carefully on the use of the "by faith alone" formula may be that this formula had been used previously by some sources in Catholic history, including some very notable names.

Robert Bellarmine listed eight earlier authors who used *sola fide* (*Disputatio de controversiis: De justificatione* 1.25 [Naples: G. Giuliano, 1856], 4.501–3):

- Origen, *Commentarius in Ep. ad Romanos*, cap. 3 (PG 14.952)
- Hilary, *Commentarius in Matthaeum* 8:6 (PL 9.961)
- Basil, *Hom. de humilitate* 20.3 (PG 31.529C)
- Ambrosiaster, *In Ep. ad Romanos* 3.24 (CSEL 81.1.119): "*sola fide justificati sunt dono Dei,*" through faith alone they have been justified by a gift of God; 4.5 (CSEL 81.1.130)

- John Chrysostom, *Hom. in Ep. ad Titum* 3.3 (PG 62.679 [not in Greek text])
- Cyril of Alexandria, *In Joannis Evangelium* 10.15.7 (PG 74.368 [but alludes to James 2:19])
- Bernard, *In Canticum serm.* 22.8 (PL 183.881): "*solam justificatur per fidem*," is justified by faith alone
- Theophylact, *Expositio in ep. ad Galatas* 3.12–13 (PG 124.988)[47]

St. Thomas Aquinas also uses it:

Therefore the hope of justification is not found in them (the moral and ceremonial requirements of the law), but *in faith alone* (*Commentary on 1 Timothy*, ch. 1, lect. 3).

[W]ith respect to being made just by the works of the Law, a man does not seem to be justified by them, because the sacraments of the Old Law did not confer grace. . . . Again, if there were any in the Old Law who were just, they were not made just by the works of the Law but *only by the faith of Christ* (*Commentary on Galatians*, ch. 2, lect. 4).

So, is there a way in which "by faith alone" could be understood in a Catholic sense?

Faith, Hope, and Charity
The Council of Trent also taught that in justification man receives "with the remission of sins all these infused at the same time: faith, hope, and charity. For faith, unless hope and charity be added to it, neither unites one perfectly with Christ, nor makes him a living member of his body. For this reason it is most truly said that 'faith without works is dead' (James 2:17 ff.), and is of no profit, and 'in Christ Jesus neither circumcision availeth anything, nor uncircumcision, but faith, which worketh by charity' (Gal. 5:6; 6:15)" (DJ ch. 7).

The Council thus teaches that the three theological virtues—faith, hope, and charity—are given to us in justification, and they are necessary to it. Following St. Paul, it teaches that the virtue of faith, if not accompanied by charity, is not effective.

Charity—the supernatural love of God—is what ultimately unites the soul to God. It therefore is recognized as the "form" of the virtues, that which binds them together and gives them their fullest expression. Catholic theologians have historically talked about virtues being "formed" or "unformed," based on whether they are united with charity. If a person has both faith and charity, for example, he is said to have "formed faith by charity" (*fides formata caritate*); if he has faith without charity, he has "unformed faith" (*fides informis*).

St. Paul indicates that anyone who has charity also has faith and hope, for charity "believes all things, hopes all things" (1 Cor. 13:7). Thus, if one has formed faith, one has not only faith and charity but also hope.

This has implications for the formula "by faith alone." Is the faith in this formula formed or unformed? If it is unformed—lacking charity—then it falls under the condemnation of Trent. But if it is understood as formed faith—faith accompanied by charity and hope—then it would not.

Recent Developments
The possibility that the formula "by faith alone" can be understood in a Catholic sense has been recognized for some time. For example, the 1985 German Conference of Bishops' adult catechism states:

> Catholic doctrine . . . says that only a faith alive in graciously bestowed love can justify. Having "mere" faith without love, merely considering something true, does not justify us. But if one understands faith in the full and comprehensive biblical sense, then faith includes conversion, hope, and love—and the Lutheran ("faith alone") formula can have a *good Catholic sense*.[48]

Similarly, the 1986 ecumenical study in which Cardinal Ratzinger took part drew this conclusion:

If we translate from one language to another, then . . . Protestant doctrine understands substantially under the one word "faith" what Catholic doctrine (following 1 Cor. 13:13) sums up in the triad of "faith, hope, and love." But in this case the mutual rejections in this question can be viewed as no longer applicable today (Lehmann and Pannenberg, *The Condemnations of the Reformation*).

The Joint Declaration and Its Annex

Different groups of Protestants mean different things by the "faith alone" formula:

- A few really do seem to mean that one is justified by intellectual belief alone, without hope or charity.
- Others, many American Evangelicals among them, appear to believe one is justified by faith plus hope, "by which we desire the kingdom of heaven and eternal life as our happiness, placing our trust in Christ's promises and relying not on our own strength, but on the help of the grace of the Holy Spirit" (CCC 1817).
- Others, including the Lutherans who signed the Joint Declaration, believe that charity, the principle behind good works, always accompanies justifying faith.

This last is the sense reflected in the Joint Declaration, which states that "justifying faith . . . includes hope in God and love for him. Such a faith is active in love and thus the Christian cannot and should not remain without works" (JD 25).

The same understanding lies behind such statements in the Joint Declaration as "We confess together that persons are justified by faith in the gospel 'apart from works prescribed by the law' (Rom. 3:28)" (JD 31).

Finally, the understanding of justifying faith as formed faith also lies behind the passage in the Annex where the "by faith alone" formula is used in a mutual statement: "Justification takes place 'by grace alone' (JD 15 and 16), by faith alone; the

person is justified 'apart from works' (Rom. 3:28, cf. JD 25)"
(Annex 2C).

Pope Benedict XVI on "Faith Alone"

After his election as Pope Benedict XVI, the former Cardinal
Ratzinger returned to the subject of the "by faith alone" formula:

> Luther's phrase "*faith alone*" is true, if it is not opposed to
> faith in charity, in love. Faith is looking at Christ, entrusting
> oneself to Christ, being united to Christ, conformed to
> Christ, to his life. And the form, the life of Christ, is love;
> hence to believe is to conform to Christ and to enter into
> his love. So it is that in the Letter to the Galatians in which
> he primarily developed his teaching on justification St. Paul
> speaks of faith that works through love (cf. Gal 5: 14) (General
> Audience, November 19, 2008).

We thus have acknowledgment from multiple sources, including a pope, that the "by faith alone" formula *can* have an
acceptable meaning.

Does this mean that Catholics should start using it?

Reasons for Caution

The signing of the Joint Declaration, and even Pope Benedict's
statement, do not mean that Catholics should begin using this
formula. There is a big difference between it being *possible* for a
formula to be given an acceptable meaning and it being *prudent*
to use it in common practice. It is one thing to note in ecumenical dialogue that a phrase can be understood in an acceptable
sense; it is another to start using it on a regular basis.

There are several reasons why Catholics should not do the latter.

One is that the formula is not the language that Scripture
uses to describe how we are justified. The phrase, *ek pisteos
monon* ("by faith alone"), appears only once in the New Testament, in James 2:24, where it is rejected. Using this formula,
whatever meaning it is given, creates an automatic tension with

the language that Scripture itself uses, and that is bound to cause confusion.

A second reason is that, even apart from its rejection in Scripture, the formula is inherently open to confusion. In common parlance, the term *faith* is a synonym for *belief.* When coupled with the word *alone* and used to describe the method of our justification, it communicates to most people the erroneous idea that we can be saved by intellectual belief alone. This has been a danger since the apostolic age. Some in the first century didn't read Paul's language carefully enough when he said in Romans 3:28 that we are justified by faith and not by works of the Law. They misunderstood him to be saying that we are saved by faith alone (rather than by faith in Christ apart from the Law of Moses), and it was this misunderstanding of Paul that James was condemning in his epistle. That is the reason James goes into the subject.

It is also a problem for modern Protestants. The phrase "faith alone" is so confusing that in evangelistic appeals, Evangelicals must frequently explain that we are *not* saved by belief apart from trust (or, for some Protestants, that we will not be saved if we do not truly repent of our sins).

A third reason is that, even though there are precedents for its use in Catholic history, it is not the primary or even a common way that Catholic theology expresses itself on justification. Taking a rare, uncommon usage and trying to use it on an everyday basis is sure to cause confusion.

A fourth reason, related to this, is that the magisterium does not use the expression on a regular basis. If you look in the *Catechism of the Catholic Church*, for instance, you will not find it. Nor will you find it used regularly in other magisterial documents. There are a handful of such documents that acknowledge that the formula *can* have a Catholic sense, but there are *none* that use it regularly or that recommend that Catholics use it.

We must recognize that the situation of documents like the Joint Declaration is special. It strikes a delicate balance regarding the formula. It acknowledges—rightly—that the formula is being used by the Lutheran World Federation in a sense that does not fall under the condemnations of Trent, because the LWF has defined the term *faith* broadly enough that justifying faith is always accompanied by hope and charity; but that doesn't mean Catholics should start using it among ourselves.

4. The Justified as Sinner

The section of the Joint Declaration that most concerned the Holy See was not the part dealing with justification by grace and faith. Indeed, the Holy See did not ask for any clarifications on that subject. The most problematic section was the one dealing with the Lutheran expression that man is "at once righteous and a sinner" (Latin, *simul iustus et peccator*).

The Holy See was concerned to uphold the Catholic teaching that "in baptism everything that is really sin is taken away, and so, in those who are born anew there is nothing that is hateful to God. It follows that the concupiscence that remains in the baptized is not, properly speaking, sin" (Response, Clarification 1).

The controversy goes back to the time of the Reformation, when Lutherans wished to say that the concupiscence (disordered desire) that remains in the individual after justification still has the character of sin. The Catholic Church taught what it always had: concupiscence "has never (been) understood to be called sin in the sense that it is truly and properly sin in those born again, but in the sense that it is from sin and inclines to sin" (Trent, *Decree on Original Sin* 5).

The *Annex to the Joint Declaration* responds by conceding that "it can be recognized from a Lutheran perspective that [concupiscent] desire can become the opening through which sin attacks" (Annex 2B). Concupiscence is a vulnerability that leads to sin, but is not itself sin.

Because concupiscence can lead to sin:

we would be wrong were we to say that we are without sin (1 John 1:8–10, cf. JD 28). "All of us make many mistakes"

(James 3:2). This recalls to us the persisting danger that comes from the power of sin and its action in Christians. To this extent, Lutherans and Catholics can together understand the Christian as *simul iustus et peccator*, despite their different approaches to this subject as expressed in JD 29–30 (Annex 2A).

Christians remain sinners in the sense that they are inclined to sin by concupiscence, but they do not remain sinners in the sense that God's forgiveness and justification takes away from them all that is properly called sin. Our sins really are taken away when we are forgiven. They do not remain in us. Annex 2A further says:

> We are truly and inwardly renewed by the action of the Holy Spirit, remaining always dependent on his work in us. "So if anyone is in Christ, there is a new creation: everything old has passed away; see, everything has become new!" (2 Cor. 5:17). The justified do not remain sinners in this sense.

5. Law and Gospel

Lutherans historically have drawn a sharp distinction between law and gospel to the point that, in Lutheran theology, these can become abstract philosophical ideas that are opposed to each other. However, as we have seen, this is not the way the terms are used in Scripture. When the Bible refers to "the Law," it almost always means the Torah, the Law of Moses, which not only makes legal demands but promises God's grace. Similarly, when the Bible speaks about "the gospel," it does not envision a set of unconditional promises; salvation in Christ is conditional on faith and sincere conversion from sin.

A consequence of Lutheranism's sharp divide between law and gospel is that Lutherans have at times used language suggesting that Christ is given to us only as a Savior to be believed in, not also as a Lawgiver to be obeyed. To correct this, the Joint Declaration contains this affirmation:

We also confess that God's commandments retain their validity for the justified and that Christ has by his teaching and example expressed God's will, which is a standard for the conduct of the justified also (JD 31).

Because of the sharp division made between law and gospel, Lutherans at times have been suspicious of Catholic discussion of Christ as Lawgiver, thinking that this may reduce Christ to being just another Moses, bringing legal demands rather than salvation. The Joint Declaration addresses this concern:

> Because the law as a way to salvation has been fulfilled and overcome through the gospel, Catholics can say that Christ is not a lawgiver in the manner of Moses. When Catholics emphasize that the righteous are bound to observe God's commandments, they do not thereby deny that through Jesus Christ God has mercifully promised to his children the grace of eternal life (JD 33).

6. Assurance of Salvation

Whether we can have assurance of salvation has been one of the most polarizing topics since the time of the Reformation.

Lutherans have sometimes made it sound as if one can have absolute assurance that one is or will be saved. But even they will admit that, because of the fallenness of the human intellect and the capacity for self-deception (not to mention the possibility of falling from grace, which Luther acknowledged), one cannot have infallible certitude regarding salvation.

By contrast, Catholics have sometimes made it sound as if it is not possible to have any assurance of salvation. They have even appealed to passages from the Council of Trent, but these have been misread. What the Council stated was that a person cannot "know with the certainty of faith, *which cannot be subject to error,* that he has obtained the grace of God" (DJ 9). It also said that he cannot know "with an *absolute and infallible certainty,* (that he will) have that great gift of perseverance even to the end, unless he shall have learned this by a special revelation" (DJ 16).

It is one thing to say that one ordinarily cannot be assured of present or future salvation with "absolute and infallibly certainty" in a way "which cannot be subject to error." But that is very different than saying one cannot have any assurance *at all*.

Consequently, the two sides today find themselves in more agreement than they have historically perceived. The Joint Declaration affirms:

> We confess together that the faithful can rely on the mercy and promises of God. In spite of their own weakness and the manifold threats to their faith, on the strength of Christ's death and resurrection they can build on the effective promise of God's grace in Word and Sacrament and so be sure of this grace. . . . In trust in God's promise [believers] are assured of their salvation, but are never secure looking at themselves. . . . No one may doubt God's mercy and Christ's merit. Every person, however, may be concerned about his salvation when he looks upon his own weaknesses and shortcomings (JD 34–36).

7. The Good Works of the Justified

Lutherans have been suspicious that the Church holds that one must do good works in order to enter a state of justification. This has never been the case. In Catholic teaching, one is not capable of doing supernaturally good works outside of a state of justification, because one's soul lacks the virtue of charity—the thing that makes good works supernaturally good. Consequently, the Council of Trent taught that "none of those things that precede justification, whether faith or works, merit the grace of justification" (DJ 8).

The Joint Declaration stresses that good works are a consequence of entering a state of justification, not the cause of entering it:

> We confess together that good works—a Christian life lived in faith, hope, and love—follow justification and are its fruits.

When the justified live in Christ and act in the grace they receive, they bring forth, in biblical terms, good fruit. . . .

According to Catholic understanding, good works, made possible by grace and the working of the Holy Spirit, contribute to growth in grace, so that the righteousness that comes from God is preserved and communion with Christ is deepened. When Catholics affirm the "meritorious" character of good works, they wish to say that, according to the biblical witness, a reward in heaven is promised to these works. Their intention is to emphasize the responsibility of persons for their actions, not to contest the character of those works as gifts, or far less to deny that justification always remains the unmerited gift of grace (JD 37–38).

General Appraisal of the Joint Declaration

The Joint Declaration clears away a significant number of misunderstandings regarding justification, but at times the language it uses is confusing. The Holy See acknowledged this when it issued the *Response to the Joint Declaration*, insisting on a number of further clarifications before the Joint Declaration could be signed.

The Joint Declaration also gives very little attention to, or simply omits, some aspects of the doctrine of justification. I very much would have liked to see the Joint Declaration further explain the sense in which Scripture describes eternal life as a reward for "perseverance in working good" (Rom. 2:6–7). More attention could have been devoted to the subject of progressive justification, by which we grow in righteousness over the course of the Christian life. And we could have done with a fuller treatment of the way justification is lost through sin and then regained.

One of the most conspicuous absences from the Joint Declaration is a discussion of the language James uses in chapter 2 of his epistle. James is cited only once, a reference to 3:2, which simply acknowledges that "we all stumble in many things."

Despite these limitations, the Joint Declaration is significant for ecumenical dialogue and worthy of close study, even if it is not a complete treatment of the subject and more work needs to be done.

This attitude seems to have been expressed by Benedict XVI in an address to representatives of the Lutheran World Federation in which he stated:

> For many years the Catholic Church and the Lutheran World Federation have enjoyed close contacts and participated in intensive ecumenical dialogue. This exchange of ideas has been most productive and promising. Indeed, one of the results of this fruitful dialogue is the *Joint Declaration on Justification*, which constitutes a significant milestone on our common path to full visible unity. This is an important achievement. In order to build on this accomplishment, we must accept that differences remain regarding the central question of justification; these need to be addressed, together with the ways in which God's grace is communicated in and through the Church (Address, November 7, 2005).

Outside the Church, No Salvation?

Is salvation connected with one's religious identity? Does it matter to God whether you are a Christian—or whether you are a Catholic in particular? Do you have to be a baptized, card-carrying member of a particular church in order to get into heaven? Will God cast you into hell if you're not?

These are sensitive questions, but they are questions that cannot be avoided. Since the beginning of Church history, Christians have announced the gospel and the offer of salvation through Jesus Christ. Rejecting this offer has been regarded as rejecting salvation itself.

Furthermore, Christ established a Church, and he wills his followers to belong to it. To refuse to become or remain a member of his Church imperils one's salvation. Historically, this has been summed up in the phrase *Extra Ecclesiam, nulla sallus*, which is Latin for "Outside the Church, no salvation."

To non-Christians, the claim that one must be a Christian in order to be saved can sound arrogant. In the same way, to non-Catholics, the claim that one needs to be a Catholic to be saved can sound arrogant. In both cases, though, the truth is otherwise.

Christians do not believe that they are saved because they are superior people. They acknowledge that they are sinners and are saved only by the mercy of God. The same is true of Catholic Christians in particular.

To say that salvation may be found in the Christian Faith and in the Catholic Church is not to make an arrogant boast of superiority. It is to identify the channels of God's mercy and to invite others to receive it as well.

"But surely there are many people who are neither Christian nor Catholic through no fault of their own!" one may protest.

"Doesn't God care for them, too? Won't he make it possible for them to be saved?"

We thus see two, related insights at work. On the one hand, there is the insight that God has intervened in history to give us the means to be saved. On the other hand, there is the insight that salvation should still be possible for those who have not embraced these means through no fault of their own.

How these two insights are to be squared has a history dating back to the Bible.

EXCLUSIVITY IN SCRIPTURE

As we saw in chapter 3, the Old Testament is principally concerned with temporal salvation. There is very little material in it concerning eternal salvation. While the ancient Israelites believed in an afterlife (otherwise they would not have had to have been warned against using mediums; Deut. 18:10–12), the details of it were unclear, and the hope of the resurrection was revealed in the later phases of the Old Testament's composition.

As a result, there is no clear vision of how to achieve a favorable state in the afterlife, although worshipping God and obeying his will would surely have been understood as contributing to that.

There was not, however, an expectation that people needed to become Jewish in order to be saved. The Israelites were God's chosen people, and they had been blessed by him giving them his Law, but there was no expectation that everyone in the world should become Jewish. Judaism was not meant to be a universal faith. It was the religion of a particular people that God had chosen, but it was not meant for all peoples.

Instead, it was meant to reveal the true God to all peoples. This is the expectation when God tells Abraham, "by you all the families of the earth shall bless themselves" (Gen. 12:3), and, later, when he tells him, "by your descendants shall all the nations of the earth bless themselves" (Gen. 22:18).

Thus, when Na´aman the leper, who was a Syrian by birth, came to worship the true God, he was not required to become a Jew, and the prophet Elisha told him to "Go in peace" (2 Kings 5:1–19).

By the first century, there were many such "God-fearers," Gentiles who reverenced the true God though they did not become Jews (cf. Acts 13:16, 26), and it was from among these that the first Gentile converts were made.

Mere conversion to the Christian faith was not enough for some Jewish Christians, however, and some mistakenly claimed, "Unless you are circumcised according to the custom of Moses, you cannot be saved" (Acts 15:1). In other words, they held that people needed to become Jewish in order to be saved. This view was rejected at the Council of Jerusalem, but the subject continued to be controversial, as illustrated by Paul's letters to the Galatians and the Romans.

While this kind of *ethnic* exclusivism was rejected, the early Christians did recognize a form of *theological* exclusivism based on the unique role of Jesus Christ in God's plan.

After all, Jesus himself declared: "I am the way, and the truth, and the life; no one comes to the Father, but by me" (John 14:6). Consequently, the apostles preached that "there is salvation in no one else, for there is no other name under heaven given among men by which we must be saved" (Acts 4:12).

If someone rejected this message of salvation, it was taken as a sign that he had rejected eternal life. Thus, when Paul's preaching was rejected by the Jews of Pisidian Antioch, he told them, "It was necessary that the word of God should be spoken first to you. Since you thrust it from you, and judge yourselves unworthy of eternal life, behold, we turn to the Gentiles" (Acts 13:46).

Taken together, passages like these could be understood as meaning that salvation is available on an exclusive basis to Christians alone. If you don't accept the Christian message, you're lost, and that's all there is to it. Many Christians, throughout history, have drawn this conclusion.

But there are nagging questions. For example, what about those who have never heard the Christian message? They would not seem to be at fault for their failure to embrace it. Without knowledge of it, they *couldn't* embrace it! And there were millions of people in the world in that condition, including *all* of the Gentiles who lived before the time of Christ.

Does the New Testament give us any indication that salvation might be possible for them?

It does. In Acts 17, Paul makes a speech to the Aeropagus, which was a kind of discussion society in Athens. During the course of the speech, he tells the Athenians:

> [God] made from one every nation of men to live on all the face of the earth, having determined allotted periods and the boundaries of their habitation, that they should seek God, in the hope that they might feel after him and find him. Yet he is not far from each one of us, for "In him we live and move and have our being"; as even some of your poets have said, "For we are indeed his offspring."
>
> Being then God's offspring, we ought not to think that the Deity is like gold, or silver, or stone, a representation by the art and imagination of man. The times of ignorance God overlooked, but now he commands all men everywhere to repent, because he has fixed a day on which he will judge the world in righteousness by a man whom he has appointed, and of this he has given assurance to all men by raising him from the dead (Acts 17:26–31).

Here Paul refers to the period of history in which men worshipped idols as "times of ignorance," and he says that "God overlooked" these times. Although men could fall into idolatry through a deliberate suppression of the truth, leading to a culpable spiral of degradation and sin (Rom. 1:18–31), Paul acknowledges that in the midst of an idolatrous culture, men "might feel after him and find him."

Indeed, some of the Greek philosophers had arrived at a limited knowledge of God based on natural theology, and Paul notes that "some of your own poets" have acknowledged that men can be regarded the children of God. (The line Paul quotes is from the poet Aratus of Cilicia—where Paul's home city of Tarsus is located—though similar thoughts were expressed by other Greek literary figures, including Cleanthes and Epimenides).

This raises the possibility that God might be willing to "overlook" the elements of falsehood in their knowledge of God, provided they were otherwise seeking him. Paul raises a similar possibility in Romans:

> When Gentiles who have not the Law do by nature what the Law requires, they are a law to themselves, even though they do not have the Law. They show that what the Law requires is written on their hearts, while their conscience also bears witness and their conflicting thoughts accuse or perhaps excuse them on that day when, according to my gospel, God judges the secrets of men by Christ Jesus (Rom. 2:14–16).

Here Paul speaks of "Gentiles who have not the Law," who are presumably Gentiles who do not have knowledge of the Jewish Torah, which would indicate non-Christian Gentiles. Despite the fact that they do not have the Jewish Law, they still have the moral law of God written on their hearts, and so they may find that their consciences will "perhaps excuse them" on judgment day. This seems to hold out the possibility of salvation for some non-Christian Gentiles.

Exclusivity in the Church Fathers

The Church Fathers wrestled with the same kind of questions we have been considering.

On the one hand, they were quite clear about the fact that salvation is to be found in Jesus Christ and his Church in a unique sense. The latter point—salvation being found in the Church—was forced to the surface by the appearance of two phenomena that wounded the unity of the Church: heresy and schism.

It was clear that, to respond to the proclamation of the gospel, one needed to be baptized, and that this brought with it salvation (1 Pet. 3:21). Baptism also placed one in the Church, the mystical body of Christ (1 Cor. 12:13, 27, Gal. 3:27, Col. 1:18). Attaining salvation was thus linked to becoming a member of Christ's Church.

But already in the first century, problems arose with some who had become members. Some insisted on believing things that were fundamentally contrary to the Christian message, while others formed factions and separated themselves. The first of these came to be known as *heresy* and the latter as *schism*.

In the fourth century, St. Jerome explained it this way:

> Between heresy and schism there is this difference: heresy involves perverse doctrine, while schism separates one from the Church on account of disagreement with the bishop (*Commentaries on Titus* 3:10).

Both of these strike at one's union with the Church. The Church could not allow people to remain within it who were teaching things fundamentally contrary to the Christian Faith, and so they were expelled or they left on their own to form heretical churches. Similarly, schismatics withdrew from communion with the Church to form their own groups.

To knowingly and deliberately do either of these things— embrace teachings contrary to the Faith or to withdraw from communion with Christ's Church—would be a mortal sin, and the Fathers warned against them. For example, at the beginning of the second century, St. Ignatius of Antioch wrote:

> If any man follows him that makes a schism in the Church, he shall not inherit the kingdom of God. If anyone walks according to a strange opinion [i.e., a heresy], he does not agree with the Passion [of Christ]. Take heed, then, to have but one Eucharist. For there is one flesh of our Lord Jesus Christ, and one cup to [show forth] the unity of his blood; one altar; as there is one bishop, along with the presbytery and deacons, my fellow servants (*Letter to the Philadelphians* 3–4).

Separating oneself from Christ's Church—either by the mortal sin of heresy or schism—was to reject the salvation that Christ offers.

But the Church Fathers also faced questions like, "What about those who died before Christ and had no opportunity to hear the gospel? What about those who were martyred for their faith in Christ before they were baptized? And what about those who believe in Jesus but die before they can be baptized?"

The Fathers shared the same intuition that we do—that it seems salvation should be possible for those who through no fault of their own are not able to be baptized, and so in answering these questions, the Fathers acknowledge the possibility of salvation for those who were not baptized members of the Church.

For example, on the question of those who lived before the time of Christ, St. Justin Martyr, writing in the mid-100s, had something very interesting to say:

We have been taught that Christ is the first-born of God, and we have declared above that He is the Word [logos] of whom every race of men were partakers (cf. John 1:1–9); and those who lived reasonably [meta logou] are Christians, even though they have been thought atheists; as, among the Greeks, Socrates and Heraclitus, and men like them; and among the barbarians, Abraham, and Ananiah, and Azariah, and Mishael, and Elijah, and many others whose actions and names we now decline to recount, because we know it would be tedious. So that even they who lived before Christ, and lived without reason [aneu logou], were wicked and hostile to Christ, and slew those who lived reasonably [meta logou] (First Apology 46).

Here St. Justin relies on the fact that the Greek word logos can mean both "word" and "reason." As revealed in the prologue to John's Gospel, Jesus Christ is the Logos—the "Word" or "Reason" of God. Since "every race of men" have been partakers in the divine Reason, there is a sense in which Christ has come to all men as "true light that enlightens every man" (John 1:9).

People then have a choice as to how they respond. They can either live "reasonably" (*meta logou* = "with reason") or "without reason" (*aneu logou*).

"Those who lived reasonably (*meta logou*) are Christians," Justin says, even if they lived before the time of Christ and were thought to be atheists because of their attitude toward the pagan gods. As examples, he names the Greek philosophers Socrates and Heraclitus and Jewish figures like Abraham, the three Hebrew children of Daniel, and Elijah. All these figures lived before the time of Christ, yet because they lived according to Reason, Justin regards them as being Christians in a sense.

By contrast, those who "lived without reason (*aneu logou*) were wicked," and they were implicitly "hostile to Christ, and slew those who lived reasonably." They thus included the persecutors of people like the pre-Christian figures Justin has named, and by living without reason and persecuting them, they implicitly rejected the divine Reason, or Christ.

Justin thus sees the possibility of salvation for individuals who do not know the gospel of Jesus, so long as they otherwise live according to the Logos or Reason that God has given them.

When it came to those who *did* know the gospel but who were martyred before they could be baptized, the Church Fathers also acknowledge the possibility of salvation. They referred to such individuals as being baptized in their own blood. Thus St. Cyprian of Carthage wrote, in the mid-200s, when the age of persecution was still going on:

> Those catechumens hold the sound faith and truth of the Church, and advance from the divine camp to do battle with the devil, with a full and sincere acknowledgment of God the Father, and of Christ, and of the Holy Ghost; then, that they certainly are not deprived of the sacrament of baptism who are baptized with the most glorious and greatest baptism of blood, concerning which the Lord also said, that He had another baptism to be baptized with (Luke 12:50).

But the same Lord declares in the Gospel, that those who are baptized in their own blood, and sanctified by suffering, are perfected, and obtain the grace of the divine promise, when He speaks to the thief believing and confessing in His very passion, and promises that he should be with Himself in paradise (Luke 23:40–43) (*Letters* 72:22).

Even after the age of persecutions, there was still the problem of catechumens who died—without martyrdom—before they could be baptized. What of them? Here, too, the Fathers recognized the possibility of their salvation.

In the late 300s, St. Ambrose of Milan stated:

I hear you lamenting because (the Emperor Valentinian) had not received the sacrament of baptism. Tell me, what else could we have, except the will to it, the asking for it? He too now had this desire, and after he came into Italy it was begun, and a short time ago he signified that he wished to be baptized by me. Did he not have the grace he desired? Did he not have what he eagerly sought? Certainly, because he sought it, he received it. What else does it mean: "Whatever just man shall be overtaken by death, his soul shall be at rest" (Wis. 4:7)? (*Sympathy at the Death of Valentinian*).

And Ambrose's protégé, St. Augustine, similarly wrote:

If unbaptized persons die confessing Christ, this confession is of the same efficacy for the remission of sins as if they were washed in the sacred font of baptism. For he who said, "Except a man be born of water and of the Spirit, he cannot enter into the kingdom of God" (John 3:5) also made an exception in their favor, in that other sentence in which he clearly said, "Whosoever shall confess me before men, him will I confess also before my Father which is in heaven" (Matt. 10:32) (*City of God* 13:7).

Elsewhere, he wrote:

When we speak of within and without in relation to the Church, it is the position of the heart that we must consider, not of the body. . . . All who are within [the Church] in heart are saved in the unity of the ark (*On Baptism, Against the Donatists* 5:28:39).

Therefore, while in the age of the Church Fathers we find a recognition that baptism and the formal membership in the Church are ordinarily required for salvation, we also find a recognition of the possibility of salvation for those who have not heard the gospel but who live according to Reason and for those who have faith in Christ but who die before baptism.

Exclusivity in the Middle Ages

The teaching that baptism of blood and the desire for baptism could make salvation possible continued to be recognized in the Middle Ages. In the 1200s, St. Thomas Aquinas taught:

The sacrament or Baptism may be wanting to someone in two ways. First, both in reality and in desire; as is the case with those who neither are baptized, nor wished to be baptized: which clearly indicates contempt of the sacrament, in regard to those who have the use of the free-will. Consequently those to whom Baptism is wanting thus, cannot obtain salvation: since neither sacramentally nor mentally are they incorporated in Christ, through Whom alone can salvation be obtained.

Secondly, the sacrament of Baptism may be wanting to anyone in reality but not in desire: for instance, when a man wishes to be baptized, but by some ill-chance he is forestalled by death before receiving Baptism. And such a man can obtain salvation without being actually baptized, on account of his desire for Baptism, which desire is the outcome of "faith that worketh by charity," whereby God, Whose power is not tied to visible sacraments, sanctifies man inwardly. Hence

Ambrose says of Valentinian, who died while yet a catechu-men: "I lost him whom I was to regenerate: but he did not lose the grace he prayed for" (*Summa Theologiae* III:68:2).

However, during this period, the idea that someone could be saved who had not heard the gospel went into something of an eclipse.

The reason was that, unlike the age of the Church Fathers, there were very few unevangelized people in Europe. There were a few, residual pagans in Scandinavia, but even they had heard of Christ. There were heretics, who were to be stamped out if they refused to recant. In the East there were schismat-ics. There were Jews in some locations who knew the gospel of Christ but rejected it. And there were Muslims who were vio-lent enemies of the cross.

The fact that there were whole continents full of people who had never heard the gospel was unknown. To medieval Euro-pean Catholics, it seemed there were very few people who had no knowledge whatsoever of the Christian Faith, and it was easy to view those who weren't members of the Church as being in bad faith. After all, they could convert if they wanted, and the fact that they did not was taken as evidence of their hostility to the Faith.

Still, theologians did recognize the theoretical possibility of a person not having heard the gospel, as in the case of feral chil-dren brought up in the forest or by wild animals. What would God do in such a person's case?

According to one theory, if the person otherwise lived as he should, God would arrange it for a missionary (or even an an-gel!) to come and evangelize him before he died—or else God himself would give him a direct, personal revelation so that he could believe the gospel. St. Thomas Aquinas wrote:

Granted that everyone is bound to believe something ex-plicitly, no untenable conclusion follows even if someone is brought up in the forest or among wild beasts. For it per-tains to divine providence to furnish everyone with what is necessary for salvation, provided that on his part there is no hindrance. Thus, if someone so brought up followed the direction of natural reason in seeking good and avoiding evil, we must most certainly hold that God would either reveal to him through internal inspiration what had to be believed, or would send some preacher of the faith to him as he sent Peter to Cornelius (Acts 10:20) (*De Veritate* 14:11 ad 1).

St. Thomas held that explicit belief in the gospel was necessary for salvation, though it could be obtained by those who were not baptized through no fault of their own.

It was during this period that some of the most famous—and sharply worded—formulations of the need to belong to the Church were framed. For example, in 1215 the Fourth Lateran Council issued a profession of faith against the Albigensians and other heretics, which stated:

One indeed is the universal Church of the faithful, outside which no one at all is saved (D 430 [DS 802]).

Almost a century later, in 1302, Pope Boniface VIII issued the bull *Unam Sanctam*, in which he made the following dogmatic definition:

We declare, say, define, and proclaim to every human creature that they by necessity for salvation are entirely subject to the Roman Pontiff (D 469 [DS 873]).

And, in 1442, the Council of Florence taught:

It [the Church] firmly believes, professes, and proclaims that those not living within the Catholic Church, not only pagans, but also Jews and heretics and schismatics cannot become participants in eternal life, but will depart "into everlasting fire which was prepared for the devil and his angels" (Matt. 25:41), unless before the end of life the same have been added to the flock; and that the unity of the ecclesiastical body is so strong that only to those remaining in it are the sacraments of the Church of benefit for salvation, and do fastings, almsgiving, and other functions of piety and exercises of Christian service produce eternal reward, and that no one, whatever almsgiving he has practiced, even if he has shed blood for the name of Christ, can be saved, unless he has remained in the bosom and unity of the Catholic Church (*Decree for the Jacobites*, D 714 [DS 1351]).

These statements are to be understood in terms of the context in which they were written. As we have noted, the theology of the day recognized the possibility of salvation for those who consciously desired baptism but were prevented from receiving it through no fault of their own.

It was also understood at this time that the only people who were outside the Church (pagans, Jews, heretics, and schismatics) were *not* outside of the Church through no fault of their own. They were thought to be *culpable* for their failure to join it.

That assumption was called into question by the discovery of the New World.

Exclusivity in the Age of Exploration

The discovery that there were whole continents of people who had never heard the gospel caused a major rethinking of the question of whether explicit faith was needed for salvation. As Francis A. Sullivan, S.J., explained:

The Decree for the Jacobites, which declared that all pagans were destined for the fires of hell, was enacted in the year 1442. Just fifty years later, Columbus discovered America, shattering what had been the assumption of the medieval mind that the world was practically co-extensive with Christendom. Now Christian thinkers had to ask themselves: How can we continue to judge all pagans guilty of sinful unbelief, when we know that countless people have been living without the knowledge of the gospel, though no fault of their own? And how can we reconcile our belief in the universality of God's salvific will with the fact that he apparently has left all those people without any possibility of becoming members of the Church, outside of which they could not be saved? (*Salvation Outside the Church?*, 69).

Although Christianity was the dominant religion in Europe, suddenly theologians realized that the world was a much bigger place. They were forced to confront the fact that they were living in an age more like that of the Church Fathers than they had realized. The Fathers lived in an age when Christians were not a majority and when there were vast numbers of unevangelized people, many of whom seemed virtuous. Now theologians had to grapple with the fact that this was still true.

The discovery of the New World eventually would lead to a retrieval of the kind of thinking about the unevangelized that St. Justin Martyr and other Fathers had explored. Cardinal Avery Dulles, S.J., explained:

A major theological development occurred in the sixteenth and seventeenth centuries. The voyages of discovery had by this time disclosed that there were large populations in North and South America, Africa, and Asia who had lived since the time of Christ and had never had access to the preaching of the gospel. The missionaries found no sign that even the most upright among these peoples had learned the mysteries of the Trinity and the Incarnation by interior inspirations or angelic visitations.

Luther, Calvin, and the Jansenists professed the strict Augustinian doctrine that God did not will to save everyone, but the majority of Catholic theologians rejected the idea that God had consigned all these unevangelized persons to hell without giving them any possibility of salvation. A series of theologians proposed more hopeful theories that they took to be compatible with Scripture and Catholic tradition.

The Dominican Melchior Cano argued that these populations were in a situation no different from that of the pre-Christian pagans praised by Justin and others. They could be justified in this life (but not saved in the life to come) by implicit faith in the Christian mysteries. Another Dominican, Domingo de Soto, went further, holding that, for the unevangelized, implicit faith in Christ would be sufficient for salvation itself. Their contemporary, Albert Pighius, held that for these unevangelized persons the only faith required would be that mentioned in Hebrews 11:6: "Without faith it is impossible to please him. For whoever would draw near to God must believe that he exists and that he rewards those who seek him." They could therefore be saved by general revelation and grace even though no missionary came to evangelize them.

The Jesuit Francisco Suarez, following these pioneers, argued for the sufficiency of implicit faith in the Trinity and the Incarnation, together with an implicit desire for baptism on the part of the unevangelized. Cardinal Juan de Lugo agreed, but he added that such persons could not be saved if they had committed serious sins, unless they obtained forgiveness by an act of perfect contrition ("Who Can Be Saved?" *First Things*, February 2008).

In the age of the Fathers, St. Justin Martyr had proposed that unevangelized people could be related to Christ, the Logos, if they lived according to reason (*meta logou*). Now, theologians were proposing something similar—that the unevangelized could be related to Christ through *implicit* rather than *explicit* faith. The concept of implicit faith would be a key part of the eventual solution to the question.

Another key part would be the concept of invincible ignorance. It had been recognized for centuries that people cannot be held accountable for what they could not have known. Aquinas referred to this type of ignorance as "invincible" because "it cannot be known by study" (*Summa Theologiae* I–II:76:2).

Initially, it was assumed that the only way for a person to be invincibly ignorant of the gospel was if he had never heard it. If the gospel had been proclaimed to him, he was at fault if he did not accept it. But among the new insights that came out of the discussion over the New World natives was the fact that the question of *how* the gospel was presented was *also* relevant to whether a person was responsible for not accepting it.

The sixteenth-century Spanish Dominican theologian Francisco de Vitoria proposed that more than merely hearing the gospel announced was required to make a person culpable for disbelieving it. Motives of credibility, such as miracles or demonstrable holiness of life, were needed, and—in fact—the conquistadors were doing things that positively scandalized the recently discovered Indians and drove them away from the Faith. He wrote:

> It is not sufficiently clear to me that the Christian faith has yet been so put before the aborigines and announced to them that they are bound to believe it or commit fresh sin. I say this because (as appears from my second proposition) they are not bound to believe unless the faith be put before them with persuasive demonstration. Now, I hear of no miracles or signs or religious patterns of life; nay, on the other hand, I hear of many scandals and cruel crimes and acts of impiety. Hence it does not appear that the Christian religion has been preached to them with such sufficient propriety and piety that they are bound to acquiesce in it, although many religious and other ecclesiastics seem both by their lives and example and their diligent preaching to have bestowed sufficient pains and industry in this business, had they not been hindered therein by others who had other matters in their charge (*De Indis* I:2:14).

This was an important conceptual advance for, as Fr. Sullivan noted:

> During the middle ages, it does not seem to have occurred to Christians to ask whether the Christian message had been

proclaimed to the Jews in a convincing way, or whether the evil actions of Christians might have proved an obstacle to their being persuaded of the truth of Christianity (op. cit., 73).

As this insight began to sink in, theologians came to recognize that the natives in newly discovered parts of the world might not be at fault if they didn't immediately embrace the gospel because of the way it had been presented to them. The same insight was applied to other non-Catholics, such as Jews, Muslims, and even Christian heretics.

For example, Cardinal Juan de Lugo wrote in the 1600s:

> He who is baptized as an infant by heretics, and is brought up by them in false doctrine, when he reaches adulthood, could for some time not be guilty of sin against the Catholic Faith, as long as this had not been proposed to him in a way sufficient to oblige him to embrace it. However, if the Catholic Faith were subsequently proposed to him in a way sufficient to oblige him to embrace it and to abandon errors contrary to it, and he still persisted in his errors, then he would be a heretic (*De Virtute Fidei Divinae*, disp. 20, n. 149, pp. 566–567; cited in Sullivan, op. cit., 97).

Over time, the first kind of case—where the person baptized and brought up by heretics does not sin against the Catholic Faith—came to be included under the heading of invincible ignorance. It was not that the person *could not* have overcome his ignorance by study (the definition offered of invincible ignorance by Aquinas, see above). It is that the person could not be expected to change his view since the Faith "had not been proposed to him in a way sufficient to oblige him to embrace it."

This fits a more contemporary understanding of invincible ignorance:

> Ignorance is said to be invincible when a person is unable to rid himself of it notwithstanding the employment of moral diligence, that is, such as under the circumstances is, morally

speaking, possible and obligatory (*Catholic Encyclopedia*, 1910 ed., s.v. "Ignorance").

If the Faith has not been proposed in a way that would oblige one to accept it, then one could fail to accept it while still employing the moral diligence that, "under the circumstances is, morally speaking, possible and obligatory." A person in such a situation is thus invincibly ignorant of the truth of the Catholic Faith.

The discovery of the New World thus prompted a reconsideration of the status of non-Catholics in the Old World and whether they might be outside of the Church through no fault of their own.

Exclusivity in the Modern Age

The efforts of theologians in exploring the concepts of implicit faith and invincible ignorance led to the eventual solution that was endorsed by the magisterium, or teaching authority, of the Church. This also happened in stages.

Pius IX

On December 9, 1854—the day after he defined the dogma of the Immaculate Conception—Pope Pius IX delivered an address on the subject of invincible ignorance. In this address, he expressed caution regarding the salvation of most non-Catholics, but he also refused to deny the possibility, saying:

> Far be it from us, venerable brethren, to presume on the limits of the divine mercy which is infinite; far from us, to wish to scrutinize the hidden counsel and "judgments of God" which are "a great deep" (Ps. 35:7) and cannot be penetrated by human thought (*Singulari Quadem*; D 1646).

He condemned, however, the view that "the way of eternal salvation can be found in any religion whatsoever."

Pius IX thus held open the possibility of salvation for non-Catholics while at the same time resisting the claim that one's religion is in no way related to one's faith.

How these two principles can be harmonized was explored in what he said next:

> For, it must be held by faith that outside the Apostolic Roman Church, no one can be saved; that this is the only ark of salvation; that he who shall not have entered therein will perish in the flood; but, on the other hand, it is necessary to hold for certain that they who labor in ignorance of the true religion, if this ignorance is invincible, are not stained by any guilt in this matter in the eyes of God (op. cit.; D 1647).

Pius IX thus acknowledged that those who are in invincible ignorance of the truth of the Catholic Faith "are not stained by any guilt in this matter in the eyes of God."

He went even further and declared that the extent of invincible ignorance might, in fact, be very great, stating:

> Now, in truth, who would arrogate so much to himself as to mark the limits of such an ignorance, because of the nature and variety of peoples, regions, innate dispositions, and of so many other things? (ibid.)

Pius IX was thus prepared to acknowledge that those in invincible ignorance of the truth of the Catholic Faith would not be held accountable by God, that the number of these people might be very great, and that we are not to presume on "the limits of the divine mercy which is infinite."

Later, in 1863, he went further. Still expressing caution against the idea of simply thinking, *without any qualifications*, that those alienated from the Catholic Church could attain eternal salvation, he went on to acknowledge that those in invincible ignorance could "attain eternal life" if they lived honest lives, responding to "divine light and grace":

There are, of course, those who are struggling with invincible ignorance about our most holy religion. Sincerely observing the natural law and its precepts inscribed by God on all hearts and ready to obey God, they live honest lives and are able to attain eternal life by the efficacious virtue of divine light and grace. Because God knows, searches and clearly understands the minds, hearts, thoughts, and nature of all, his supreme kindness and clemency do not permit anyone at all who is not guilty of deliberate sin to suffer eternal punishments (*Quanto Conficiamur Moerore* 7).

Early Twentieth Century

Reflecting these developments, the early twentieth-century edition of the *Catholic Encyclopedia* noted:

This saying ("Outside the Church, no salvation") has been the occasion of so many objections that some consideration of its meaning seems desirable. It certainly does not mean that none can be saved except those who are in visible communion with the Church. The Catholic Church has ever taught that nothing else is needed to obtain justification than an act of perfect charity and of contrition. Whoever, under the impulse of actual grace, elicits these acts receives immediately the gift of sanctifying grace, and is numbered among the children of God (s.v. "The Church").

It further noted:

Should he die in these dispositions, he will assuredly attain heaven. It is true such acts could not possibly be elicited by one who was aware that God has commanded all to join the Church, and who nevertheless should willfully remain outside her fold. For love of God carries with it the practical desire to fulfill His commandments. But of those who die without visible communion with the Church, not all are guilty of willful disobedience to God's commands. Many are kept from the Church by ignorance. Such may be the case of numbers among those who have been brought up in heresy. To others the external means of grace may be unattainable. Thus an excommunicated person may have no opportunity of seeking reconciliation at the last, and yet may repair his faults by inward acts of contrition and charity.

It should be observed that those who are thus saved are not entirely outside the pale of the Church. The will to fulfill all God's commandments is, and must be, present in all of them. Such a wish implicitly includes the desire for incorporation with the visible Church: for this, though they know it not, has been commanded by God. They thus belong to the Church by desire ([Latin,] *voto*). Moreover, there is a true sense in which they may be said to be saved through the Church.

However useful it may be, the *Catholic Encyclopedia* is a witness to the Catholic thought of its time; it is not an expression of the Church's magisterium.

Pius XII

Pope Pius XII did exercise the magisterium, and in 1943, he issued the encyclical *Mystici Corporis*, which addressed the subject:

As you know, Venerable Brethren, from the very beginning of Our Pontificate, We have committed to the protection and guidance of heaven those who do not belong to the visible Body of the Catholic Church, solemnly declaring that after the example of the Good Shepherd We desire nothing more ardently than that they may have life and have it more abundantly. Imploring the prayers of the whole Church We wish to repeat this solemn declaration in this Encyclical Letter in which We have proclaimed the praises of the "great and glorious Body of Christ" and from a heart overflowing

with love We ask each and every one of them to correspond
to the interior movements of grace, and to seek to withdraw
from that state in which they cannot be sure of their salvation.
For even though by an unconscious desire and longing they
have a certain relationship with the Mystical Body of the
Redeemer, they still remain deprived of those many heavenly
gifts and helps which can only be enjoyed in the Catholic
Church. Therefore may they enter into Catholic unity and,
joined with Us in the one, organic Body of Jesus Christ, may
they together with us run on to the one Head in the Society
of glorious love. Persevering in prayer to the Spirit of love and
truth, We wait for them with open and outstretched arms to
come not to a stranger's house, but to their own, their father's
home (*Mystici Corporis* 103).

Here Pius XII acknowledges that non-Catholics can "have
a certain relationship" to the Church, the Mystical Body of the
Redeemer, by "an unconscious desire and longing."

Like the statements made by Pius IX, this statement does not
rule out the possibility of salvation for non-Catholics. Instead, it
appears to envision it, though it notes that outside of the Church
they "cannot be sure of their salvation" since they "remain deprived of those many heavenly gifts and helps which can only be
enjoyed in the Catholic Church."

The text also notes that they can have "a certain relationship"
with the Church "by an unconscious desire or longing." This gave
papal support to the solution proposed by theologians that non-
Catholics could have a saving union with Christ and his Mystical
Body, the Church, in an implicit rather than explicit way.

The Leonard Feeney Controversy

Pius XII's statement was not persuasive to everyone that non-
Catholics could be saved, and, in particular, it was not convincing
to a Boston-based American Jesuit named Leonard Feeney. In
the ensuing years, his St. Benedict Center issued a number of

publications that advocated a strict view of *Extra Ecclesiam, nulla salus*, arguing that all non-Catholics are damned. He even went so far as to deny that those who had baptism of blood or even the explicit desire for baptism could be saved.

The matter was eventually addressed by the Holy Office in Rome, which is today known as the Congregation for the Doctrine of the Faith. It sent a letter to the Cardinal Archbishop of Boston, Richard Cushing, which it ordered him to publish.

This letter was personally approved by Pope Pius XII, and it serves as an official clarification of his statements in *Mystici Corporis*. According to the Holy Office:

> In His infinite mercy God has willed that the effects, necessary for one to be saved, of those helps to salvation which are directed toward man's final end, not by intrinsic necessity, but only by divine institution, can also be obtained in certain circumstances when those helps are used only in desire and longing. This we see clearly stated in the Sacred Council of Trent, both in reference to the sacrament of regeneration (baptism) and in reference to the sacrament of penance (Denzinger, *Sources of Catholic Dogma*, nn. 797, 807).
>
> The same in its own degree must be asserted of the Church, in as far as she is the general help to salvation. Therefore, that one may obtain eternal salvation, it is not always required that he be incorporated into the Church actually as a member, but it is necessary that at least he be united to her by desire and longing.
>
> However, this desire need not always be explicit, as it is in catechumens; but when a person is involved in invincible ignorance God accepts also an implicit desire, so called because it is included in that good disposition of soul whereby a person wishes his will to be conformed to the will of God.
>
> These things are clearly taught in that dogmatic letter which was issued by the Sovereign Pontiff, Pope Pius XII, on June 29, 1943, *On the Mystical Body of Jesus Christ* (i.e., *Mystici Corporis*) (AAS, Vol. 35, an. 1943, p. 193 ff.). For in this letter

the Sovereign Pontiff clearly distinguishes between those who are actually incorporated into the Church as members, and those who are united to the Church only by desire.

The letter also contains an important clarification about the kind of implicit desire that is sufficient for salvation:

> But it must not be thought that any kind of desire of entering the Church suffices that one may be saved. It is necessary that the desire by which one is related to the Church be animated by perfect charity. Nor can an implicit desire produce its effect, unless a person has supernatural faith: "For he who comes to God must believe that God exists and is a rewarder of those who seek Him" (Heb. 11:6). The Council of Trent declares (Session VI, chap. 8): "Faith is the beginning of man's salvation, the foundation and root of all justification, without which it is impossible to please God and attain to the fellowship of His children" (Denzinger, n. 801).

Here the Holy Office indicated two requirements for a person to have an implicit desire that would allow salvation.

First, the person must have the theological virtue of charity, whereby God is loved above all things (CCC 1822). Charity and mortal sin cannot exist together; one excludes the other. Thus a person with the right kind of implicit desire could not be in mortal sin. In the absence of the sacraments of baptism or confession, he would be able to return to a state of grace through an act of perfect contrition (CCC 1452), being excused from the requirement of going to the sacrament by invincible ignorance.

Second, the person must have the theological virtue of faith, whereby what God reveals is believed because he is truth itself (CCC 1814).

A person with an implicit desire sufficient for salvation would thus have the theological virtues of faith and charity, meaning that they had "faith working by charity" (Gal. 5:6).

Vatican II

In the 1960s, the Second Vatican Council made several statements bearing on the question of salvation outside the visible boundaries of the Church. One was in the pastoral constitution *Gaudium et Spes*:

> Since Christ died for all men, and since the ultimate vocation of man is in fact one, and divine, we ought to believe that the Holy Spirit in a manner known only to God offers to every man the possibility of being associated with this paschal mystery (*Gaudium et Spes* 22).

The "paschal mystery" refers to the death of Christ on the cross and the graces that flow from this event. This statement suggests that, even if it is in a mysterious way that we do not perceive, God offers the possibility of salvation to every person.

Vatican II's dogmatic constitution *Lumen Gentium* contained a more detailed statement on the subject of salvation outside the Church. It explained:

> Basing itself upon Sacred Scripture and Tradition, [this Council] teaches that the Church, now sojourning on earth as an exile, is necessary for salvation. Christ, present to us in His Body, which is the Church, is the one Mediator and the unique way of salvation. In explicit terms He Himself affirmed the necessity of faith and baptism (cf. Mark 16:16, John 3:5) and thereby affirmed also the necessity of the Church, for through baptism as through a door men enter the Church. Whosoever, therefore, knowing that the Catholic Church was made necessary by Christ, would refuse to enter or to remain in it, could not be saved (*Lumen Gentium* 14).

The Council went on to explain:

> All the Church's children should remember that their exalted status is to be attributed not to their own merits but to the

special grace of Christ. If they fail moreover to respond to that grace in thought, word and deed, not only shall they not be saved but they will be the more severely judged.

It then discussed the various classes of people who are not formal members of the Church, beginning with catechumens:

Catechumens who, moved by the Holy Spirit, seek with explicit intention to be incorporated into the Church are by that very intention joined with her. With love and solicitude Mother Church already embraces them as her own.

The Council then notes the ways that non-Catholic Christians are linked to the Church (LG 15) and how they are related in various ways to those who have not yet received the gospel, including Jews and Muslims (LG 16). The Council concludes:

Nor is God far distant from those who in shadows and images seek the unknown God, for it is He who gives to all men life and breath and all things (cf. Acts 17:25–28), and as Savior wills that all men be saved (cf. 1 Tim. 2:4). Those also can attain to salvation who through no fault of their own do not know the Gospel of Christ or His Church, yet sincerely seek God and moved by grace strive by their deeds to do His will as it is known to them through the dictates of conscience (LG 16).

This would cover people who have explicit faith in God, but what about those who don't? Concerning them, the Council said:

Nor does Divine Providence deny the helps necessary for salvation to those who, without blame on their part, have not yet arrived at an explicit knowledge of God and with His grace strive to live a good life. Whatever good or truth is found amongst them is looked upon by the Church as a preparation for the Gospel. She knows that it is given by Him who enlightens all men so that they may finally have life.

The Council also warned that, despite the possibility of salvation for so many, this does not make it a reality. Consequently, it stated:

> But often men, deceived by the Evil One, have become vain in their reasonings and have exchanged the truth of God for a lie, serving the creature rather than the Creator (cf. Rom. 1:21, 25). Or some there are who, living and dying in this world without God, are exposed to final despair.

Because of this, the Council indicated, the Church must continue to fulfill its mission of evangelization:

> Wherefore to promote the glory of God and procure the salvation of all of these, and mindful of the command of the Lord, "Preach the Gospel to every creature" (Mark 16:16), the Church fosters the missions with care and attention.

John Paul II

After the Council, the subject of salvation outside the Church continued to be discussed. Unfortunately, in the doctrinal confusion of this period, some ignored what the Council had said about the necessity and unique role of the Church and began to propose that it does not matter at all what one's religion is and that other religions are equivalent to Christianity as means of approaching God.

St. John Paul II dealt with this issue a number of times during his pontificate. He wrote:

> The fact that the followers of other religions can receive God's grace and be saved by Christ apart from the ordinary means which he has established does not thereby cancel the call to faith and baptism which God wills for all people. It is a contradiction of the Gospel and of the Church's very nature to assert, as some do, that the Church is only one way

of salvation among many, and that her mission towards the followers of other religions should be nothing more than to help them be better followers of those religions (*Letter to the Fifth Plenary Assembly of the Asian Bishops' Conference* 4).

Similarly, during his pontificate, the Congregation for the Doctrine of the Faith issued a document known as *Dominus Iesus*, which reasserted the unique role of Christ and the Christian Faith in God's plan of salvation. Among other things, the document stated:

> With the coming of the Savior Jesus Christ, God has willed that the Church founded by him be the instrument for the salvation of all humanity (cf. Acts 17:30–31). This truth of faith does not lessen the sincere respect which the Church has for the religions of the world, but at the same time, it rules out, in a radical way, that mentality of indifferentism characterized by a religious relativism which leads to the belief that "one religion is as good as another." If it is true that the followers of other religions can receive divine grace, it is also certain that objectively speaking they are in a gravely deficient situation in comparison with those who, in the Church, have the fullness of the means of salvation.

The Catechism of the Catholic Church

It was during the pontificate of John Paul II that the *Catechism of the Catholic Church* was released. This document contained a number of passages bearing on the question of salvation outside the Church.

Under the heading "Outside the Church there is no salvation," it stated:

> How are we to understand this affirmation, often repeated by the Church Fathers? Re-formulated positively, it means that all salvation comes from Christ the Head through the Church which is his Body:

Basing itself on Scripture and Tradition, the Council teaches that the Church, a pilgrim now on earth, is necessary for salvation: the one Christ is the mediator and the way of salvation; he is present to us in his body which is the Church. He himself explicitly asserted the necessity of faith and Baptism, and thereby affirmed at the same time the necessity of the Church which men enter through Baptism as through a door. Hence they could not be saved who, knowing that the Catholic Church was founded as necessary by God through Christ, would refuse either to enter it or to remain in it (*Lumen Gentium* 14).

This affirmation is not aimed at those who, through no fault of their own, do not know Christ and his Church:

Those who, through no fault of their own, do not know the Gospel of Christ or his Church, but who nevertheless seek God with a sincere heart, and, moved by grace, try in their actions to do his will as they know it through the dictates of their conscience—those too may achieve eternal salvation (*Lumen Gentium* 16) (CCC 846–847).

The *Catechism* also contains several paragraphs dealing with the subjective state of some of those outside the Church. For example, in discussing the divisions that have arisen in the Christian community over the centuries, the *Catechism* states:

[O]ne cannot charge with the sin of the separation those who at present are born into these communities [that resulted from such separation] and in them are brought up in the faith of Christ, and the Catholic Church accepts them with respect and affection as brothers. . . . All who have been justified by faith in Baptism are incorporated into Christ; they therefore have a right to be called Christians, and with good reason are accepted as brothers in the Lord by the children of the Catholic Church.

Furthermore, many elements of sanctification and of truth are found outside the visible confines of the Catholic Church: the written Word of God; the life of grace; faith, hope, and charity, with the other interior gifts of the Holy Spirit, as well as visible elements. Christ's Spirit uses these Churches and ecclesial communities as means of salvation, whose power derives from the fullness of grace and truth that Christ has entrusted to the Catholic Church. All these blessings come from Christ and lead to him, and are in themselves calls to "Catholic unity" (CCC 818–819).

The *Catechism* also states that "many righteous people in all religions" walk with God in prayer:

Prayer is lived in the first place beginning with the realities of creation. The first nine chapters of Genesis describe this relationship with God as an offering of the first-born of Abel's flock, as the invocation of the divine name at the time of Enosh, and as "walking with God" (cf. Gen. 4:4, 26, 5:24). Noah's offering is pleasing to God, who blesses him and through him all creation, because his heart was upright and undivided; Noah, like Enoch before him, "walks with God" (Gen. 6:9, 8:20, 9:17). This kind of prayer is lived by many righteous people in all religions (CCC 2569).

Summary

As we have seen, the question of salvation outside the Church has historically involved the attempt to square two themes:

- The unique role in salvation of Jesus Christ and his requirement of becoming a member of his Mystical Body, the Church, by baptism.
- The sense that salvation also ought to be possible for those who are unable to respond to the Christian message through no fault of their own.

The first theme is clearly emphasized in the New Testament in a variety of passages, such as Jesus' declaration that he is "the way, and the truth, and the life," and that no one comes to the Father except by him. It is also emphasized by his mandate to the apostles to baptize those who would be his disciples and by passages indicating that baptism imparts salvation, that we become members of his body through baptism, and that his body is the Church.

The second theme, though less prominent in the New Testament, is suggested by St. Paul's statement to the Athenians that God "overlooked" the times of idolatry in the hopes that men would "feel after him and find him," and that some of their own thinkers had arrived at a partial knowledge of God. It is also suggested by his statement that Gentiles who do not know the Law of Moses have God's moral law written on their hearts and that they may find that their consciences excuse them on the day of judgment.

In the era of the Church Fathers, both themes continued to be stressed. The Fathers were quite clear about the need to embrace the Christian Faith, to enter the Church by baptism, and to remain in it rather than veering into heresy or schism. It was at this time that variants on the phrase "Outside the Church, no salvation" came into use.

At the same time, the second theme was also present, as the Fathers recognized that sacramental baptism was not always required for one to be saved. The phenomenon of unbaptized martyrs shedding their blood for Christ led to a recognition that "baptism of blood" can save, and the phenomenon of holy and zealous catechumens dying before baptism led to the view that explicit desire for baptism could lead to salvation.

The Fathers also recognized that not everyone had heard the gospel and that there were non-Christians who seemed to live virtuously. Some Fathers, notably St. Justin Martyr, held that those who had not heard the gospel, including various figures before the time of Christ, could be saved if they lived "according to reason" (*meta logou*), with Reason being identified as the Logos that enlightens every man, this Logos in turn being identified with Christ.

They thus pioneered the theory that people could have a saving relationship with Christ without an explicit knowledge of Christ. It remained true that no one would come to the Father except by Christ, but a conscious knowledge of Christ was not always required.

While the views that baptism of blood and the desire for baptism could save remained in the Middle Ages, the idea that one might be saved through Christ without an explicit knowledge of Christ went into eclipse. At the time, there were very few unevangelized people in Europe, and those who did not accept the Catholic Faith (schismatics, heretics, Jews, Muslims, and the few remaining pagans) seemed to European Catholics to have rejected the gospel in bad faith.

It was at this time that some of the most famous and sharply worded magisterial statements on salvation outside the Church were framed. These represented magisterial formulations of the first of the two major themes—the unique, saving role of Jesus Christ and his requirement of baptism and membership in his Church.

The Age of Exploration and the discovery of the New World led to the realization that there were enormous numbers of people around the globe who had never heard the gospel. This forced a major rethinking of the subject, as theologians realized that the idea that virtually everyone had been evangelized was false and that they were actually living in an age much like that of the Church Fathers in that Christians were a minority and many had no opportunity to respond to the gospel.

Over the course of a few centuries, theologians spurred by an awareness of God's universal salvific will (cf. 1 Tim. 2:4), began to retrieve the thought of those Fathers, such as St. Justin, who held that it was possible for individuals to have a saving relationship with Christ without an explicit knowledge of him.

It was proposed that those who were innocently ignorant of the gospel could be seen as having an implicit faith and an implicit desire for baptism and membership in the Church if they otherwise responded to the grace God had given them, e.g., by writing his law on their hearts.

It was also proposed that even those who had heard the gospel, but who had received an inadequate presentation of it or who had even been scandalized by the actions of Catholics, could also refuse to embrace the Catholic message without being personally at fault. This would allow the possibility of salvation for them as well, if they otherwise lived up to the grace they had received.

By the time of Pius IX in the nineteenth century, the papal magisterium was willing to affirm that those in innocent ignorance of the Catholic Faith would not automatically be lost on this account and that God's "supreme kindness and clemency do not permit anyone at all who is not guilty of deliberate sin to suffer eternal punishments."

In the mid-twentieth century, Pius XII taught even more definitively that it was possible for those in innocent ignorance to be saved through an implicit desire for baptism and membership in the Church. This implicit desire puts them in a saving relationship with the Church even if they are not, properly speaking, members of it. Pius XII's teaching was clarified further through the response of the Holy Office that Pius XII approved regarding the Leonard Feeney controversy.

In making their statements, both Pius IX and Pius XII strongly warned against the danger of religious indifferentism—the idea that one's religious affiliation makes no difference at all.

The Second Vatican Council took up the theme of salvation outside the Church in several passages, most notably in *Lumen Gentium*, which taught, "Those also can attain to salvation who through no fault of their own do not know the Gospel of Christ or His Church, yet sincerely seek God and moved by grace strive by their deeds to do His will as it is known to them through the dictates of conscience" (LG 16). The Council applied the same reasoning to those who "without blame on their part, have not yet arrived at an explicit knowledge of God" (ibid).

Vatican II spoke of people in this condition as being savingly "related" to the Church even though they are not "fully incorporated" into it.

The Council also warned that failure to achieve salvation is a real possibility for individuals and that the Church must pursue its missionary mandate of evangelization, as a result.

Following the Council, there was widespread outbreak of indifferentism, and the pontificate of St. John Paul II saw several interventions attempting to correct this. Most notable was the release in the year 2000 of the document *Dominus Iesus*, which the Congregation for the Doctrine of the Faith prepared on the unique role of Christ and his Church in salvation.

The *Catechism of the Catholic Church* was also released during the pontificate of John Paul II, and it contained a number of passages summarizing the Church's teaching on the question. In addition to offering a positive rephrasing of the "Outside the Church, no salvation" formula ("all salvation comes from Christ the Head through the Church which is his Body"), it reviewed the teaching of Vatican II and noted that "many righteous people in all religions" walk with God in prayer.

The magisterial interventions of the nineteenth and twentieth centuries served to give official form to the second of the two major themes: the idea that salvation should also be possible for those who, though no fault of their own, have not responded to the Catholic message but who otherwise respond to the grace that God has given them.

We thus find ourselves in an age in which both of the major themes concerning the possibility of salvation outside the Church have been the subject of developed magisterial teaching. While it is possible for those outside the formal boundaries of the Church to be saved, they are still saved through a connection with Jesus Christ and his Mystical Body, and we are still called to fulfill the Church's constant mission of preaching Jesus Christ and winning souls to him.

Now, let's go forth and evangelize!

BONUS MATERIALS
I

The Council of Trent's Decree
Concerning Justification

The following decree, along with the canons that follow it, was issued by the Council of Trent in 1547. It remains the longest, most authoritative treatment of the doctrine of justification that the Church's Magisterium has issued. For commentary on its interpretation, see chapter 7.

Preface

Whereas there is, at this time, not without the casting away of many souls, and grievous detriment to the unity of the Church, a certain erroneous doctrine disseminated concerning Justification; with a view to the praise and glory of Almighty God, the tranquilizing of the Church, and the salvation of souls, the sacred and holy, ecumenical and general Synod of Trent, lawfully assembled in the Holy Spirit—the most reverend lords, the lords Giammaria del Monte, bishop of Palestrina, and Marcellus of the title of the Holy Cross in Jerusalem, priest, cardinals of the holy Romish Church, and legates apostolic *a latere*, presiding therein, in the name of our most holy father and lord in Christ, Paul III, by the providence of God, Pope,—purposes to expound to all the faithful of Christ the true and sound doctrine of the said Justification; which the sun of righteousness,[49] Jesus Christ, *the author and finisher of our faith*[50] taught, the apostles transmitted, and the Catholic Church, the Holy Spirit reminding her thereof,[51] has continually retained; most strictly forbidding that any henceforth presume to believe, preach, or teach, otherwise than as by the present decree is ordained and declared.

CHAPTER I
On the inability of nature and of the law to justify man

The holy synod declares first, that, for the correct and sound understanding of the doctrine of Justification, it behoves that each one recognize and confess, that, whereas all men had lost their innocence in the prevarication of Adam,[52] having become unclean,[53] and, as the apostle says, *by nature the children of wrath,*[54] as (this synod) has set forth in the decree on original sin, they were so far *the servants of sin,*[55] and under the power of the devil and of death, that not only the Gentiles by the force of nature, but not even the Jews by the very letter itself of the law of Moses, were able to be liberated, or to arise, from thence; although in them free will, attenuated and bent down as it was in its powers, was by no means extinguished.

CHAPTER II
Touching the dispensation and mystery of the advent of Christ

Whence it came to pass, that the heavenly Father, *the Father of mercies and the God of all comfort,*[56] when that blessed *fullness of the time was come,*[57] *sent* unto men Jesus Christ, his own Son, who had been, both before the Law, and during the time of the Law, declared and promised to many of the holy fathers, that he might both redeem the Jews who were under the Law,[58] and that *the Gentiles, who followed not after justice,*[59] might attain to justice, and that all might receive the adoption of sons. Him hath God set forth *as a propitiator, through faith in his blood,*[60] *for our sins; and not for our sins only, but also for those of the whole world.*[61]

CHAPTER III
Who are justified through Christ

But, though *he died for all,*[62] yet do not all receive the benefit of his death; but those only, unto whom the merit of his Passion is communicated. For as in truth men, if they were not born propagated from the seed of Adam, would not be born unjust; whereas, by that propagation, they contract through the same (Adam) when they are conceived, injustice as their own; so, if they were not born again in Christ, they would never be justified; seeing that in that new birth there is bestowed upon them, through the merit of his Passion, the grace whereby they are made just. For this benefit the apostle exhorts us evermore *to give thanks to the Father, who hath made us meet to be partakers of the inheritance of the saints in light, and hath delivered us from the power of darkness, and hath translated us into the kingdom of the Son of his love, in whom we have redemption, and remission of sins.*[63]

CHAPTER IV
A description is interwoven[64] of the justification of the impious, and of the manner thereof under the state of grace

By which words a description of the justification of the impious is interwoven, to the effect that it is a translation from that state in which man is born a child of the first Adam, into the state of grace, and of *the adoption of the sons of God,*[65] through the second Adam, Jesus Christ, our Savior. And this translation, since the Gospel has been promulgated, cannot be effected, without the *laver of regeneration,*[66] or the desire thereof, as it is written; *Unless a man be born again of water and of the Holy Spirit, he cannot enter into the kingdom of God.*[67]

CHAPTER V
On the necessity of preparation for justification, in the case of adults, and whence it proceeds

[This synod] furthermore declares, that, in adults, the beginning of the said justification is to be taken from the preventing[68] grace of God, through Jesus Christ, that is to say, from his vocation, by which, without the existence of any merits on their parts, they are called; that so they, who through sins were turned away from God, may, through his quickening and assisting grace,

be disposed to turn themselves unto their own justification, by
freely assenting to, and co-operating with that said grace: so
that, while God toucheth the heart of man by the illumination
of the Holy Spirit, neither is man himself utterly inactive while
he receives that inspiration, inasmuch as he is also able to reject
it; yet is he not able, without the grace of God, by his own free
will to move himself unto justice in his sight. Whence, when it
is said in the sacred writings: *Turn ye unto me, and I will turn unto
you,*[69] we are admonished of our liberty, when we answer, *Turn
us, O Lord, unto thee, and we shall be turned,*[70] we confess that we
are prevented by the grace of God.

CHAPTER VI
The manner of preparation

Now they are disposed unto the said justice, when, quickened,
and assisted by divine grace, conceiving *faith by hearing*[71] they
are freely moved towards God, believing those things to be true
which have been divinely revealed and promised, and this especially, that the impious is justified of God *by his grace, through
the redemption that is in Christ Jesus;*[72] and when, understanding
themselves to be sinners, they, through the fear of divine justice,
whereby they are profitably agitated by turning themselves to
consider the mercy of God, are raised unto hope, trusting that
God will be propitious to them for Christ's sake; and they begin
to love him as the fountain of all justice; and are for that reason
moved against sins by a certain hatred and detestation, that is to
say, by that penitence[73] which must be performed before baptism: lastly, when they propose to receive baptism, to begin a
new life, and to keep the divine commandments. Concerning
this disposition it is written, *He that cometh to God, must believe
that he is, and is a rewarder to them that seek him;*[74] and, *Be of good
cheer, son, thy sins be forgiven thee;*[75] and, *The fear of the Lord driveth
away sin;*[76] and, *Do penance, and be baptized, every one of you in the
name of Jesus Christ, for the remission of your sins, and you shall receive
the gift of the Holy Spirit;*[77] and, *Going, therefore, teach ye all nations,*

baptizing them in the name of the Father, and of the Son, and of the Holy Spirit;[78] finally, *Prepare your hearts unto the Lord.*[79]

CHAPTER VII
What is the justification of the impious, and what are its causes

This disposition, or preparation, justification itself follows, which is not merely the remission of sins, but also the sanctification and renewal of the inward man, through the voluntary reception of the grace and gifts, whereby man from unjust becomes just, and from an enemy a friend, that so he may be *an heir according to the hope of eternal life.*[80]

Of this justification the causes are these: the final [cause] indeed is the glory of God and of Christ, and eternal life; while the efficient cause is the merciful God, who gratuitously *washes and sanctifies,*[81] *sealing,* and anointing *with* the holy *Spirit of promise, who is the earnest of our inheritance;*[82] but the meritorious cause is his most beloved only-begotten, our Lord Jesus Christ, who, when we were *enemies,*[83] *for the great charity wherewith he loved us,*[84] merited justification for us by his most holy Passion on the wood of the cross, and for us made satisfaction unto God the Father; the instrumental cause, moreover, is the sacrament of baptism, which is the sacrament of faith, without which justification never befell any man; lastly, the sole formal cause is the justice of God; not that by which he himself is just, but that by which he maketh us just, that, to wit, with which *we,* being endowed by him, *are renewed in the spirit of our mind,*[85] and we are not only reputed, but are truly called, and are, just, receiving justice within us, each one according to his own measure, *which the Holy Spirit divides to every man severally as he will,*[86] and according to each one's proper disposition and co-operation. For, although no one can be just, but he to whom the merits of the Passion of our Lord Jesus Christ are communicated, yet is this brought to pass in this justification of the impious, when, by the merit of that same most holy Passion, *the charity of God is shed abroad,* by the Holy Spirit, *in the hearts*[87] of those who are justi-

fied, and is inherent in them; whence man, in the said justification through Jesus Christ, into whom he is ingrafted, receives,
together with the remission of sins, all these things infused at
once, faith, hope, and charity. For faith, unless to it be added
hope and charity, neither unites [man] perfectly with Christ, nor
makes him a living member of his body. For which reason it is
most truly said, that *Faith without works is dead*,[88] and idle; and *In
Christ Jesus neither circumcision availeth anything, nor uncircumcision,
but faith which worketh by charity*.[89] This faith catechumens beg of
the Church, agreeably to a tradition of the apostles, previously
to the sacrament of baptism; when they beg for the faith which
bestoweth life everlasting, which, without hope and charity,
faith cannot bestow. Whence also do they straightway hear that
word of Christ: *If thou wilt enter into life, keep the commandments*.[90]
Wherefore, when receiving true and Christian justice, they, immediately on being born again, are commanded to preserve it
pure and spotless, as *the first robe*,[91] given unto them through Jesus
Christ, instead of that which Adam, by his disobedience, lost for
himself and for us, that so they may bear it before the tribunal of
our Lord Jesus Christ, and may have life everlasting.

CHAPTER VIII
*In what manner it must be understood that the impious is justified by
faith, and freely*

But whereas the apostle saith, that man is *justified by faith*, and *freely*,[92] those words are to be understood in that sense which the per-
petual consent of the Catholic Church hath held and expressed; to
wit, that we be therefore said to be *justified by faith*, because faith
is the beginning of human salvation, the foundation, and the root
of all justification; *without which it is impossible to please God*,[93] and
to come unto the fellowship of his sons; but we are therefore said
to be justified *freely*, because none of those things which precede
justification, whether faith or works, merit the grace itself of justification. For, *if it be a grace, then it is no more by works, otherwise*, as
the same apostle saith, *grace is no more grace*.[94]

CHAPTER IX
Against the vain confidence of heretics

But, although it be necessary to believe that sins neither are remitted, nor ever have been remitted, save *freely*, by the divine
mercy for Christ's sake; yet is it not to be said, that sins are
forgiven, or have been forgiven, to anyone who boasts of his
confidence and certainty of the remission of his sins, and rests
on that alone; since it may exist, yea, does in our time exist,
among heretics and schismatics; and with great earnestness is
this confidence, vain, and remote from all piety, preached up
in opposition to the Catholic Church. But neither is this to be
asserted—that it behoves them who are truly justified, without
any doubting whatever, to settle within themselves that they are
justified, and that no one is absolved from sins and justified, but
he who for certain believes that he is absolved and justified; and
that absolution and justification are effected by this faith alone;
as though whosoever believeth not this, doubts respecting the
promises of God, and the efficacy of the death and resurrection
of Christ. For, as no pious person ought to doubt respecting the
mercy of God, the merit of Christ, and the virtue and efficacy
of the sacraments, so each one, when he regards himself, and
his own peculiar weakness and indisposition, may entertain fear
and apprehension concerning his own grace; inasmuch as no one
can know with a certainty of faith, which cannot be subject to
mistake, that he has obtained the grace of God.

CHAPTER X
On the increase of justification received

Having, therefore, been thus justified, and made the friends
and domestics *of the household of God*,[95] advancing *from strength to
strength*,[96] they are *renewed*, as the apostle says, *day by day*;[97] that
is, *by mortifying the members*[98] of their own flesh, and by *yielding
them as instruments of righteousness unto holiness*,[99] they, through the
observance of the commandments of God and of the Church,

faith co-operating with good works, increase in the justice received through the grace of Christ, and are still more justified, as is written,—*He that is righteous, let him be made righteous still*;[100] and again, *Be not afraid to be justified even to death*;[101] and also, *Ye see how that by works a man is justified, and not by faith only.*[102] And this increase of justification, the Holy Church begs, when she prays, "Give unto us, O Lord, increase of faith, hope, and charity."[103]

CHAPTER XI
On the keeping of the commandments, and on the necessity and possibility thereof

But no one, how much soever justified, ought to think himself free from the observance of the commandments; no one ought to make use of that rash saying, prohibited by the fathers under an anathema; that the commandments of God are impossible for one that is justified to observe. For God commands not impossibilities, but, by commanding, admonishes thee both to do what thou art able, and to pray for what thou art not able,[104] and aids thee that thou mayest be able; *whose commandments are not grievous*;[105] *whose yoke is sweet and whose burden light.*[106] For whosoever are the sons of God, love Christ; but *they who love him*, as himself doth testify, *keep his commandments*;[107] which, assuredly, with the divine assistance, they can do. For, although in this mortal life, men, how holy and just soever, at times fall into at least light and daily sins, which are also called venial; yet they do not therefore cease to be just. For that cry of the just, *Forgive us our trespasses*,[108] is both humble and true; whence it happens, the just themselves ought to feel themselves the more obliged to walk in the way of Justice, in that, *being* already *freed from sins, but made servants unto God*,[109] they are able, *living soberly, righteously, and godly*,[110] to proceed onwards *through Jesus Christ, by whom they have had access unto that grace.*[111] For God deserts not those who have been once justified by his grace, unless he be first deserted by them. Wherefore, no one ought to flatter himself upon faith alone, deeming that by faith alone he is made an heir, and will obtain the inheritance, even though *he suffer* not *with Christ, that* so *he may be also glorified together (with him).*[112] For even *Christ* himself, as the apostle saith, *though he was the son* of God, *learned obedience by the things which he suffered, and being made perfect,*[113] *he became the cause of eternal salvation unto all who obey him.*[114] For which reason the same apostle admonishes the justified, saying: *Know ye not that they which run in the race, run all indeed, but one receiveth the prize? So run, that ye may obtain. I therefore so run, not as uncertainly: so fight I, not as one that beateth the air; but I chastise my body, and bring it into subjection; lest that by any means, when I have preached to others, I myself should become a cast-away.*[115] So also the prince of the apostles, Peter: *Then rather give diligence, that by good works ye may make sure your calling and election. For if ye do these things, you shall not sin at any time.*[116] Whence it is certain, that those who are opposed to the orthodox doctrine of religion,[117] who say that the just man sins, venially at least, in every good work: or, which is still more insupportable, that he merits eternal punishments; as also those who state,[118] that the just sin in all their works, if in those (works) they, in order to stimulate their own sloth, and to encourage themselves *to run in the course,* besides this chief aim, that God be glorified, regard also the eternal reward; whereas it is written, *I have inclined my heart to do all thy justifications for the reward;*[119] and, concerning Moses, the apostle saith, that *he had respect unto the reward.*[120]

CHAPTER XII
That a rash presumption in regard to predestination is to be avoided

No one, moreover, so long as he exists in this mortal state, ought so far to presume concerning the secret mystery of divine pre-destination, as to determine for certain that he is assuredly in the number of the predestinated; as if it were true, that he who is justified, either cannot sin any more, or if he do sin, that he ought to promise himself a certain repentance; for except by a special revelation, it cannot be known whom God hath chosen unto himself.

CHAPTER XIII
Touching the gift of perseverance

In like manner touching the gift of perseverance, of which it is written, *He that shall endure to the end, he shall be saved*[121]—which [gift] cannot indeed be obtained from any other save him, who is able to establish him who standeth,[122] that he stand perseveringly, and to restore him who falleth—let no one promise himself anything as certain with absolute certainty; though all ought to place and repose the most firm hope in God's help. For God, unless men themselves be wanting to his grace, *as he has begun the good work, so will he perfect it, working* (in them) *to will and to do.*[123] Nevertheless, let those who *think they stand, take heed lest they fall,*[124] and, *with fear and trembling work out their salvation,*[125] in labors, in watchings, in almsgivings, in prayers and oblations, in fastings and in chastity. For, knowing that they are born again unto a hope of glory,[126] and not as yet unto glory, they ought to fear for the combat which remains, with the flesh, with the world, with the devil, wherein they cannot be victors, unless they, with God's grace, obey the apostle, who says; *We are debtors, not to the flesh, to live after the flesh; for if ye live after the flesh, ye shall die; but if ye through the spirit do mortify the deeds of the flesh, ye shall live.*[127]

CHAPTER XIV
On the fallen, and their restoration

But those who through sin have fallen away from the received grace of justification, may again be justified, when, God exciting them, through the sacrament of penance, they, by the merit of Christ, shall have obtained the recovery of the grace lost. For this manner of justification is unto the fallen the reparation, which the holy fathers have aptly called a second plank after the shipwreck of grace lost.[128] For, on behalf of those who after baptism fall into sins, Christ Jesus instituted the sacrament of penance, when he said, *Receive ye the Holy Spirit; whosoever sins ye shall remit, they are remitted unto them, and whosesoever sins ye shall retain, they are retained.*[129] Whence it is to be taught, that the penitence of a Christian man after his fall, is very different from that at his baptism; and that therein are included not only a cessation from sins, and a detestation thereof, or, *a contrite and humble heart,*[130] but also the sacramental confession of the same sins, at least in desire, and to be made in its season, and sacerdotal absolution; and likewise satisfaction by fasts, almsgivings, prayers, and the other pious exercises of a spiritual life; not indeed for the eternal punishment, which is, together with the guilt, remitted, either by the sacrament, or by the desire of the sacrament; but for the temporal punishment, which, as the sacred writings teach, is not always wholly remitted, as is done in baptism, unto those who, ungrateful to the grace of God which they have received, have *grieved the Holy Spirit,*[131] and have not feared *to defile the temple of God.*[132] Concerning which penitence it is written: *Remember from whence thou art fallen; do penance, and do the first works.*[133] And again: *The sorrow that is according to God worketh penance steadfast unto salvation.*[134] And again: *Do penance, and bring forth fruits worthy of penance.*[135]

CHAPTER XV
That, by every mortal sin, grace is lost, but not faith

In opposition also to the cunning wits of certain men, who, *by good works and fair speeches, deceive the hearts of the innocent,*[136] it is to be maintained, that the received grace of justification is lost, not only by infidelity, in which even faith itself is lost, but also by any other mortal sin soever, though faith be not lost; thereby defending the doctrine of the divine law, which excludes from the kingdom of God not only the unbelieving, but also the faithful who are *fornicators, adulterers, effeminate, abusers of themselves with mankind, thieves, covetous, drunkards, revilers, extortioners,*[137] and all others who commit deadly sins; from which, with the help of divine grace, they are able to refrain, and on account of which they are separated from the grace of Christ.

CHAPTER XVI
*On the fruit of justification, that is, on the merit of good works
and on the manner of that same merit*

Unto men, therefore, who have been justified after this manner, whether they have preserved uninterruptedly the grace received, or have recovered it when lost, are to be set the words
of the apostle: *Abound in every good work, knowing that your labor
is not in vain in the Lord;*[138] *for God is not unrighteous to forget your
work, and the love which ye have showed in his name;*[139] and, *cast not
away your confidence, which hath a great recompense.*[140] And, for this
cause, unto them who work well *unto the end,*[141] and hoping in
God, life eternal is to be proposed, both as a grace mercifully
promised to the sons of God through Jesus Christ, and as a recompense which is to be faithfully rendered to their good works
and merits according to the promise of God himself. For this
is that *crown of righteousness* which the apostle asserted was, after
his *fight* and *course, laid up for him, to be given to him by the righteous
judge, and not only to him, but unto all that love his coming,*[142] For,
whereas Jesus Christ himself, as the head into the members,
and the vine into the branches, continually causes his virtue to
flow into the said justified, which virtue always precedes and
accompanies and follows after their good works, and without
which it could not in anywise be pleasing and meritorious before God, we must needs believe that to the justified nothing
further is wanting, but that they be accounted to have, by those
very works which have been done in God, fully satisfied the
divine law according to the state of this life, and truly to have
merited eternal life, to be obtained also in its due time; if so
be, however, that they shall have departed in grace: forasmuch
as Christ, our Savior, saith: *If anyone shall drink of the water that
I shall give him, he shall not thirst for ever; but it shall become in him
a well of water springing up into everlasting life.*[143] Thus, neither is
our own *righteousness established as our own*[144] as from ourselves;
nor is the righteousness of God denied or repudiated: for that
righteousness which is called ours, because we are justified

from its being inherent in us, that same is [the righteousness] of God, because it is infused into us of God, through the merit of Christ. Nor is this to be omitted, that, although, in the sacred writings, so much is attributed to good works, that Christ promises, that even *he that shall give a drink of cold water to one of his least ones, shall not lose his reward;*[145] and the apostle bears witness that, *That which is at present but for a moment and light of our tribulation, worketh for us a far more exceeding eternal weight of glory;*[146] nevertheless far be it that a Christian man should either trust or glory in himself, and not *in the Lord,*[147] whose goodness towards all men is so great, that he will have the things which are his own gifts to be their own merits.[148] And whereas *in many things we all offend,*[149] each one ought to have before his eyes, as well severity and judgment, as mercy and goodness; neither ought any one *to judge himself,* even though he be not conscious to himself of anything;[150] inasmuch as the whole life of man is to be examined and judged, not by the judgment of men, but of God, *who will bring to light the hidden things of darkness, and will make manifest the counsels of the hearts, and then shall every man have praise of God,*[151] who, as it is written, *will render to every man according to his works.*[152]

After this Catholic doctrine on justification, which whosoever receiveth not faithfully and firmly cannot be justified, it hath pleased the holy synod to subjoin these canons, that all may Know not only what they ought to hold and follow, but also what to avoid and shun.

On Justification
Canon I. If anyone shall say, that man may be justified before God by his own works, whether done through the strength of human nature, or through the teaching of the law, without the divine grace through Jesus Christ; let him be anathema.

Canon II. If anyone shall say, that the divine grace through Jesus Christ is given only unto this, that man may more easily be able to live justly, and to merit eternal life, as if, by free will without

grace, he were able (to do) both, though hardly and with difficulty; let him be anathema.

Canon III. If anyone shall say, that without the preventing inspiration of the Holy Spirit, and his help, man can believe, hope,
love, or be penitent, as he ought, so that the grace of justification
may be conferred upon him; let him be anathema.

Canon IV. If anyone shall say, that the free will of man moved
and excited by God, by assenting to God exciting and calling,
nowise co-operates to the end that it should dispose and prepare
itself for obtaining the grace of justification; and that it cannot
refuse consent, if it would, but that, like something inanimate,
it does nothing whatever, and is merely in a passive state; let him
be anathema.

Canon V. If anyone shall say, that, since Adam's sin, the free will
of man is lost and extinguished; or, that it is a thing with a name
only, yea, a title without a reality, a figment, in fine, brought
into the Church by Satan; let him be anathema.

Canon VI. If anyone shall say, that it is not in the power of man
to make his ways evil, but that God worketh the works that are
evil as well as those that are good, not by permission only, but
properly, and of himself, in such wise that the treason of Judas
be no less his own proper work than the calling of Paul; let him
be anathema.

Canon VII. If anyone shall say, that all works which are done before justification, in what manner soever they be done, are truly
sins, or deserve the hatred of God; or that, the more earnestly
one strive to dispose himself for grace, so much the more griev-
ously he sins; let him be anathema.

Canon VIII. If anyone shall say, that the fear of hell, through
which, by grieving for our sins, we flee unto the mercy of God,

or refrain from sinning, is a sin, or makes sinners worse; let him be anathema.

Canon IX. If anyone shall say, that by faith alone the impious is justified; so as to mean that nothing else is required to co-operate in order unto the obtaining the grace of justification, and that it is not in any respect necessary that he be prepared and disposed by the movement of his own will; let him be anathema.

Canon X. If anyone shall say, that men are justified without the righteousness of Christ, by which he merited for us to be justi-fied; or that it is by that [justice] itself that they are formally just; let him be anathema.

Canon XI. If anyone shall say, that men are justified either by the sole imputation of the righteousness of Christ, or by the sole re-mission of sins, to the exclusion of the grace and *the charity which is shed abroad in their hearts by the Holy Spirit*,[153] and is inherent in them; or even that the grace, by which we are justified, is only the favor of God; let him be anathema.

Canon XII. If anyone shall say, that justifying faith is nought else but confidence in the divine mercy which remits sins for Christ's sake; or that it is this confidence alone by which we are justified; let him be anathema.

Canon XIII. If anyone shall say, that it is necessary unto every one, for the obtaining the remission of sins, that he believe for certain, and without any hesitation arising from his own infir-mity and indisposition, that his sins are remitted unto him; let him be anathema.

Canon XIV. If anyone shall say, that man is absolved from his sins and justified, because that he assuredly believed himself to be absolved and justified; or that no one is truly justified save he who believes himself justified; and that, by this faith alone, absolution and justification are perfected; let him be anathema.

Canon XV. If anyone shall say, that a man, who is born again and justified, is bound of faith to believe that he is assuredly in the number of the predestinated; let him be anathema.

Canon XVI. If anyone shall say, that he will for certain, of an absolute and infallible certainty, have that great gift of perseverance unto the end, unless that he have learnt this by a special revelation; let him be anathema.

Canon XVII. If anyone shall say, that the grace of justification only befalleth those who are predestined unto life; but that all others who are called, are called indeed, but receive not grace, as being, by the divine power, predestined unto evil; let him be anathema.

Canon XVIII. If anyone shall say, that the commandments of God are, even for a man that is justified and constituted in grace, impossible to keep; let him be anathema.

Canon XIX. If anyone shall say that nothing besides faith is commanded in the Gospel; that other things are indifferent, neither commanded nor prohibited, but free; or, that the ten commandments in nowise appertain to Christians; let him be anathema.

Canon XX. If anyone shall say, that a man who is justified and how perfect soever, is not bound to the observance of the commandments of God and of the Church, but only to believe; as if, forsooth, the Gospel were a bore and absolute promise of eternal life, without the condition of observation of the commandments; let him be anathema.

Canon XXI. If anyone shall say, that Christ Jesus was given of God unto men, as a redeemer, in whom they should trust, and not also as a legislator, whom they should obey; let him be anathema.

Canon XXII. If anyone shall say, that the justified is able either to persevere, without the special assistance of God, in the justice received; or that, with that [assistance], he is not able; let him be anathema.

Canon XXIII. If anyone shall say, that a man once justified can sin no more, nor lose grace, and that therefore he that falls and sins was never truly justified; or, on the other hand, that he is able, throughout his whole life, to avoid all sins, even those that are venial, except by a special privilege from God, as the Church holds respecting the Blessed Virgin;[154] let him be anathema.

Canon XXIV. If anyone shall say, that the justice received is not preserved, and also increased in the sight of God through good works; but that the said works are merely the fruits and signs of justification received, but not a cause of the increase thereof; let him be anathema.

Canon XXV. If anyone shall say, that, in every good work, the just sins venially at least, or, which is still more intolerable, mortally, and therefore deserves eternal punishments; and that it is only for this cause he is not damned, because God does not impute those works unto damnation; let him be anathema.

Canon XXVI. If anyone shall say, that the just ought not, for their good works which have been done in God, to expect and hope for an eternal recompense from God, through his mercy and the merit of Jesus Christ, if they persevere *unto the end*[155] in well doing and in keeping the divine commandments; let him be anathema.

Canon XXVII. If anyone shall say, that there is no deadly sin but that of infidelity; or, that grace once received is not lost by any other sin, however grievous and enormous, save only by that of infidelity; let him be anathema.

Canon XXVIII. If anyone shall say, that, grace being lost through sin, faith also is always lost with it; or that the faith which remains is not a true faith, though it be not a lively faith; or, that he, who has faith without charity, is not a Christian; let him be anathema.

Canon XXIX. If anyone shall say, that he, who has fallen after baptism, is not able by the grace of God to rise again; or, that he is able indeed to recover the justice lost, but by faith alone, without the sacrament of penance, contrary to what the holy Roman and universal Church, instructed by Christ and his apostles, has hitherto professed, observed and taught; let him be anathema.

Canon XXX. If anyone shall say, that, after the grace of justification received, unto every penitent sinner the guilt is so remitted, and the penalty[156] of eternal punishment so blotted out, that there remains not any penalty of temporal punishment, to be discharged either in this world, or in the next in purgatory,[157] before the entrance to the kingdom of heaven can be laid open; let him be anathema.

Canon XXXI. If anyone shall say, that the justified sins when he doeth good works with a view to an eternal recompense; let him be anathema.

Canon XXXII. If anyone shall say, that the good works of a man that is justified are in such wise the gifts of God, as that they are not also the good merits of him that is justified; or, that the said justified, by the good works which are performed by him through the grace of God and the merit of Jesus Christ, whose living member he is, does not truly merit increase of grace, eternal life, and the attainment of that eternal life, if so be, however, that he depart in grace, and, moreover, an increase of glory; let him be anathema.

Canon XXXIII. If anyone shall say, that, by this Catholic doctrine touching justification, set forth by this holy synod in this present decree, aught is derogated from the glory of God, or the merits of our Lord Jesus Christ, and not rather that the truth of our faith, and the glory in fine of God and of Christ Jesus are rendered illustrious; let him be anathema.[158]

Letter of the Holy Office
on Salvation Outside the Church

The following letter was sent by the Holy Office (now known as the Congregation for the Doctrine of the Faith) to the Cardinal Archbishop of Boston in 1949. It concerns the controversial claims made by Fr. Leonard Feeney, S.J. For further information, see chapter 9.

LETTER OF THE SACRED CONGREGATION
OF THE HOLY OFFICE
Archbishop Richard J. Cushing

Given on August 8, 1949, explaining the true sense of Catholic doctrine that there is no salvation outside the Church.

This important Letter of the Holy Office is introduced by a letter of the Most Reverend Archbishop of Boston.

The Supreme Sacred Congregation of the Holy Office has examined again the problem of Father Leonard Feeney and St. Benedict Center. Having studied carefully the publications issued by the Center, and having considered all the circumstances of this case, the Sacred Congregation has ordered me to publish, in its entirety, the letter which the same Congregation sent me on the 8th of August, 1949. The Supreme Pontiff, His Holiness, Pope Pius XII, has given full approval to this decision. In due obedience, therefore, we publish, in its entirety, the Latin text of the letter as received from the Holy Office with an English translation of the same approved by the Holy See.

Given at Boston, Mass., the fourth day of September, 1952.
Walter J. Furlong, Chancellor
Richard J. Cushing, Archbishop of Boston.

LETTER OF THE HOLY OFFICE
From the Headquarters of the Holy Office, Aug. 8, 1949.

Your Excellency:

This Supreme Sacred Congregation has followed very atten-
tively the rise and the course of the grave controversy stirred
up by certain associates of "St. Benedict Center" and "Boston
College" in regard to the interpretation of that axiom: "Outside
the Church there is no salvation."

After having examined all the documents that are necessary or useful in this matter, among them information from your
Chancery, as well as appeals and reports in which the associates of
"St. Benedict Center" explain their opinions and complaints, and
also many other documents pertinent to the controversy, officially
collected, the same Sacred Congregation is convinced that the
unfortunate controversy arose from the fact that the axiom, "outside the Church there is no salvation," was not correctly understood and weighed, and that the same controversy was rendered
more bitter by serious disturbance of discipline arising from the
fact that some of the associates of the institutions mentioned above
refused reverence and obedience to legitimate authorities.

Accordingly, the most eminent and most reverend cardinals of this supreme congregation, in a plenary session held on
Wednesday, July 27, 1949, decreed, and the august pontiff in an
audience on the following Thursday, July 28, 1949, deigned to
give his approval, that the following explanations pertinent to
the doctrine, and also that invitations and exhortations relevant
to discipline be given:

We are bound by divine and Catholic Faith to believe all
those things which are contained in the word of God, whether
it be Scripture or Tradition, and are proposed by the Church to
be believed as divinely revealed, not only through solemn judgment but also through the ordinary and universal teaching office
(Denzinger, n. 1792).

Now, among those things which the Church has always
preached and will never cease to preach is contained also that

infallible statement by which we are taught that there is no salvation outside the Church.

However, this dogma must be understood in that sense in which the Church herself understands it. For, it was not to private judgments that our Savior gave for explanation those things that are contained in the deposit of faith, but to the teaching authority of the Church.

Now, in the first place, the Church teaches that in this matter there is question of a most strict command of Jesus Christ. For he explicitly enjoined on his apostles to teach all nations to observe all things whatsoever he himself had commanded (Matt. 28:19–20).

Now, among the commandments of Christ, that one holds not the least place by which we are commanded to be incorporated by baptism into the Mystical Body of Christ, which is the Church, and to remain united to Christ and to his vicar, through whom he himself in a visible manner governs the Church on earth.

Therefore, no one will be saved who, knowing the Church to have been divinely established by Christ, nevertheless refuses to submit to the Church or withholds obedience from the Roman pontiff, the vicar of Christ on earth.

Not only did the Savior command that all nations should enter the Church, but he also decreed the Church to be a means of salvation without which no one can enter the kingdom of eternal glory.

In his infinite mercy God has willed that the effects, necessary for one to be saved, of those helps to salvation which are directed toward man's final end, not by intrinsic necessity, but only by divine institution, can also be obtained in certain circumstances when those helps are used only in desire and longing. This we see clearly stated in the Sacred Council of Trent, both in reference to the sacrament of regeneration and in reference to the sacrament of penance (Denzinger, nn. 797, 807).

The same in its own degree must be asserted of the Church, in as far as she is the general help to salvation. Therefore, that one may obtain eternal salvation, it is not always required that he be incorporated into the Church actually as a member, but it is necessary that at least he be united to her by desire and longing.

However, this desire need not always be explicit, as it is in catechumens; but when a person is involved in invincible ignorance God accepts also an implicit desire, so called because it is included in that good disposition of soul whereby a person wishes his will to be conformed to the will of God.

These things are clearly taught in that dogmatic letter which was issued by the sovereign pontiff, Pope Pius XII, on June 29, 1943, On the Mystical Body of Jesus Christ (AAS, vol. 35, an. 1943, p. 193 ff.). For in this letter the sovereign pontiff clearly distinguishes between those who are actually incorporated into the Church as members, and those who are united to the Church only by desire.

Discussing the members of which the Mystical Body is composed here on earth, the same august pontiff says: "Actually only those are to be included as members of the Church who have been baptized and profess the true faith, and who have not been so unfortunate as to separate themselves from the unity of the Body, or been excluded by legitimate authority for grave faults committed."

Toward the end of this same encyclical letter, when most affectionately inviting to unity those who do not belong to the body of the Catholic Church, he mentions those who "are related to the Mystical Body of the Redeemer by a certain unconscious yearning and desire," and these he by no means excludes from eternal salvation, but on the other hand states that they are in a condition "in which they cannot be sure of their salvation" since "they still remain deprived of those many heavenly gifts and helps which can only be enjoyed in the Catholic Church" (AAS, 1. c., p. 243). With these wise words he reproves both those who exclude from eternal salvation all united to the Church only by implicit desire, and those who falsely assert that men can be saved equally well in every religion (cf. Pope Pius IX, Allocution, *Singulari quadam*, in Denzinger, n. 1641 ff.; also Pope Pius IX in the encyclical letter, *Quanto conficiamur moerore*, in Denzinger, n. 1677).

But it must not be thought that any kind of desire of entering the Church suffices that one may be saved. It is necessary that the desire by which one is related to the Church be animated by perfect charity. Nor can an implicit desire produce its effect, unless a person has supernatural faith: "For he who comes to God must believe that God exists and is a rewarder of those who seek him" (Heb. 11:6). The Council of Trent declares (Session VI, chapter 8): "Faith is the beginning of man's salvation, the foundation and root of all justification, without which it is impossible to please God and attain to the fellowship of his children" (Denzinger, n. 801).

From what has been said it is evident that those things which are proposed in the periodical *From the Housetops*, fascicle 3, as the genuine teaching of the Catholic Church are far from being such and are very harmful both to those within the Church and those without.

From these declarations which pertain to doctrine, certain conclusions follow which regard discipline and conduct, and which cannot be unknown to those who vigorously defend the necessity by which all are bound of belonging to the true Church and of submitting to the authority of the Roman pontiff and of the Bishops "whom the Holy Spirit has placed . . . to rule the Church" (Acts 20:28).

Hence, one cannot understand how the St. Benedict Center can consistently claim to be a Catholic school and wish to be accounted such, and yet not conform to the prescriptions of canons 1381 and 1382 of the Code of Canon Law, and continue to exist as a source of discord and rebellion against ecclesiastical authority and as a source of the disturbance of many consciences.

Furthermore, it is beyond understanding how a member of a religious Institute, namely Father Feeney, presents himself as a "Defender of the Faith," and at the same time does not hesitate to attack the catechetical instruction proposed by lawful authorities, and has not even feared to incur grave sanctions threatened by the sacred canons because of his serious violations of his duties as a religious, a priest, and an ordinary member of the Church.

Finally, it is in no wise to be tolerated that certain Catholics shall claim for themselves the right to publish a periodical, for the purpose of spreading theological doctrines, without the permission of competent Church authority, called the "imprimatur," which is prescribed by the sacred canons.

Therefore, let them who in grave peril are ranged against the Church seriously bear in mind that after "Rome has spoken" they cannot be excused even by reasons of good faith. Certainly, their bond and duty of obedience toward the Church is much graver than that of those who as yet are related to the Church "only by an unconscious desire." Let them realize that they are children of the Church, lovingly nourished by her with the milk of doctrine and the sacraments, and hence, having heard the clear voice of their Mother, they cannot be excused from culpable ignorance, and therefore to them apply without any restriction that principle: submission to the Catholic Church and to the sovereign pontiff is required as necessary for salvation.

In sending this letter, I declare my profound esteem, and remain, Your Excellency's most devoted,
F. Cardinal Marchetti-Selvaggiani.
A. Ottaviani, Assessor.
(Private); Holy Office, 8 Aug., 1949.

BONUS MATERIALS
III

The Catechism of the Catholic Church
on Grace and Justification

The following material is taken from the Catechism of the Catholic
Church *and contains the most recent, highly authoritative statement of
the Magisterium on justification.*

I. JUSTIFICATION

1987. The grace of the Holy Spirit has the power to justify us,
that is, to cleanse us from our sins and to communicate to us
"the righteousness of God through faith in Jesus Christ" and
through Baptism:[159]

> But if we have died with Christ, we believe that we shall also
> live with him. For we know that Christ being raised from the
> dead will never die again; death no longer has dominion over
> him. The death he died he died to sin, once for all, but the life
> he lives he lives to God. So you also must consider yourselves
> as dead to sin and alive to God in Christ Jesus.[160]

1988. Through the power of the Holy Spirit we take part in
Christ's Passion by dying to sin, and in his Resurrection by be-
ing born to a new life; we are members of his Body which is the
Church, branches grafted onto the vine which is himself:[161]

> (God) gave himself to us through his Spirit. By the participation
> of the Spirit, we become communicants in the divine nature. . . .
> For this reason, those in whom the Spirit dwells are divinized.[162]

1989. The first work of the grace of the Holy Spirit is *conversion,* effecting justification in accordance with Jesus' proclamation at the beginning of the Gospel: "Repent, for the kingdom of heaven is at hand."[163] Moved by grace, man turns toward God and away from sin, thus accepting forgiveness and righteousness from on high. "Justification is not only the remission of sins, but also the sanctification and renewal of the interior man."[164]

1990. Justification *detaches man from sin* which contradicts the love of God, and purifies his heart of sin. Justification follows upon God's merciful initiative of offering forgiveness. It reconciles man with God. It frees from the enslavement to sin, and it heals.

1991. Justification is at the same time *the acceptance of God's righteousness* through faith in Jesus Christ. Righteousness (or "justice") here means the rectitude of divine love. With justification, faith, hope, and charity are poured into our hearts, and obedience to the divine will is granted us.

1992. Justification has been *merited for us by the Passion of Christ* who offered himself on the cross as a living victim, holy and pleasing to God, and whose blood has become the instrument of atonement for the sins of all men. Justification is conferred in Baptism, the sacrament of faith. It conforms us to the righteousness of God, who makes us inwardly just by the power of his mercy. Its purpose is the glory of God and of Christ, and the gift of eternal life:[165]

> But now the righteousness of God has been manifested apart from law, although the law and the prophets bear witness to it, the righteousness of God through faith in Jesus Christ for all who believe. For there is no distinction: since all have sinned and fall short of the glory of God, they are justified by his grace as a gift, through the redemption which is in Christ Jesus, whom God put forward as an expiation by his

blood, to be received by faith. This was to show God's righteousness, because in his divine forbearance he had passed over former sins; it was to prove at the present time that he himself is righteous and that he justifies him who has faith in Jesus.[166]

1993. Justification establishes *cooperation between God's grace and man's freedom*. On man's part it is expressed by the assent of faith to the Word of God, which invites him to conversion, and in the cooperation of charity with the prompting of the Holy Spirit who precedes and preserves his assent:

> When God touches man's heart through the illumination of the Holy Spirit, man himself is not inactive while receiving that inspiration, since he could reject it; and yet, without God's grace, he cannot by his own free will move himself toward justice in God's sight.[167]

1994. Justification is the *most excellent work of God's love* made manifest in Christ Jesus and granted by the Holy Spirit. It is the opinion of St. Augustine that "the justification of the wicked is a greater work than the creation of heaven and earth," because "heaven and earth will pass away but the salvation and justification of the elect . . . will not pass away."[168] He holds also that the justification of sinners surpasses the creation of the angels in justice, in that it bears witness to a greater mercy.

1995. The Holy Spirit is the master of the interior life. By giving birth to the "inner man,"[169] justification entails the *sanctification* of his whole being:

> Just as you once yielded your members to impurity and to greater and greater iniquity, so now yield your members to righteousness for sanctification. . . . But now that you have been set free from sin and have become slaves of God, the return you get is sanctification and its end, eternal life.[170]

II. GRACE

1996. Our justification comes from the grace of God. Grace is *favor*, the *free and undeserved help* that God gives us to respond to his call to become children of God, adoptive sons, partakers of the divine nature and of eternal life.[171]

1997. Grace is a *participation in the life of God.* It introduces us into the intimacy of Trinitarian life: by Baptism the Christian participates in the grace of Christ, the Head of his Body. As an "adopted son" he can henceforth call God "Father," in union with the only Son. He receives the life of the Spirit who breathes charity into him and who forms the Church.

1998. This vocation to eternal life is *supernatural.* It depends entirely on God's gratuitous initiative, for he alone can reveal and give himself. It surpasses the power of human intellect and will, as that of every other creature.[172]

1999. The grace of Christ is the gratuitous gift that God makes to us of his own life, infused by the Holy Spirit into our soul to heal it of sin and to sanctify it. It is the *sanctifying* or *deifying grace* received in Baptism. It is in us the source of the work of sanctification:[173]

> Therefore if any one is in Christ, he is a new creation; the old has passed away, behold, the new has come. All this is from God, who through Christ reconciled us to himself.[174]

2000. Sanctifying grace is a habitual gift, a stable and supernatural disposition that perfects the soul itself to enable it to live with God, to act by his love. *Habitual grace*, the permanent disposition to live and act in keeping with God's call, is distinguished from *actual graces* which refer to God's interventions, whether at the beginning of conversion or in the course of the work of sanctification.

2001. The *preparation of man* for the reception of grace is already a work of grace. This latter is needed to arouse and sustain our collaboration in justification through faith, and in sanctification through charity. God brings to completion in us what he has begun, "since he who completes his work by cooperating with our will began by working so that we might will it:"[175]

> Indeed we also work, but we are only collaborating with God who works, for his mercy has gone before us. It has gone before us so that we may be healed, and follows us so that once healed, we may be given life; it goes before us so that we may be called, and follows us so that we may be glorified; it goes before us so that we may live devoutly, and follows us so that we may always live with God: for without him we can do nothing.[176]

2002. God's free initiative demands *man's free response*, for God has created man in his image by conferring on him, along with freedom, the power to know him and love him. The soul only enters freely into the communion of love. God immediately touches and directly moves the heart of man. He has placed in man a longing for truth and goodness that only he can satisfy. The promises of "eternal life" respond, beyond all hope, to this desire:

> If at the end of your very good works . . . , you rested on the seventh day, it was to foretell by the voice of your book that at the end of our works, which are indeed "very good" since you have given them to us, we shall also rest in you on the sabbath of eternal life.[177]

2003. Grace is first and foremost the gift of the Spirit who justifies and sanctifies us. But grace also includes the gifts that the Spirit grants us to associate us with his work, to enable us to collaborate in the salvation of others and in the growth of the Body of Christ, the Church. There are *sacramental graces*, gifts proper to the different sacraments. There are furthermore *special graces*, also called *charisms* after the Greek term used by St. Paul

and meaning "favor," "gratuitous gift," "benefit."[178] Whatever
their character—sometimes it is extraordinary, such as the gift
of miracles or of tongues—charisms are oriented toward sanctifying grace and are intended for the common good of the
Church. They are at the service of charity which builds up the
Church.[179]

2004. Among the special graces ought to be mentioned the *graces
of state* that accompany the exercise of the responsibilities of the
Christian life and of the ministries within the Church:

> Having gifts that differ according to the grace given to us, let us
> use them: if prophecy, in proportion to our faith; if service, in
> our serving; he who teaches, in his teaching; he who exhorts, in
> his exhortation; he who contributes, in liberality; he who gives
> aid, with zeal; he who does acts of mercy, with cheerfulness.[180]

2005. Since it belongs to the supernatural order, grace *escapes
our experience* and cannot be known except by faith. We cannot therefore rely on our feelings or our works to conclude that
we are justified and saved.[181] However, according to the Lord's
words—"Thus you will know them by their fruits"[182]—reflection on God's blessings in our life and in the lives of the saints
offers us a guarantee that grace is at work in us and spurs us on
to an ever greater faith and an attitude of trustful poverty.

> A pleasing illustration of this attitude is found in the reply of
> St. Joan of Arc to a question posed as a trap by her ecclesiasti-
> cal judges: "Asked if she knew that she was in God's grace,
> she replied: 'If I am not, may it please God to put me in it; if
> I am, may it please God to keep me there.'"[183]

III. MERIT

You are glorified in the assembly of your Holy Ones, for in
crowning their merits you are crowning your own gifts.[184]

2006. The term "merit" refers in general to the *recompense owed* by a community or a society for the action of one of its members, experienced either as beneficial or harmful, deserving reward or punishment. Merit is relative to the virtue of justice, in conformity with the principle of equality which governs it.

2007. With regard to God, there is no strict right to any merit on the part of man. Between God and us there is an immeasurable inequality, for we have received everything from him, our Creator.

2008. The merit of man before God in the Christian life arises from the fact that *God has freely chosen to associate man with the work of his grace.* The fatherly action of God is first on his own initiative, and then follows man's free acting through his collaboration, so that the merit of good works is to be attributed in the first place to the grace of God, then to the faithful. Man's merit, moreover, itself is due to God, for his good actions proceed in Christ, from the predispositions and assistance given by the Holy Spirit.

2009. Filial adoption, in making us partakers by grace in the divine nature, can bestow *true merit* on us as a result of God's gratuitous justice. This is our right by grace, the full right of love, making us "co-heirs" with Christ and worthy of obtaining "the promised inheritance of eternal life."[185] The merits of our good works are gifts of the divine goodness.[186] "Grace has gone before us; now we are given what is due. . . . Our merits are God's gifts."[187]

2010. Since the initiative belongs to God in the order of grace, *no one can merit the initial grace* of forgiveness and justification, at the beginning of conversion. Moved by the Holy Spirit and by charity, *we can then merit* for ourselves and for others the graces needed for our sanctification, for the increase of grace and charity, and for the attainment of eternal life. Even temporal goods like health and friendship can be merited in accordance with God's wisdom. These graces and goods are the object of Christian prayer. Prayer attends to the grace we need for meritorious actions.

2011. The charity of Christ is the source in us of all our merits before God. Grace, by uniting us to Christ in active love, ensures the supernatural quality of our acts and consequently their merit before God and before men. The saints have always had a lively awareness that their merits were pure grace.

> After earth's exile, I hope to go and enjoy you in the fatherland, but I do not want to lay up merits for heaven. I want to work for your *love alone*. . . . In the evening of this life, I shall appear before you with empty hands, for I do not ask you, Lord, to count my works. All our justice is blemished in your eyes. I wish, then, to be clothed in your own *justice* and to receive from your *love* the eternal possession of *yourself*.[188]

IN BRIEF

2017. The grace of the Holy Spirit confers upon us the righteousness of God. Uniting us by faith and Baptism to the Passion and Resurrection of Christ, the Spirit makes us sharers in his life.

2018. Like conversion, justification has two aspects. Moved by grace, man turns toward God and away from sin, and so accepts forgiveness and righteousness from on high.

2019. Justification includes the remission of sins, sanctification, and the renewal of the inner man.

2020. Justification has been merited for us by the Passion of Christ. It is granted us through Baptism. It conforms us to the righteousness of God, who justifies us. It has for its goal the glory of God and of Christ, and the gift of eternal life. It is the most excellent work of God's mercy.

2021. Grace is the help God gives us to respond to our vocation of becoming his adopted sons. It introduces us into the intimacy of the Trinitarian life.

2022. The divine initiative in the work of grace precedes, prepares, and elicits the free response of man. Grace responds to the deepest yearnings of human freedom, calls freedom to cooperate with it, and perfects freedom.

2023. Sanctifying grace is the gratuitous gift of his life that God makes to us; it is infused by the Holy Spirit into the soul to heal it of sin and to sanctify it.

2024. Sanctifying grace makes us "pleasing to God." Charisms, special graces of the Holy Spirit, are oriented to sanctifying grace and are intended for the common good of the Church. God also acts through many actual graces, to be distinguished from habitual grace which is permanent in us.

2025. We can have merit in God's sight only because of God's free plan to associate man with the work of his grace. Merit is to be ascribed in the first place to the grace of God, and secondly to man's collaboration. Man's merit is due to God.

2026. The grace of the Holy Spirit can confer true merit on us, by virtue of our adoptive filiation, and in accordance with God's gratuitous justice. Charity is the principal source of merit in us before God.

2027. No one can merit the initial grace which is at the origin of conversion. Moved by the Holy Spirit, we can merit for ourselves and for others all the graces needed to attain eternal life, as well as necessary temporal goods.

BONUS MATERIALS
IV

Joint Declaration on the Doctrine of Justification

The following documents—the Joint Declaration on the Doctrine of Justification, the Response of the Catholic Church, and the Annex to the Joint Declaration—represent an important milestone in ecumenical discussion and present the Church's teaching on justification in an ecumenical perspective that clears away many of the misunderstandings that have existed in the past. The Joint Declaration and its Annex are jointly issued by both the Catholic Church and the Lutheran World Federation. Later, the World Methodist Council also subscribed to them. For more information, see chapter 8.

JOINT DECLARATION ON THE DOCTRINE OF JUSTIFICATION
by the Lutheran World Federation and the Catholic Church

Preamble

1. The doctrine of justification was of central importance for the Lutheran Reformation of the sixteenth century. It was held to be the "first and chief article"[189] and at the same time the "ruler and judge over all other Christian doctrines."[190] The doctrine of justification was particularly asserted and defended in its Reformation shape and special valuation over against the Roman Catholic Church and theology of that time, which in turn asserted and defended a doctrine of justification of a different character. From the Reformation perspective, justification was the crux of all the disputes. Doctrinal condemnations were put forward both in the Lutheran Confessions[191] and by the Roman Catholic Church's Council of Trent. These condemnations are still valid today and thus have a church-dividing effect.

2. For the Lutheran tradition, the doctrine of justification has retained its special status. Consequently it has also from the beginning occupied an important place in the official Lutheran-Roman Catholic dialogue.

3. Special attention should be drawn to the following reports: "The Gospel and the Church" (1972)[192] and "Church and Justification" (1994)[193] by the Lutheran-Roman Catholic Joint Commission, "Justification by Faith" (1983)[194] of the Lutheran-Roman Catholic dialogue in the USA and "The Condemnations of the Reformation Era—Do They Still Divide?" (1986)[195] by the Ecumenical Working Group of Protestant and Catholic theologians in Germany. Some of these dialogue reports have been officially received by the churches. An important example of such reception is the binding response of the United Evangelical-Lutheran Church of Germany to the "Condemnations" study, made in 1994 at the highest possible level of ecclesiastical recognition together with the other churches of the Evangelical Church in Germany.[196]

4. In their discussion of the doctrine of justification, all the dialogue reports as well as the responses show a high degree of agreement in their approaches and conclusions. The time has therefore come to take stock and to summarize the results of the dialogues on justification so that our churches may be informed about the overall results of this dialogue with the necessary accuracy and brevity, and thereby be enabled to make binding decisions.

5. The present Joint Declaration has this intention: namely, to show that on the basis of their dialogue the subscribing Lutheran churches and the Roman Catholic Church[197] are now able to articulate a common understanding of our justification by God's grace through faith in Christ. It does not cover all that either church teaches about justification; it does encompass a consensus on basic truths of the doctrine of justification and shows that the remaining differences in its explication are no longer the occasion for doctrinal condemnations.

6. Our Declaration is not a new, independent presentation alongside the dialogue reports and documents to date, let alone a replacement of them. Rather, as the appendix of sources shows, it makes repeated reference to them and their arguments.

7. Like the dialogues themselves, this Joint Declaration rests on the conviction that in overcoming the earlier controversial questions and doctrinal condemnations, the churches neither take the condemnations lightly nor do they disavow their own past. On the contrary, this Declaration is shaped by the conviction that in their respective histories our churches have come to new insights. Developments have taken place which not only make possible, but also require the churches to examine the divisive questions and condemnations and see them in a new light.

1. BIBLICAL MESSAGE OF JUSTIFICATION

8. Our common way of listening to the word of God in Scripture has led to such new insights. Together we hear the gospel that "God so loved the world that he gave his only Son, so that everyone who believes in him may not perish but may have eternal life" (John 3:16). This good news is set forth in Holy Scripture in various ways. In the Old Testament we listen to God's word about human sinfulness (Ps. 51:1–5; Dan. 9:5f; Eccles. 8:9f; Ezra 9:6f) and human disobedience (Gen. 3:1–19; Neh. 9:16f, 26) as well as of God's "righteousness" (Isa. 46:13; 51:5–8; 56:1 [cf. 53:11]; Jer. 9:24) and "judgment" (Eccles. 12:14; Ps. 9:5f; 76:7–9).

9. In the New Testament diverse treatments of "righteousness" and "justification" are found in the writings of Matthew (5:10; 6:33; 21:32), John (16:8–11), Hebrews (5:3; 10:37f), and James (2:14–26).[198] In Paul's letters also, the gift of salvation is described in various ways, among others: "for freedom Christ has set us

free" (Gal. 5:1–13; cf. Rom. 6:7), "reconciled to God" (2 Cor. 5:18–21; cf. Rom. 5:11), "peace with God" (Rom. 5:1), "new creation" (2 Cor. 5:17), "alive to God in Christ Jesus" (Rom. 6:11, 23), or "sanctified in Christ Jesus" (cf. 1 Cor. 1:2; 1:30; 2 Cor. 1:1). Chief among these is the "justification" of sinful human beings by God's grace through faith (Rom. 3:23–25), which came into particular prominence in the Reformation period.

10. Paul sets forth the gospel as the power of God for salvation of the person who has fallen under the power of sin, as the message that proclaims that "the righteousness of God is revealed through faith for faith" (Rom. 1:16f) and that grants "justification" (Rom. 3:21–31). He proclaims Christ as "our righteousness" (1 Cor. 1:30), applying to the risen Lord what Jeremiah proclaimed about God himself (Jer. 23:6). In Christ's death and resurrection all dimensions of his saving work have their roots for he is "our Lord, who was put to death for our trespasses and raised for our justification" (Rom. 4:25). All human beings are in need of God's righteousness, "since all have sinned and fall short of the glory of God" (Rom. 3:23; cf. Rom. 1:18–3:20; 11:32; Gal. 3:22). In Galatians (3:6) and Romans (4:3–9), Paul understands Abraham's faith (Gen. 15:6) as faith in the God who justifies the sinner (Rom. 4:5) and calls upon the testimony of the Old Testament to undergird his gospel that this righteousness will be reckoned to all who, like Abraham, trust in God's promise. "For the righteous will live by faith (Heb. 2:4; cf. Gal. 3:11; Rom. 1:17). In Paul's letters, God's righteousness is also God's power for those who have faith (Rom. 1:16f; 2 Cor. 5:21). In Christ he makes it our righteousness (2 Cor. 5:21). Justification becomes ours through Christ Jesus "whom God put forward as a sacrifice of atonement by his blood, effective through faith" (Rom. 3:25; see 3:21–28). "For by grace you have been saved through faith, and this is not your own doing; it is the gift of God—not the result of works" (Eph. 2:8f).

11. Justification is the forgiveness of sins (cf. Rom. 3:23–25; Acts 13:39; Luke 18:14), liberation from the dominating power of sin and death (Rom. 5:12–21) and from the curse of the law (Gal. 3:10–14). It is acceptance into communion with God: already now, but then fully in God's coming kingdom (Rom. 5:1f). It unites with Christ and with his death and resurrection (Rom. 6:5). It occurs in the reception of the Holy Spirit in baptism and incorporation into the one body (Rom. 8:1f, 9f; 1 Cor. 12:12f). All this is from God alone, for Christ's sake, by grace, through faith in "the gospel of God's Son" (Rom. 1:1–3).

12. The justified live by faith that comes from the Word of Christ (Rom. 10:17) and is active through love (Gal. 5:6), the fruit of the Spirit (Gal. 5:22f). But since the justified are assailed from within and without by powers and desires (Rom. 8:35–39; Gal. 5:16–21) and fall into sin (1 John 1:8, 10), they must constantly hear God's promises anew, confess their sins (1 John 1:9), participate in Christ's body and blood, and be exhorted to live righteously in accord with the will of God. That is why the apostle says to the justified: "Work out your own salvation with fear and trembling; for it is God who is at work in you, enabling you both to will and to work for his good pleasure" (Phil. 2:12f). But the good news remains: "there is now no condemnation for those who are in Christ Jesus" (Rom. 8:1), and in whom Christ lives (Gal. 2:20). Christ's "act of righteousness leads to justification and life for all" (Rom. 5:18).

2. THE DOCTRINE OF JUSTIFICATION AS ECUMENICAL PROBLEM

13. Opposing interpretations and applications of the biblical message of justification were in the sixteenth century a principal cause of the division of the Western church and led as well to doctrinal condemnations. A common understanding of justification is therefore fundamental and indispensable to overcoming that division. By appropriating insights of recent biblical studies and drawing on modern investigations of the history of theology and dogma, the post-Vatican II ecumenical dialogue has led to

a notable convergence concerning justification, with the result that this Joint Declaration is able to formulate a consensus on basic truths concerning the doctrine of justification. In light of this consensus, the corresponding doctrinal condemnations of the sixteenth century do not apply to today's partner.

3. THE COMMON UNDERSTANDING OF JUSTIFICATION

14. The Lutheran churches and the Roman Catholic Church have together listened to the good news proclaimed in Holy Scripture. This common listening, together with the theological conversations of recent years, has led to a shared understanding of justification. This encompasses a consensus in the basic truths; the differing explications in particular statements are compatible with it.

15. In faith we together hold the conviction that justification is the work of the triune God. The Father sent his Son into the world to save sinners. The foundation and presupposition of justification is the incarnation, death, and resurrection of Christ. Justification thus means that Christ himself is our righteousness, in which we share through the Holy Spirit in accord with the will of the Father. Together we confess: By grace alone, in faith in Christ's saving work and not because of any merit on our part, we are accepted by God and receive the Holy Spirit, who renews our hearts while equipping and calling us to good works.[199]

16. All people are called by God to salvation in Christ. Through Christ alone are we justified, when we receive this salvation in faith. Faith is itself God's gift through the Holy Spirit who works through word and sacrament in the community of believers and who, at the same time, leads believers into that renewal of life which God will bring to completion in eternal life.

17. We also share the conviction that the message of justification directs us in a special way towards the heart of the New Testament

witness to God's saving action in Christ: it tells us that as sinners our new life is solely due to the forgiving and renewing mercy that God imparts as a gift and we receive in faith, and never can merit in any way.

18. Therefore the doctrine of justification, which takes up this message and explicates it, is more than just one part of Christian doctrine. It stands in an essential relation to all truths of faith, which are to be seen as internally related to each other. It is an indispensable criterion which constantly serves to orient all the teaching and practice of our churches to Christ. When Lutherans emphasize the unique significance of this criterion, they do not deny the interrelation and significance of all truths of faith. When Catholics see themselves as bound by several criteria, they do not deny the special function of the message of justification. Lutherans and Catholics share the goal of confessing Christ in all things, who alone is to be trusted above all things as the one Mediator (1 Tim. 2:5f) through whom God in the Holy Spirit gives himself and pours out his renewing gifts. (cf. Sources for section 3).

4. EXPLICATING THE COMMON UNDERSTANDING OF JUSTIFICATION

4.1 Human Powerlessness and Sin in Relation to Justification

19. We confess together that all persons depend completely on the saving grace of God for their salvation. The freedom they possess in relation to persons and the things of this world is no freedom in relation to salvation, for as sinners they stand under God's judgment and are incapable of turning by themselves to God to seek deliverance, of meriting their justification before God, or of attaining salvation by their own abilities. Justification takes place solely by God's grace. Because Catholics and Lutherans confess this together, it is true to say:

20. When Catholics say that persons "cooperate" in preparing for and accepting justification by consenting to God's justifying

action, they see such personal consent as itself an effect of grace, not as an action arising from innate human abilities.

21. According to Lutheran teaching, human beings are incapable of cooperating in their salvation, because as sinners they actively oppose God and his saving action. Lutherans do not deny that a person can reject the working of grace. When they emphasize that a person can only receive (mere passive) justification, they mean thereby to exclude any possibility of contributing to one's own justification, but do not deny that believers are fully involved personally in their faith, which is effected by God's Word. (cf. Sources for 4.1).

4.2 Justification as Forgiveness of Sins and Making Righteous

22. We confess together that God forgives sin by grace and at the same time frees human beings from sin's enslaving power and imparts the gift of new life in Christ. When persons come by faith to share in Christ, God no longer imputes to them their sin and through the Holy Spirit effects in them an active love. These two aspects of God's gracious action are not to be separated, for persons are by faith united with Christ, who in his person is our righteousness (1 Cor. 1:30): both the forgiveness of sin and the saving presence of God himself. Because Catholics and Lutherans confess this together, it is true to say that:

23. When Lutherans emphasize that the righteousness of Christ is our righteousness, their intention is above all to insist that the sinner is granted righteousness before God in Christ through the declaration of forgiveness and that only in union with Christ is one's life renewed. When they stress that God's grace is forgiving love ("the favor of God"[200]), they do not thereby deny the renewal of the Christian's life. They intend rather to express that justification remains free from human cooperation and is not dependent on the life-renewing effects of grace in human beings.

24. When Catholics emphasize the renewal of the interior person through the reception of grace imparted as a gift to the believer,[201] they wish to insist that God's forgiving grace always brings with it a gift of new life, which in the Holy Spirit becomes effective in active love. They do not thereby deny that God's gift of grace in justification remains independent of human cooperation. (cf. Sources for section 4.2).

4.3 Justification by Faith and through Grace

25. We confess together that sinners are justified by faith in the saving action of God in Christ. By the action of the Holy Spirit in baptism, they are granted the gift of salvation, which lays the basis for the whole Christian life. They place their trust in God's gracious promise by justifying faith, which includes hope in God and love for him. Such a faith is active in love and thus the Christian cannot and should not remain without works. But whatever in the justified precedes or follows the free gift of faith is neither the basis of justification nor merits it.

26. According to Lutheran understanding, God justifies sinners in faith alone (*sola fide*). In faith they place their trust wholly in their Creator and Redeemer and thus live in communion with him. God himself effects faith as he brings forth such trust by his creative word. Because God's act is a new creation, it affects all dimensions of the person and leads to a life in hope and love. In the doctrine of "justification by faith alone," a distinction but not a separation is made between justification itself and the renewal of one's way of life that necessarily follows from justification and without which faith does not exist. Thereby the basis is indicated from which the renewal of life proceeds, for it comes forth from the love of God imparted to the person in justification. Justification and renewal are joined in Christ, who is present in faith.

27. The Catholic understanding also sees faith as fundamental in justification. For without faith, no justification can take place. Persons are justified through baptism as hearers of the word and believers in it. The justification of sinners is forgiveness of sins and being made righteous by justifying grace, which makes us children of God. In justification the righteous receive from Christ faith, hope, and love and are thereby taken into communion with him.[202] This new personal relation to God is grounded totally on God's graciousness and remains constantly dependent on the salvific and creative working of this gracious God, who remains true to himself, so that one can rely upon him. Thus justifying grace never becomes a human possession to which one could appeal over against God. While Catholic teaching emphasizes the renewal of life by justifying grace, this renewal in faith, hope, and love is always dependent on God's unfathomable grace and contributes nothing to justification about which one could boast before God (Rom. 3:27). (cf. Sources for section 4.3).

4.4 The Justified as Sinner

28. We confess together that in baptism the Holy Spirit unites one with Christ, justifies, and truly renews the person. But the justified must all through life constantly look to God's unconditional justifying grace. They also are continuously exposed to the power of sin still pressing its attacks (cf. Rom. 6:12–14) and are not exempt from a lifelong struggle against the contradiction to God within the selfish desires of the old Adam (cf. Gal. 5:16; Rom. 7:7–10). The justified also must ask God daily for forgiveness as in the Lord's Prayer (Matt. 6:12; 1 John 1:9), are ever again called to conversion and penance, and are ever again granted forgiveness.

29. Lutherans understand this condition of the Christian as a being "at the same time righteous and sinner." Believers are totally righteous, in that God forgives their sins through Word and Sacrament and grants the righteousness of Christ which they appropriate in faith. In Christ, they are made just before God. Looking at themselves through the law, however, they

JOINT DECLARATION ON THE DOCTRINE OF JUSTIFICATION 269

recognize that they remain also totally sinners. Sin still lives in them (1 John 1:8; Rom. 7:17, 20), for they repeatedly turn to false gods and do not love God with that undivided love which God requires as their Creator (Deut. 6:5; Matt. 22:36–40 pr.). This contradiction to God is as such truly sin. Nevertheless, the enslaving power of sin is broken on the basis of the merit of Christ. It no longer is a sin that "rules" the Christian for it is itself "ruled" by Christ with whom the justified are bound in faith. In this life, then, Christians can in part lead a just life. Despite sin, the Christian is no longer separated from God, because in the daily return to baptism, the person who has been born anew by baptism and the Holy Spirit has this sin forgiven. Thus this sin no longer brings damnation and eternal death.[203] Thus, when Lutherans say that justified persons are also sinners and that their opposition to God is truly sin, they do not deny that, despite this sin, they are not separated from God and that this sin is a "ruled" sin. In these affirmations, they are in agreement with Roman Catholics, despite the difference in understanding sin in the justified.

30. Catholics hold that the grace of Jesus Christ imparted in baptism takes away all that is sin "in the proper sense" and that is "worthy of damnation" (Rom. 8:1).[204] There does, however, re- main in the person an inclination (concupiscence) which comes from sin and presses toward sin. Since, according to Catholic conviction, human sins always involve a personal element and since this element is lacking in this inclination, Catholics do not see this inclination as sin in an authentic sense. They do not thereby deny that this inclination does not correspond to God's original design for humanity and that it is objectively in contradiction to God and remains one's enemy in lifelong struggle. Grateful for deliverance by Christ, they underscore that this inclination in contradiction to God does not merit the punishment of eternal death[205] and does not separate the justi- fied person from God. But when individuals voluntarily separate themselves from God, it is not enough to return to observing the

commandments, for they must receive pardon and peace in the Sacrament of Reconciliation through the word of forgiveness imparted to them in virtue of God's reconciling work in Christ. (cf. Sources for section 4.4).

4.5 Law and Gospel

31. We confess together that persons are justified by faith in the gospel "apart from works prescribed by the law" (Rom. 3:28). Christ has fulfilled the law and by his death and resurrection has overcome it as a way to salvation. We also confess that God's commandments retain their validity for the justified and that Christ has by his teaching and example expressed God's will which is a standard for the conduct of the justified also.

32. Lutherans state that the distinction and right ordering of law and gospel is essential for the understanding of justification. In its theological use, the law is demand and accusation. Throughout their lives, all persons, Christians also, in that they are sinners, stand under this accusation which uncovers their sin so that, in faith in the gospel, they will turn unreservedly to the mercy of God in Christ, which alone justifies them.

33. Because the law as a way to salvation has been fulfilled and overcome through the gospel, Catholics can say that Christ is not a lawgiver in the manner of Moses. When Catholics emphasize that the righteous are bound to observe God's commandments, they do not thereby deny that through Jesus Christ God has mercifully promised to his children the grace of eternal life.[206] (cf. Sources for section 4.5).

4.6 Assurance of Salvation

34. We confess together that the faithful can rely on the mercy and promises of God. In spite of their own weakness and the manifold threats to their faith, on the strength of Christ's death and resurrection they can build on the effective promise of God's grace in Word and Sacrament and so be sure of this grace.

35. This was emphasized in a particular way by the Reformers: in the midst of temptation, believers should not look to themselves but look solely to Christ and trust only him. In trust in God's promise they are assured of their salvation, but are never secure looking at themselves.

36. Catholics can share the concern of the Reformers to ground faith in the objective reality of Christ's promise, to look away from one's own experience, and to trust in Christ's forgiving word alone (cf. Matt. 16:19; 18:18). With the Second Vatican Council, Catholics state: to have faith is to entrust oneself totally to God,[207] who liberates us from the darkness of sin and death and awakens us to eternal life.[208] In this sense, one cannot believe in God and at the same time consider the divine promise untrustworthy. No one may doubt God's mercy and Christ's merit. Every person, however, may be concerned about his salvation when he looks upon his own weaknesses and shortcomings. Recognizing his own failures, however, the believer may yet be certain that God intends his salvation. (cf. Sources for section 4.6).

4.7 The Good Works of the Justified

37. We confess together that good works—a Christian life lived in faith, hope and love—follow justification and are its fruits. When the justified live in Christ and act in the grace they receive, they bring forth, in biblical terms, good fruit. Since Christians struggle against sin their entire lives, this consequence of justification is also for them an obligation they must fulfill. Thus both Jesus and the apostolic Scriptures admonish Christians to bring forth the works of love.

38. According to Catholic understanding, good works, made possible by grace and the working of the Holy Spirit, contribute

to growth in grace, so that the righteousness that comes from God is preserved and communion with Christ is deepened. When Catholics affirm the "meritorious" character of good works, they wish to say that, according to the biblical witness, a reward in heaven is promised to these works. Their intention is to emphasize the responsibility of persons for their actions, not to contest the character of those works as gifts, or far less to deny that justification always remains the unmerited gift of grace.

39. The concept of a preservation of grace and a growth in grace and faith is also held by Lutherans. They do emphasize that righteousness as acceptance by God and sharing in the righteousness of Christ is always complete. At the same time, they state that there can be growth in its effects in Christian living. When they view the good works of Christians as the fruits and signs of justification and not as one's own "merits," they nevertheless also understand eternal life in accord with the New Testament as unmerited "reward" in the sense of the fulfillment of God's promise to the believer. (cf. Sources for section 4.7).

5. THE SIGNIFICANCE AND SCOPE OF THE CONSENSUS REACHED

40. The understanding of the doctrine of justification set forth in this Declaration shows that a consensus in basic truths of the doctrine of justification exists between Lutherans and Catholics. In light of this consensus the remaining differences of language, theological elaboration, and emphasis in the understanding of justification described in paras. 18 to 39 are acceptable. Therefore the Lutheran and the Catholic explications of justification are in their difference open to one another and do not destroy the consensus regarding the basic truths.

41. Thus the doctrinal condemnations of the sixteenth century, in so far as they relate to the doctrine of justification, appear in a new light: The teaching of the Lutheran churches presented in this Declaration does not fall under the condemnations from the Council of Trent. The condemnations in the Lutheran Confessions do not apply to the teaching of the Roman Catholic Church presented in this Declaration.

42. Nothing is thereby taken away from the seriousness of the condemnations related to the doctrine of justification. Some were not simply pointless. They remain for us "salutary warnings" to which we must attend in our teaching and practice.[209]

43. Our consensus in basic truths of the doctrine of justification must come to influence the life and teachings of our churches. Here it must prove itself. In this respect, there are still questions of varying importance which need further clarification. These include, among other topics, the relationship between the Word of God and church doctrine, as well as ecclesiology, ecclesial authority, church unity, ministry, the sacraments, and the relation between justification and social ethics. We are convinced that the consensus we have reached offers a solid basis for this clarification. The Lutheran churches and the Roman Catholic Church will continue to strive together to deepen this common understanding of justification and to make it bear fruit in the life and teaching of the churches.

44. We give thanks to the Lord for this decisive step forward on the way to overcoming the division of the church. We ask the Holy Spirit to lead us further toward that visible unity which is Christ's will.

APPENDIX
Resources for the Joint Declaration on the Doctrine of Justification

In parts 3 and 4 of the "Joint Declaration" formulations from different Lutheran-Catholic dialogues are referred to. They are the following documents:

"All Under One Christ," Statement on the Augsburg Confession by the Roman Catholic/Lutheran Joint Commission, 1980, in: *Growth in Agreement*, edited by Harding Meyer and Lukas Vischer, New York/Ramsey, Geneva, 1984, 241–247.

Denzinger-Schönmetzer, *Enchiridion symbolorum*, 32nd to 36th edition (hereafter: DS).

Denzinger-Hünermann, *Enchiridion symbolorum*, since the 37th edition (hereafter: DH).

Evaluation of the Pontifical Council for Promoting Christian Unity of the Study Lehrverurteilungen-kirchentrennend?, Vatican, 1992, unpublished document (hereafter: PCPCU).

Justification by Faith, Lutherans and Catholics in Dialogue VII, Minneapolis, 1985 (hereafter: USA).

Position Paper of the Joint Committee of the United Evangelical Lutheran Church of Germany and the LWF German National Committee regarding the document "The Condemnations of the Reformation Era. Do They Still Divide?" in: Lehrverurteilungen im Gespräch, Göttingen, 1993 (hereafter: VELKD).

The Condemnations of the Reformation Era. Do they Still Divide? Edited by Karl Lehmann and Wolfhart Pannenberg, Minneapolis, 1990 (hereafter: LV:E).

For 3: The Common Understanding of Justification (paras. 17 and 18) (LV:E 68f; VELKD 95).

—"… a faith centered and forensically conceived picture of justification is of major importance for Paul and, in a sense, for the Bible as a whole, although it is by no means the only biblical or Pauline way of representing God's saving work" (USA, no. 146).

—"Catholics as well as Lutherans can acknowledge the need to test the practices, structures, and theologies of the church by the extent to which they help or hinder 'the proclamation of God's free and merciful promises in Christ Jesus which can be rightly received only through faith' (para. 28)" (USA, no. 153).

Regarding the "fundamental affirmation" (USA, no. 157; cf. 4) it is said:

—"This affirmation, like the Reformation doctrine of justification by faith alone, serves as a criterion for judging all church practices, structures, and traditions precisely because its counterpart is 'Christ alone' (*solus Christus*). He alone is to be ultimately trusted as the one mediator through whom God in the Holy Spirit pours out his saving gifts. All of us in this dialogue affirm that all Christian teachings, practices, and offices should so function as to foster 'the obedience of faith' (Rom. 1:5) in God's saving action in Christ Jesus alone through the Holy Spirit, for the salvation of the faithful and the praise and honor of the heavenly Father" (USA, no. 160).

—"For that reason, the doctrine of justification—and, above all, its biblical foundation—will always retain a special function in the church. That function is continually to remind Christians that we sinners live solely from the forgiving love of God, which we merely allow to be bestowed on us, but which we in no way—in however modified a form—'earn' or are able to tie down to any preconditions or postconditions. The doctrine of justification therefore becomes the touchstone for testing at all times whether a particular interpretation of our relationship to God can claim the name of 'Christian.' At the same time, it becomes the touchstone for the church, for testing at all times whether its proclamation and its praxis correspond to what has been given to it by its Lord" (LV:E 69).

—"An agreement on the fact that the doctrine of justification is significant not only as one doctrinal component within the whole of our church's teaching, but also as the touchstone for testing the whole doctrine and practice of our churches, is—from a Lutheran point of view—fundamental progress in the ecumenical dialogue between our churches. It cannot be welcomed enough" (VELKD 95, 20–26; cf. 157).

—"For Lutherans and Catholics, the doctrine of justification has a different status in the hierarchy of truth; but both sides agree that the doctrine of justification has its specific function in the fact that it is 'the touchstone for testing at all times whether a particular interpretation of our relationship to God can claim the name of "Christian." At the same time it becomes the touchstone for the church, for testing at all times whether its proclamation and its praxis correspond to what has been given to it by its Lord' (LV:E 69). The criteriological significance of the doctrine of justification for sacramentology, ecclesiology and ethical teachings still deserves to be studied further" (PCPCU 96).

For 4.1: Human Powerlessness and Sin in Relation to Justification (paras 19–21) (LV:E 42ff; 46; VELKD 77–81; 83f)

—"Those in whom sin reigns can do nothing to merit justification, which is the free gift of God's grace. Even the beginnings of justification, for example, repentance, prayer for grace, and desire for forgiveness, must be God's work in us" (USA, no. 156.3).

—"*Both* are concerned to make it clear that . . . human beings cannot . . . cast a sideways glance at their own endeavors . . . But a response is not a 'work.' The response of faith is itself brought about through the uncoercible word of promise which comes to human beings from outside themselves. There can be '*co*operation' only in the sense that in faith the heart is involved, when the Word touches it and creates faith" (LV:E 46f).

—"Where, however, Lutheran teaching construes the relation of God to his human creatures in justification with such emphasis on the divine 'monergism' or the sole efficacy of Christ in such a way, that the person's willing acceptance of God's grace—which is itself a gift of God—has no essential role in justification, then the Tridentine canons 4, 5, 6 and 9 still constitute a notable doctrinal difference on justification" (PCPCU 22).

—"The strict emphasis on the passivity of human beings concerning their justification never meant, on the Lutheran side, to contest the full personal participation in believing; rather it meant to exclude any cooperation in the event of justification itself. Justification is the work of Christ alone, the work of grace alone" (VELKD 84, 3–8).

For 4.2: Justification as Forgiveness of Sins and Making Righteous (paras. 22–24) (USA, nos. 98–101; LV:E 47ff; VELKD 84ff; cf. also the quotations for 4.3)

—"By justification we are both declared and made righteous. Justification, therefore, is not a legal fiction. God, in justifying, effects what he promises; he forgives sin and makes us truly righteous" (USA, no. 156.5).

—"Protestant theology does not overlook what Catholic doctrine stresses: the creative and renewing character of God's love; nor does it maintain God's impotence toward a sin which is 'merely' forgiven in justification but which is not truly abolished in its power to divide the sinner from God" (LV:E 49).

—"The Lutheran doctrine has never understood the 'crediting of Christ's justification' as without effect on the life of the faithful, because Christ's word achieves what it promises. Accordingly the Lutheran doctrine understands grace as God's favor, but nevertheless as effective power, 'for where there is forgiveness of sins, there is also life and salvation'" (VELKD 86, 15–23).

—"Catholic doctrine does not overlook what Protestant theology stresses: the personal character of grace, and its link with the

Word; nor does it maintain grace as an objective 'possession' (even if a conferred possession) on the part of the human being— something over which he can dispose" (LV:E 49).

For 4.3: Justification by Faith and through Grace (paras. 25–27) (USA, nos. 105ff; LV:E 49–53; VELKD 87–90)

—"If we translate from one language to another, then Protestant talk about justification through faith corresponds to Catholic talk about justification through grace; and on the other hand, Protestant doctrine understands substantially under the one word 'faith' what Catholic doctrine (following 1 Cor. 13:13) sums up in the triad of 'faith, hope, and love'" (LV:E 52).

—"We emphasize that faith in the sense of the first commandment always means love to God and hope in him and is expressed in the love to the neighbor" (VELKD 89, 8–11).

—"Catholics teach as do Lutherans, that nothing prior to the free gift of faith merits justification and that all of God's saving gifts come through Christ alone" (USA, no. 105).

—"The Reformers understood faith as the forgiveness and fellowship with Christ effected by the word of promise itself. . . . This is the ground for the new being, through which the flesh is dead to sin and the new man or woman in Christ has life (*sola fide per Christum*). But even if this faith necessarily makes the human being new, the Christian builds his confidence, not on his own new life, but solely on God's gracious promise. Acceptance in Christ is sufficient, if 'faith' is understood as 'trust in the promise' (*fides promissionis*)" (LV:E 50).

—Cf. The Council of Trent, Session 6, Chap. 7: "Consequently, in the process of justification, together with the forgiveness of sins a person receives, through Jesus Christ into whom he is grafted, all these infused at the same time: faith, hope and charity" (DH 1530).

—"According to Protestant interpretation, the faith that clings unconditionally to God's promise in Word and Sacrament is sufficient for righteousness before God, so that the renewal of the human being, without which there can be no faith, does not in itself make any contribution to justification" (LV:E 52).

—"As Lutherans we maintain the distinction between justification and sanctification, of faith and works, which however implies no separation" (VELKD 89, 6–8).

—"Catholic doctrine knows itself to be at one with the Protestant concern in emphasizing that the renewal of the human being does not 'contribute' to justification, and is certainly not a contribution to which he could make any appeal before God. Nevertheless it feels compelled to stress the renewal of the human being through justifying grace, for the sake of acknowledging God's newly creating power; although this renewal in faith, hope, and love is certainly nothing but a response to God's unfathomable grace" (LV:E 52f).

—"Insofar as the Catholic doctrine stresses that grace is personal and linked with the Word, that renewal . . . is certainly nothing but a response effected by God's word itself, and that the renewal of the human being does not contribute to justification, and is certainly not a contribution to which a person could make any appeal before God, our objection . . . no longer applies" (VELKD 89, 12–21).

For 4.4: The Justified as Sinner (paras. 28–30) (USA, nos. 102ff; LV:E 44ff; VELKD 81ff)

—"For however just and holy, they fall from time to time into the sins that are those of daily existence.

What is more, the Spirit's action does not exempt believers from the lifelong struggle against sinful tendencies. Concupiscence and other effects of original and personal sin, according to Catholic doctrine, remain in the justified, who therefore must pray daily to God for forgiveness" (USA, no. 102).

—"The doctrines laid down at Trent and by the Reformers are at one in maintaining that original sin, and also the concupiscence that remains, are in contradiction to God . . . object of the life-long struggle against sin . . . [A]fter baptism, concupiscence in the person justified no longer cuts that person off from God; in Tridentine language, it is 'no longer sin in the real sense'; in Lutheran phraseology, it is *peccatum regnatum*, 'controlled sin'" (LV:E 46).

—"The question is how to speak of sin with regard to the justified without limiting the reality of salvation. While Lutherans express this tension with the term 'controlled sin' (*peccatum regnatum*) which expresses the teaching of the Christian as 'being justified and sinner at the same time' (*simul iustus et peccator*), Roman Catholics think the reality of salvation can only be maintained by denying the sinful character of concupiscence. With regard to this question a considerable rapprochement is reached if LV:E calls the concupiscence that remains in the justified a 'contradiction to God' and thus qualifies it as sin" (VELKD 82, 29–39).

For 4.5: Law and Gospel (paras. 31–33)

—According to Pauline teaching this topic concerns the Jewish law as means of salvation. This law was fulfilled and overcome in Christ. This statement and the consequences from it have to be understood on this basis.

—With reference to Canons 19f of the Council of Trent, the VELKD (89, 28–36) says as follows:

"The ten commandments of course apply to Christians as stated in many places of the confessions. . . . If Canon 20 stresses that a person . . . is bound to keep the commandments of God, this canon does not strike to us; if however Canon 20 affirms that faith has salvific power only on condition of keeping the commandments this applies to us. Concerning the reference of the Canon regarding the commandments of the church, there is no difference between us if these commandments are only expressions of the commandments of God; otherwise it would apply to us."

—The last paragraph is related factually to 4.3, but emphasizes the "convicting function" of the law which is important to Lutheran thinking.

For 4.6: Assurance of Salvation (paras. 34–36) (LV:E 53–56; VELKD 90ff)

—"The question is: How can, and how may, human beings live before God in spite of their weakness, and with that weakness?" (LV:E 53).

—"The foundation and the point of departure [of the Reformers is] . . . the reliability and sufficiency of God's promise, and the power of Christ's death and resurrection; human weakness, and the threat to faith and salvation which that involves" (LV:E 56).

—The Council of Trent also emphasizes that "it is necessary to believe that sins are not forgiven, nor have they ever been forgiven, save freely by the divine mercy on account of Christ"; and that we must not doubt "the mercy of God, the merit of Christ and the power and efficacy of the sacraments; so it is possible for anyone, while he regards himself and his own weakness and lack of dispositions, to be anxious and fearful about his own state of grace" (Council of Trent, Session 6, chapter 9, DH 1534).

—"Luther and his followers go a step farther. They urge that the uncertainty should not merely be endured. We should avert our eyes from it and take seriously, practically, and personally the objective efficacy of the absolution pronounced in the sacrament of penance, which comes 'from outside.' . . . Since Jesus said, 'Whatever you loose on earth shall be loosed in heaven' (Matt. 16:19), the believer . . . would declare Christ to be a liar . . . if he did not rely with a rock-like assurance on the forgiveness of God uttered in the absolution. . . . This reliance can itself be subjectively uncertain—that the assurance of forgiveness is not a security of forgiveness (*securitas*); but this must not be turned into yet another problem, so to speak: the believer should turn his eyes away from it, and should look only to Christ's word of forgiveness" (LV:E 53f).

—"Today Catholics can appreciate the Reformer's efforts to ground faith in the objective reality of Christ's promise, 'whatsoever you loose on earth . . .' and to focus believers on the specific word of absolution from sins. . . . Luther's original concern to teach people to look away from their experience, and to rely on Christ alone and his word of forgiveness [is not to be condemned]" (PCPCU 24).

—A mutual condemnation regarding the understanding of the assurance of salvation "can even less provide grounds for mutual objection today—particularly if we start from the foundation of a biblically renewed concept of faith. For a person can certainly lose or renounce faith, and self-commitment to God and his word of promise. But if he believes in this sense, he *cannot at the same time* believe that God is unreliable in his word of promise. In this sense it is true today also that—in Luther's words—faith *is* the assurance of salvation" (LV:E 56).

—With reference to the concept of faith of Vatican II, see Dogmatic Constitution on Divine Revelation, no. 5: "'The obedience of faith' . . . must be given to God who reveals, an obedience by which man entrusts his whole self freely to God, offering 'the full submission of intellect and will to God who reveals,' and freely assenting to the truth revealed by him."

—"The Lutheran distinction between the certitude (*certitudo*) of faith which looks alone to Christ and earthly security (*securitas*), which is based on the human being, has not been dealt with clearly enough in the LV. The question whether a Christian 'has believed fully and completely' (LV:E 53) does not arise for the Lutheran understanding, since faith never reflects on itself, but depends completely on God, whose grace is bestowed through word and sacrament, thus from outside (*extra nos*)" (VELKD 92, 2–9).

For 4.7: The Good Works of the Justified (paras. 37–39) (LV:E 66ff, VELKD 90ff)

—"But the Council excludes the possibility of earning *grace*—that is, justification—(can. 2; DS 1552) and bases the earning or merit of *eternal life* on the gift of grace itself, through membership in Christ (can. 32: DS 1582). Good works are 'merits' as a *gift*. Although the Reformers attack 'Godless trust' in one's own works, the Council explicitly excludes any notion of a claim or any false security (cap. 16: DS 1548f). It is evident . . . that the Council wishes to establish a link with Augustine, who introduced the concept of merit, in order to express the responsibility of human beings, in spite of the 'bestowed' character of good works" (LV:E 66).

—If we understand the language of "cause" in Canon 24 in more personal terms, as it is done in chapter 16 of the Decree on Justification, where the idea of communion with Christ is foundational, then we can describe the Catholic doctrine on merit as it is done in the first sentence of the second paragraph of 4.7: growth in grace, perseverance in righteousness received from God and a deeper communion with Christ.

—"Many antitheses could be overcome if the misleading word 'merit' were simply to be viewed and thought about in connection with the true sense of the biblical term 'wage' or reward" (LV:E 67).

—"The Lutheran confessions stress that the justified person is responsible not to lose the grace received but to live in it. . . . Thus the confessions can speak of a preservation of grace and a growth in it. If 'righteousness' in Canon 24 is understood in the sense that it affects human beings, then it does not strike to us. But if 'righteousness' in Canon 24 refers to the Christian's acceptance by God, it strikes to us; for this righteousness is always perfect; compared with it the works of Christians are only 'fruits' and 'signs'" (VELKD 94, 2–14).

—"Concerning Canon 26, we refer to the Apology where eternal life is described as reward: '. . . We grant that eternal life is a reward because it is something that is owed—not because of our merits but because of the promise'" (VELKD 94, 20–24).

RESPONSE OF THE CATHOLIC CHURCH TO THE JOINT DECLARATION OF THE CATHOLIC CHURCH AND THE LUTHERAN WORLD FEDERATION ON THE DOCTRINE OF JUSTIFICATION

Declaration

The "Joint Declaration of the Catholic Church and the Lutheran World Federation on the Doctrine of Justification" represents a significant progress in mutual understanding and in the coming together in dialogue of the parties concerned; it shows that there are many points of convergence between the Catholic position and the Lutheran position on a question that has been for centuries so controversial. It can certainly be affirmed that a high degree of agreement has been reached, as regards both the approach to the question and the judgment it merits.[210] It is rightly stated that there is "a consensus in basic truths of the doctrine of justification."[211]

The Catholic Church is, however, of the opinion that we cannot yet speak of a consensus such as would eliminate every difference between Catholics and Lutherans in the understanding of justification. The Joint Declaration itself refers to certain of these differences. On some points the positions are, in fact, still divergent. So, on the basis of the agreement already reached on many aspects, the Catholic Church intends to contribute towards overcoming the divergencies that still exist by suggesting, below, in order of importance, a list of points that constitute still an obstacle to agreement between the Catholic Church and the Lutheran World Federation on all the fundamental truths concerning justification. The Catholic Church hopes that the following indications may be an encouragement to continue study of these questions in the same fraternal spirit that, in recent times, has characterized the dialogue between the Catholic Church and the Lutheran World Federation.

Clarifications

1. The major difficulties preventing an affirmation of total consensus between the parties on the theme of Justification arise in paragraph 4.4 *The Justified as Sinner* (nn. 28–30). Even taking into account the differences, legitimate in themselves, that come from different theological approaches to the content of faith, from a Catholic point of view the title is already a cause of perplexity. According, indeed, to the doctrine of the Catholic Church, in baptism everything that is really sin is taken away, and so, in those who are born anew there is nothing that is hateful to God.[212] It follows that the concupiscence that remains in the baptized is not, properly speaking, sin. For Catholics, therefore, the formula *"at the same time righteous and sinner,"* as it is explained at the beginning of n. 29 (*"Believers are totally righteous, in that God forgives their sins through Word and Sacrament. . . . Looking at themselves . . . however, they recognize that they remain also totally sinners. Sin still lives in them. . . ."*), is not acceptable.

This statement does not, in fact, seem compatible with the renewal and sanctification of the interior man of which the Council of Trent speaks.[213] The expression "Opposition to

God" (*Gottwidrigkeit*) that is used in nn. 28–30 is understood differently by Lutherans and by Catholics, and so becomes, in fact, equivocal. In this same sense, there can be ambiguity for a Catholic in the sentence of n. 22, ". . . *God no longer imputes to them their sin and through the Holy Spirit effects in them an active love,*" because man's interior transformation is not clearly seen. So, for all these reasons, it remains difficult to see how, in the current state of the presentation, given in the Joint Declaration, we can say that this doctrine on "*simul iustus et peccator*" is not touched by the anathemas of the Tridentine decree on original sin and justification.

2. Another difficulty arises in n. 18 of the Joint Declaration, where a clear difference appears in the importance, for Catholics and for Lutherans, of the doctrine of justification as criterion for the life and practice of the Church.

Whereas for Lutherans this doctrine has taken on an altogether particular significance, for the Catholic Church the message of justification, according to Scripture and already from the time of the Fathers, has to be organically integrated into the fundamental criterion of the "*regula fidei,*" that is, the confession of the one God in three persons, christologically centered and rooted in the living Church and its sacramental life.

3. As stated in n. 17 of the Joint Declaration, Lutherans and Catholics share the common conviction that the new life comes from divine mercy and not from any merit of ours. It must, however, be remembered—as stated in 2 Cor 5:17—that this divine mercy brings about a new creation and so makes man capable of responding to God's gift, of cooperating with grace. In this regard, the Catholic Church notes with satisfaction that n. 21, in conformity with can. 4 of the Decree on Justification of the Council of Trent (DS 1554) states that man can refuse grace; but it must also be affirmed that, with this freedom to refuse, there is also a new capacity to adhere to the divine will, a capacity rightly called "*cooperation.*" This new capacity given in

the new creation, does not allow us to use in this context the expression "mere passive" (n. 21). On the other hand, the fact that
this capacity has the character of a gift is well expressed in cap. 5
(DS 1525) of the Tridentine Decree when it says: "*ita ut tangente
Deo cor hominis per Spiritus Sancti illuminationem, neque homo ipse
nihil omnino agat, inspirationem illam recipiens, quippe qui illam et
abicere potest, neque tamen sine gratia Dei movere se ad iustitiam coram
illo libera sua voluntate possit.*"

In reality, also on the Lutheran side, there is the affirmation,
in n. 21, of a full personal involvement in faith (*"believers are fully
involved personally in their faith"*).

A clarification would, however, be necessary as to the compatibility of this involvement with the reception *"mere passive"* of justification, in order to determine more exactly the degree of consensus
with the Catholic doctrine. As for the final sentence of n. 24: "*God's
gift of grace in justification remains independent of human cooperation,*" this
must be understood in the sense that the gifts of God's grace do not
depend on the works of man, but not in the sense that justification
can take place without human cooperation. The sentence of n. 19
according to which man's freedom "*is no freedom in relation to salvation*" must, similarly, be related to the impossibility for man to reach
justification by his own efforts.

The Catholic Church maintains, moreover, that the good
works of the justified are always the fruit of grace. But at the
same time, and without in any way diminishing the totally divine initiative,[214] they are also the fruit of man, justified and
interiorly transformed. We can therefore say that eternal life is,
at one and the same time, grace and the reward given by God
for good works and merits.[215] This doctrine results from the interior transformation of man to which we referred in n. 1 of this
"Note." These clarifications are a help for a right understanding,
from the Catholic point of view, of paragraph 4.7 (nn. 37–39) on
the good works of the justified.

4. In pursuing this study further, it will be necessary to treat
also the sacrament of penance, which is mentioned in n. 30 of

the Joint Declaration. According to the Council of Trent, in fact,[216] through this sacrament the sinner can be justified anew (*rursus iustificari*): this implies the possibility, by means of this sacrament, as distinct from that of baptism, to recover lost justice.[217] These aspects are not all sufficiently noted in the abovementioned n. 30.

5. These remarks are intended as a more precise explanation of the teaching of the Catholic Church with regard to the points on which complete agreement has not been reached; they are also meant to complete some of the paragraphs explaining Catholic doctrine, in order to bring out more clearly the degree of consensus that has been reached. The level of agreement is high, but it does not yet allow us to affirm that all the differences separating Catholics and Lutherans in the doctrine concerning justification are simply a question of emphasis or language. Some of these differences concern aspects of substance and are therefore not all mutually compatible, as affirmed on the contrary in n. 40.

If, moreover, it is true that in those truths on which a consensus has been reached the condemnations of the Council of Trent no longer apply, the divergencies on other points must, on the contrary, be overcome before we can affirm, as is done generically in n. 41, that these points no longer incur the condemnations of the Council of Trent. That applies in the first place to the doctrine on "*simul iustus et peccator*" (cf. n. l, above).

6. We need finally to note, from the point of view of their representative quality, the different character of the two signataries of this Joint Declaration. The Catholic Church recognises the great effort made by the Lutheran World Federation in order to arrive, through consultation of the Synods, at a "*magnus consensus,*" and so to give a true ecclesial value to its signature; there remains, however, the question of the real authority of such a synodal consensus, today and also tomorrow, in the life and doctrine of the Lutheran community.

Prospects for Future Work

7. The Catholic Church wishes to reiterate its hope that this important step forward towards agreement in doctrine on justification may be followed by further studies that will make possible a satisfactory clarification of the divergencies that still exist. Particularly desirable would be a deeper reflection on the biblical foundation that is the common basis of the doctrine on justification both for Catholics and for Lutherans. This reflection should be extended to the New Testament as a whole and not only to the Pauline writings. If it is true, indeed, that St. Paul is the New Testament author who has had most to say on this subject, and this fact calls for a certain preferential attention, substantial references to this theme are not lacking also in the other New Testament writings. As for the various ways in which Paul describes man's new condition, as mentioned in the Joint Declaration, we could add the categories of sonship and of heirs (Gal. 4:4–7; Rom. 8:14–17). Consideration of all these elements will be a great help for mutual understanding and will make it possible to resolve the divergences that still exist in the doctrine on justification.

8. Finally, it should be a common concern of Lutherans and Catholics to find a language which can make the doctrine on justification more intelligible also for men and women of our day. The fundamental truths of the salvation given by Christ and received in faith, of the primacy of grace over every human initiative, of the gift of the Holy Spirit which makes us capable of living according to our condition as children of God, and so on. These are essential aspects of the Christian message that should be a light for the believers of all times.

ANNEX TO THE OFFICIAL COMMON STATEMENT

This note, which constitutes the official Catholic response to the text of the Joint Declaration, has been prepared by common agreement between the Congregation for the Doctrine of the Faith and the Pontifical Council for Promoting Christian Unity. It is signed by the president of the same Pontifical Council, which is directly responsible for the ecumenical dialogue.

1. The following elucidations underline the consensus reached in the *Joint Declaration on the Doctrine of Justification* (JD) regarding basic truths of justification; thus it becomes clear that the mutual condemnations of former times do not apply to the Catholic and Lutheran doctrines of justification as they are presented in the Joint Declaration.

2. "Together we confess: By grace alone, in faith in Christ's saving work and not because of any merit on our part, we are accepted by God and receive the Holy Spirit, who renews our hearts while equipping and calling us to good works"(JD 15).

A) We confess together that God forgives sin by grace and at the same time frees human beings from sin's enslaving power" (JD 22). Justification is forgiveness of sins and being made righteous, through which God "imparts the gift of new life in Christ" (JD 22). "Since we are justified by faith we have peace with God" (Rom. 5:1). We are "called children of God; and that is what we are" (1 John 3:1).We are truly and inwardly renewed by the action of the Holy Spirit, remaining always dependent on his work in us. "So if anyone is in Christ, there is a new creation: everything old has passed away; see, everything has become new!" (2 Cor. 5:17). The justified do not remain sinners in this sense.

Yet we would be wrong were we to say that we are without sin (1 John 1:8–10, cf. JD 28). "All of us make many mistakes" (James 3:2). "Who is aware of his unwitting sins? Cleanse me of many secret faults" (Ps. 19:12). And when we pray, we can only say, like the tax collector, "God, be merciful to me, a sinner" (Luke 18:13). This is expressed in a variety of ways in our liturgies. Together we hear the exhortation "Therefore, do not let sin exercise dominion in your mortal bodies, to make you obey their passions" (Rom. 6:12). This recalls to us the persisting danger which comes from the power of sin and its action in Christians. To this extent, Lutherans and Catholics can together understand the Christian as *simul justus et peccator,* despite their different approaches to this subject as expressed in JD 29–30.

B) The concept of "concupiscence" is used in different senses on the Catholic and Lutheran sides. In the Lutheran Confessional writings "concupiscence" is understood as the self-seeking desire of the human being, which in light of the Law, spiritually understood, is regarded as sin. In the Catholic understanding concupiscence is an inclination, remaining in human beings even after baptism, which comes from sin and presses towards sin. Despite the differences involved here, it can be recognized from a Lutheran perspective that desire can become the opening through which sin attacks. Due to the power of sin the entire human being carries the tendency to oppose God. This tendency, according to both Lutheran and Catholic conception, "does not correspond to God's original design for humanity" (JD 30). Sin has a personal character and, as such, leads to separation from God. It is the selfish desire of the old person and the lack of trust and love toward God.

The reality of salvation in baptism and the peril from the power of sin can be expressed in such a way that, on the one hand, the forgiveness of sins and renewal of humanity in Christ by baptism is emphasized and, on the other hand, it can be seen that the justified also "are continuously exposed to the power of sin still pressing its attacks (cf. Rom. 6:12–14) and are not exempt from a lifelong struggle against the contradiction to God. . . ." (JD 28).

C) Justification takes place "by grace alone" (JD 15 and 16), by faith alone, the person is justified "apart from works" (Rom. 3:28, cf. JD 25). "Grace creates faith not only when faith begins in a person but as long as faith lasts" (Thomas Aquinas, S. Th.II/II 4, 4 ad 3). The working of God's grace does not exclude human action: God effects everything, the willing and the achievement, therefore, we are called to strive (cf. Phil. 2:12 ff). "As soon as the Holy Spirit has initiated his work of regeneration and renewal in us through the Word and the holy sacraments, it is certain that we

can and must cooperate by the power of the Holy Spirit. . . ." (The
Formula of Concord, FC SD II, 64f; BSLK 897, 37ff).

D) Grace as fellowship of the justified with God in faith, hope
and love is always received from the salvific and creative work
of God (cf. JD 27). But it is nevertheless the responsibility of the
justified not to waste this grace but to live in it. The exhortation to do good works is the exhortation to practice the faith (cf.
BSLK 197, 45). The good works of the justified "should be done
in order to confirm their call, that is, lest they fall from their call
by sinning again" (Rev. 20, 13, BSLK 316, 18–24; with reference to 2 Pet. 1:10. Cf. also FC SD IV, 33; BSLK 948, 9–23). In
this sense Lutherans and Catholics can understand together what
is said about the "preservation of grace" in JD 38 and 39. Certainly, "whatever in the justified precedes or follows the free gift
of faith is neither the basis of justification nor merits it" (JD 25).

E) By justification we are unconditionally brought into communion with God. This includes the promise of eternal life; "If
we have been united with him in a death like his, we will certainly be united with him in a resurrection like his" (Rom. 6:5;
cf. John 3:36; Rom. 8:17). In the final judgment, the justified will
be judged also on their works (cf. Matt. 16:27, 25:31–46; Rom.
2:16; 14:12; 1 Cor. 3:8; 2 Cor. 5:10, etc.). We face a judgment in
which God's gracious sentence will approve anything in our life
and action that corresponds to his will. However, everything in
our life that is wrong will be uncovered and will not enter eternal life. The Formula of Concord also states: "It is God's will and
express command that believers should do good works which the
Holy Spirit works in them, and God is willing to be pleased with
them for Christ's sake and he promises to reward them gloriously
in this and in the future life" (FC SD IV, 38). Any reward is a
reward of grace, on which we have no claim.

3. The doctrine of justification is measure or touchstone for the
Christian faith. No teaching may contradict this criterion. In this
sense, the doctrine of justification is an "indispensable criterion
which constantly serves to orient all the teaching and practice of

our churches to Christ" (JD 18). As such, it has its truth and specific meaning within the overall context of the Church's fundamental Trinitarian confession of faith. We "share the goal of confessing Christ in all things, who is to be trusted above all things as the one Mediator (1 Tim. 2:5–6) through whom God in the Holy Spirit gives himself and pours out his renewing gifts" (JD 18).

4. The Response of the Catholic Church does not intend to put in question the authority of Lutheran Synods or of the Lutheran World Federation. The Catholic Church and the Lutheran World Federation began the dialogue and have taken it forward as partners with equal rights (*"par cum pari"*). Notwithstanding different conceptions of authority in the church, each partner respects the other partner's ordered process of reaching doctrinal decisions.

BONUS MATERIALS
V

Dominus Iesus

The following instruction was issued in 2000 by the Congregation for the Doctrine of the Faith. It concerns the unique role in salvation of Jesus Christ and his Church. For more information, see chapter 9.

Congregation for the Doctrine of the Faith

DECLARATION *"DOMINUS IESUS"* ON THE UNICITY AND SALVIFIC UNIVERSALITY OF JESUS CHRIST AND THE CHURCH

Introduction

1. The *Lord Jesus*, before ascending into heaven, commanded his disciples to proclaim the Gospel to the whole world and to baptize all nations: "Go into the whole world and proclaim the Gospel to every creature. He who believes and is baptized will be saved; he who does not believe will be condemned" (Mark 16:15–16); "All power in heaven and on earth has been given to me. Go therefore and teach all nations, baptizing them in the name of the Father, and of the Son, and of the Holy Spirit, teaching them to observe all that I have commanded you. And behold, I am with you always, until the end of the world" (Matt. 28:18–20; cf. Luke 24:46–48; John 17:18, 20, 21; Acts 1:8).

The Church's universal mission is born from the command of Jesus Christ and is fulfilled in the course of the centuries in the proclamation of the mystery of God, Father, Son, and Holy Spirit, and the mystery of the incarnation of the Son, as saving event for all humanity. The fundamental contents of the profession of the Christian faith are expressed thus: "I believe in one

God, the Father, Almighty, maker of heaven and earth, of all that is, seen and unseen. I believe in one Lord, Jesus Christ, the only Son of God, eternally begotten of the Father, God from God, Light from Light, true God from true God, begotten, not made, of one being with the Father. Through him all things were made. For us men and for our salvation, he came down from heaven: by the power of the Holy Spirit he became incarnate of the Virgin Mary, and became man. For our sake he was crucified under Pontius Pilate; he suffered death and was buried. On the third day he rose again in accordance with the Scriptures; he ascended into heaven and is seated at the right hand of the Father. He will come again in glory to judge the living and the dead, and his kingdom will have no end. I believe in the Holy Spirit, the Lord, the giver of life, who proceeds from the Father. With the Father and the Son he is worshipped and glorified. He has spoken through the prophets. I believe in one, holy, catholic, and apostolic Church. I acknowledge one baptism for the forgiveness of sins. I look for the resurrection of the dead, and the life of the world to come."[218]

2. In the course of the centuries, the Church has proclaimed and witnessed with fidelity to the Gospel of Jesus. At the close of the second millennium, however, this mission is still far from complete.[219] For that reason, Saint Paul's words are now more relevant than ever: "Preaching the Gospel is not a reason for me to boast; it is a necessity laid on me: woe to me if I do not preach the Gospel!" (1 Cor. 9:16). This explains the Magisterium's particular attention to giving reasons for and supporting the evangelizing mission of the Church, above all in connection with the religious traditions of the world.[220]

In considering the values which these religions witness to and offer humanity, with an open and positive approach, the Second Vatican Council's Declaration on the relation of the Church to non-Christian religions states: "The Catholic Church rejects nothing of what is true and holy in these religions. She has a high regard for the manner of life and conduct, the precepts and teachings, which, although differing in many ways from her own teaching, nonetheless often reflect a ray of that truth which enlightens all men."[221] Continuing in this line of thought, the Church's proclamation of Jesus Christ, "the way, the truth, and the life" (John 14:6), today also makes use of the practice of inter-religious dialogue. Such dialogue certainly does not replace, but rather accompanies the *missio ad gentes*, directed toward that "mystery of unity," from which "it follows that all men and women who are saved share, though differently, in the same mystery of salvation in Jesus Christ through his Spirit."[222] Inter-religious dialogue, which is part of the Church's evangelizing mission,[223] requires an attitude of understanding and a relationship of mutual knowledge and reciprocal enrichment, in obedience to the truth and with respect for freedom.[224]

3. In the practice of dialogue between the Christian faith and other religious traditions, as well as in seeking to understand its theoretical basis more deeply, new questions arise that need to be addressed through pursuing new paths of research, advancing proposals, and suggesting ways of acting that call for attentive discernment. In this task, the present Declaration seeks to recall to Bishops, theologians, and all the Catholic faithful, certain indispensable elements of Christian doctrine, which may help theological reflection in developing solutions consistent with the contents of the faith and responsive to the pressing needs of contemporary culture.

The expository language of the Declaration corresponds to its purpose, which is not to treat in a systematic manner the question of the unicity and salvific universality of the mystery of Jesus Christ and the Church, nor to propose solutions to questions that are matters of free theological debate, but rather to set forth again the doctrine of the Catholic faith in these areas, pointing out some fundamental questions that remain open to further development, and refuting specific positions that are erroneous or ambiguous. For this reason, the Declaration takes up what has been taught in previous Magisterial documents, in order to reiterate certain truths that are part of the Church's faith.

4. The Church's constant missionary proclamation is endangered today by relativistic theories which seek to justify religious
pluralism, not only *de facto* but also *de iure* (or *in principle*). As a
consequence, it is held that certain truths have been superseded;
for example, the definitive and complete character of the revelation of Jesus Christ, the nature of Christian faith as compared
with that of belief in other religions, the inspired nature of the
books of Sacred Scripture, the personal unity between the Eternal Word and Jesus of Nazareth, the unity of the economy of
the Incarnate Word and the Holy Spirit, the unicity and salvific
universality of the mystery of Jesus Christ, the universal salvific
mediation of the Church, the inseparability—while recognizing the distinction—of the kingdom of God, the kingdom of
Christ, and the Church, and the subsistence of the one Church
of Christ in the Catholic Church.

The roots of these problems are to be found in certain presuppositions of both a philosophical and theological nature, which
hinder the understanding and acceptance of the revealed truth.
Some of these can be mentioned: the conviction of the elusive-
ness and inexpressibility of divine truth, even by Christian revelation; relativistic attitudes toward truth itself, according to
which what is true for some would not be true for others; the
radical opposition posited between the logical mentality of the
West and the symbolic mentality of the East; the subjectivism
which, by regarding reason as the only source of knowledge,
becomes incapable of raising its "gaze to the heights, not daring
to rise to the truth of being;"[225] the difficulty in understanding and accepting the presence of definitive and eschatological
events in history; the metaphysical emptying of the historical
incarnation of the Eternal Logos, reduced to a mere appearing of
God in history; the eclecticism of those who, in theological research, uncritically absorb ideas from a variety of philosophical
and theological contexts without regard for consistency, systematic connection, or compatibility with Christian truth; finally,

the tendency to read and to interpret Sacred Scripture outside the Tradition and Magisterium of the Church.

On the basis of such presuppositions, which may evince different nuances, certain theological proposals are developed—at times presented as assertions, and at times as hypotheses—in which Christian revelation and the mystery of Jesus Christ and the Church lose their character of absolute truth and salvific universality, or at least shadows of doubt and uncertainty are cast upon them.

I. THE FULLNESS AND DEFINITIVENESS OF THE REVELATION OF JESUS CHRIST

5. As a remedy for this relativistic mentality, which is becoming ever more common, it is necessary above all to reassert the definitive and complete character of the revelation of Jesus Christ. In fact, it must be *firmly believed* that, in the mystery of Jesus Christ, the Incarnate Son of God, who is "the way, the truth, and the life" (John 14:6), the full revelation of divine truth is given: "No one knows the Son except the Father, and no one knows the Father except the Son and anyone to whom the Son wishes to reveal him" (Matt. 11:27); "No one has ever seen God; God the only Son, who is in the bosom of the Father, has revealed him" (John 1:18); "For in Christ the whole fullness of divinity dwells in bodily form" (Col. 2:9–10).

Faithful to God's word, the Second Vatican Council teaches: "By this revelation then, the deepest truth about God and the salvation of man shines forth in Christ, who is at the same time the mediator and the fullness of all revelation."[226] Furthermore, "Jesus Christ, therefore, the Word made flesh, sent 'as a man to men,' 'speaks the words of God' (John 3:34), and completes the work of salvation which his Father gave him to do (cf. John 5:36; 17:4). To see Jesus is to see his Father (cf. John 14:9). For this reason, Jesus perfected revelation by fulfilling it through his whole work of making himself present and manifesting himself: through his words and deeds, his signs and wonders, but especially through his death and glorious resurrection from the dead and finally with the sending of the Spirit of truth, he completed and perfected revelation and confirmed it with divine testimony. . . . The Christian dispensation, therefore, as the new and definitive covenant, will never pass away, and we now await no further new public revelation before the glorious manifestation of our Lord Jesus Christ (cf. 1 Tim. 6:14 and Titus 2:13)."[227]

Thus, the encyclical *Redemptoris Missio* calls the Church once again to the task of announcing the Gospel as the fullness of truth: "In this definitive Word of his revelation, God has made himself known in the fullest possible way. He has revealed to mankind who he is. This definitive self-revelation of God is the fundamental reason why the Church is missionary by her very nature. She cannot do other than proclaim the Gospel, that is, the fullness of the truth which God has enabled us to know about himself."[228] Only the revelation of Jesus Christ, therefore, "introduces into our history a universal and ultimate truth which stirs the human mind to ceaseless effort."[229]

6. Therefore, the theory of the limited, incomplete, or imperfect character of the revelation of Jesus Christ, which would be complementary to that found in other religions, is contrary to the Church's faith. Such a position would claim to be based on the notion that the truth about God cannot be grasped and manifested in its globality and completeness by any historical religion, neither by Christianity nor by Jesus Christ.

Such a position is in radical contradiction with the foregoing statements of Catholic faith according to which the full and complete revelation of the salvific mystery of God is given in Jesus Christ. Therefore, the words, deeds, and entire historical event of Jesus, though limited as human realities, have nevertheless the divine Person of the Incarnate Word, "true God and true man"[230] as their subject. For this reason, they possess in themselves the definitiveness and completeness of the revelation of God's salvific ways, even if the depth of the divine mystery in itself remains transcendent and inexhaustible. The truth about

God is not abolished or reduced because it is spoken in human language; rather, it is unique, full, and complete, because he who speaks and acts is the Incarnate Son of God. Thus, faith requires us to profess that the Word made flesh, in his entire mystery, who moves from incarnation to glorification, is the source, participated but real, as well as the fulfilment of every salvific revelation of God to humanity,[231] and that the Holy Spirit, who is Christ's Spirit, will teach this "entire truth" (John 16:13) to the apostles and, through them, to the whole Church.

7. The proper response to God's revelation is *"the obedience of faith* (Rom. 16:26; cf. Rom. 1:5; 2 Cor. 10:5–6) by which man freely entrusts his entire self to God, offering 'the full submission of intellect and will to God who reveals' and freely assenting to the revelation given by him."[232] Faith is a gift of grace: "in order to have faith, the grace of God must come first and give assistance; there must also be the interior helps of the Holy Spirit, who moves the heart and converts it to God, who opens the eyes of the mind and gives 'to everyone joy and ease in assenting to and believing in the truth.'"[233]

The obedience of faith implies acceptance of the truth of Christ's revelation, guaranteed by God, who is Truth itself.[234] "Faith is first of all a personal adherence of man to God. At the same time, and inseparably, it is a *free assent to the whole truth that God has revealed*."[235] Faith, therefore, as *"a gift of God"* and as *"a supernatural virtue infused by him,"*[236] involves a dual adherence: to God who reveals and to the truth which he reveals, out of the trust which one has in him who speaks. Thus, "we must believe in no one but God: the Father, the Son and the Holy Spirit."[237]

For this reason, the distinction between *theological faith* and *belief* in the other religions, must be *firmly held*. If faith is the acceptance in grace of revealed truth, which "makes it possible to penetrate the mystery in a way that allows us to understand it coherently,"[238] then belief, in the other religions, is that sum of experience and thought that constitutes the human treasury of wisdom and religious aspiration, which man in his search for

truth has conceived and acted upon in his relationship to God
and the Absolute.[239]

This distinction is not always borne in mind in current theological reflection. Thus, theological faith (the acceptance of the
truth revealed by the One and Triune God) is often identified
with belief in other religions, which is religious experience still
in search of the absolute truth and still lacking assent to God
who reveals himself. This is one of the reasons why the differences between Christianity and the other religions tend to be
reduced at times to the point of disappearance.

8. The hypothesis of the inspired value of the sacred writings of
other religions is also put forward. Certainly, it must be recognized that there are some elements in these texts which may be
de facto instruments by which countless people throughout the
centuries have been and still are able today to nourish and maintain their life-relationship with God. Thus, as noted above, the
Second Vatican Council, in considering the customs, precepts,
and teachings of the other religions, teaches that "although differing in many ways from her own teaching, these nevertheless
often reflect a ray of that truth which enlightens all men."[240]

The Church's tradition, however, reserves the designation of
inspired texts to the canonical books of the Old and New Testaments, since these are inspired by the Holy Spirit.[241] Taking up
this tradition, the Dogmatic Constitution on Divine Revelation
of the Second Vatican Council states: "For Holy Mother Church,
relying on the faith of the apostolic age, accepts as sacred and canonical the books of the Old and New Testaments, whole and
entire, with all their parts, on the grounds that, written under
the inspiration of the Holy Spirit (cf. John 20:31; 2 Tim. 3:16; 2
Pet. 1:19–21, 3:15–16), they have God as their author, and have
been handed on as such to the Church herself."[242] These books
"firmly, faithfully, and without error, teach that truth which
God, for the sake of our salvation, wished to see confided to the
Sacred Scriptures."[243]

Nevertheless, God, who desires to call all peoples to himself in Christ and to communicate to them the fullness of his revelation and love, "does not fail to make himself present in many ways, not only to individuals, but also to entire peoples through their spiritual riches, of which their religions are the main and essential expression even when they contain 'gaps, insufficiencies and errors.'"[244] Therefore, the sacred books of other religions, which in actual fact direct and nourish the existence of their followers, receive from the mystery of Christ the elements of goodness and grace which they contain.

II. THE INCARNATE LOGOS AND THE HOLY SPIRIT IN THE WORK OF SALVATION

9. In contemporary theological reflection there often emerges an approach to Jesus of Nazareth that considers him a particular, finite, historical figure, who reveals the divine not in an exclusive way, but in a way complementary with other revelatory and salvific figures. The Infinite, the Absolute, the Ultimate Mystery of God would thus manifest itself to humanity in many ways and in many historical figures: Jesus of Nazareth would be one of these. More concretely, for some, Jesus would be one of the many faces which the Logos has assumed in the course of time to communicate with humanity in a salvific way.

Furthermore, to justify the universality of Christian salvation as well as the fact of religious pluralism, it has been proposed that there is an economy of the eternal Word that is valid also outside the Church and is unrelated to her, in addition to an economy of the incarnate Word. The first would have a greater universal value than the second, which is limited to Christians, though God's presence would be more full in the second.

10. These theses are in profound conflict with the Christian faith. The doctrine of faith must be *firmly believed* which proclaims that Jesus of Nazareth, son of Mary, and he alone, is the Son and the Word of the Father. The Word, which "was in the beginning with God" (John 1:2) is the same as he who "became flesh"

(John 1:14). In Jesus, "the Christ, the Son of the living God" (Matt. 16:16), "the whole fullness of divinity dwells in bodily form" (Col. 2:9). He is the "only begotten Son of the Father, who is in the bosom of the Father" (John 1:18), his "beloved Son, in whom we have redemption. . . . In him the fullness of God was pleased to dwell, and through him, God was pleased to reconcile all things to himself, on earth and in the heavens, making peace by the blood of his cross" (Col. 1:13–14, 19–20).

Faithful to Sacred Scripture and refuting erroneous and reductive interpretations, the First Council of Nicaea solemnly defined its faith in: "Jesus Christ, the Son of God, the only begotten generated from the Father, that is, from the being of the Father, God from God, Light from Light, true God from true God, begotten, not made, one in being with the Father, through whom all things were made, those in heaven and those on earth. For us men and for our salvation, he came down and became incarnate, was made man, suffered, and rose again on the third day. He ascended to the heavens and shall come again to judge the living and the dead."[245] Following the teachings of the Fathers of the Church, the Council of Chalcedon also professed: "the one and the same Son, our Lord Jesus Christ, the same perfect in divinity and perfect in humanity, the same truly God and truly man . . . , one in being with the Father according to the divinity and one in being with us according to the humanity . . . , begotten of the Father before the ages according to the divinity and, in these last days, for us and our salvation, of Mary, the Virgin Mother of God, according to the humanity."[246]

For this reason, the Second Vatican Council states that Christ "the new Adam . . . 'image of the invisible God' (Col. 1:15) is himself the perfect man who has restored that likeness to God in the children of Adam which had been disfigured since the first sin. . . . As an innocent lamb he merited life for us by his blood which he freely shed. In him God reconciled us to himself and to one another, freeing us from the bondage of the devil and of sin, so that each one of us could say with the apostle: the Son of God 'loved me and gave himself up for me' (Gal. 2:20)."[247]

In this regard, John Paul II has explicitly declared: "To introduce any sort of separation between the Word and Jesus Christ is contrary to the Christian faith. . . . Jesus is the Incarnate Word— a single and indivisible person. . . . Christ is none other than Jesus of Nazareth; he is the Word of God made man for the salvation of all. . . . In the process of discovering and appreciating the manifold gifts—especially the spiritual treasures—that God has bestowed on every people, we cannot separate those gifts from Jesus Christ, who is at the center of God's plan of salvation."[248]

It is likewise contrary to the Catholic Faith to introduce a separation between the salvific action of the Word as such and that of the Word made man. With the incarnation, all the salvific actions of the Word of God are always done in unity with the human nature that he has assumed for the salvation of all people. The one subject which operates in the two natures, human and divine, is the single person of the Word.[249]

Therefore, the theory which would attribute, after the incarnation as well, a salvific activity to the Logos as such in his divinity, exercised "in addition to" or "beyond" the humanity of Christ, is not compatible with the Catholic faith.[250]

11. Similarly, the doctrine of faith regarding the unicity of the salvific economy willed by the One and Triune God must be *firmly believed,* at the source and center of which is the mystery of the incarnation of the Word, mediator of divine grace on the level of creation and redemption (cf. Col. 1:15–20), he who recapitulates all things (cf. Eph. 1:10), he "whom God has made our wisdom, our righteousness, and sanctification and redemption" (1 Cor. 1:30). In fact, the mystery of Christ has its own intrinsic unity, which extends from the eternal choice in God to the parousia: "[The Father] chose us in Christ before the foundation of the world to be holy and blameless before him in love" (Eph. 1:4); "In Christ we are heirs, having been destined according to the purpose of him who accomplishes all things according to his counsel and will" (Eph. 1:11); "For those whom he foreknew he also predestined to be conformed to the image of his Son, in

order that he might be the firstborn among many brothers; those whom he predestined he also called; and those whom he called he also justified; and those whom he justified he also glorified" (Rom. 8:29–30).

The Church's Magisterium, faithful to divine revelation, reasserts that Jesus Christ is the mediator and the universal redeemer: "The Word of God, through whom all things were made, was made flesh, so that as perfect man he could save all men and sum up all things in himself. The Lord . . . is he whom the Father raised from the dead, exalted and placed at his right hand, constituting him judge of the living and the dead."[251] This salvific mediation implies also the unicity of the redemptive sacrifice of Christ, eternal high priest (cf. Heb. 6:20, 9:11, 10:12–14).

12. There are also those who propose the hypothesis of an economy of the Holy Spirit with a more universal breadth than that of the Incarnate Word, crucified and risen. This position also is contrary to the Catholic faith, which, on the contrary, considers the salvific incarnation of the Word as a trinitarian event. In the New Testament, the mystery of Jesus, the Incarnate Word, constitutes the place of the Holy Spirit's presence as well as the principle of the Spirit's effusion on humanity, not only in messianic times (cf. Acts 2:32–36; John 7:39, 20:22; 1 Cor. 15:45), but also prior to his coming in history (cf. 1 Cor. 10:4; 1 Pet. 1:10–12).

The Second Vatican Council has recalled to the consciousness of the Church's faith this fundamental truth. In presenting the Father's salvific plan for all humanity, the Council closely links the mystery of Christ from its very beginnings with that of the Spirit.[252] The entire work of building the Church by Jesus Christ the Head, in the course of the centuries, is seen as an action which he does in communion with his Spirit.[253]

Furthermore, the salvific action of Jesus Christ, with and through his Spirit, extends beyond the visible boundaries of the Church to all humanity. Speaking of the paschal mystery, in which Christ even now associates the believer to himself in a living manner in the Spirit and gives him the hope of resurrection, the Council states: "All this holds true not only for Christians but also for all men of good will in whose hearts grace is active invisibly. For since Christ died for all, and since all men are in fact called to one and the same destiny, which is divine, we must hold that the Holy Spirit offers to all the possibility of being made partners, in a way known to God, in the paschal mystery."[254]

Hence, the connection is clear between the salvific mystery of the Incarnate Word and that of the Spirit, who actualizes the salvific efficacy of the Son made man in the lives of all people, called by God to a single goal, both those who historically preceded the Word made man, and those who live after his coming in history: the Spirit of the Father, bestowed abundantly by the Son, is the animator of all (cf. John 3:34).

Thus, the recent Magisterium of the Church has firmly and clearly recalled the truth of a single divine economy: "The Spirit's presence and activity affect not only individuals but also society and history, peoples, cultures and religions. . . . The Risen Christ 'is now at work in human hearts through the strength of his Spirit.' . . . Again, it is the Spirit who sows the 'seeds of the word' present in various customs and cultures, preparing them for full maturity in Christ."[255] While recognizing the historical-salvific function of the Spirit in the whole universe and in the entire history of humanity,[256] the Magisterium states: "This is the same Spirit who was at work in the incarnation and in the life, death, and resurrection of Jesus and who is at work in the Church. He is therefore not an alternative to Christ nor does he fill a sort of void which is sometimes suggested as existing between Christ and the Logos. Whatever the Spirit brings about in human hearts and in the history of peoples, in cultures and religions, serves as a preparation for the Gospel and can only be understood in reference to Christ, the Word who took flesh by the power of the Spirit 'so that as perfectly human he would save all human beings and sum up all things.'"[257]

In conclusion, the action of the Spirit is not outside or parallel to the action of Christ. There is only one salvific economy of the

One and Triune God, realized in the mystery of the incarnation, death, and resurrection of the Son of God, actualized with the cooperation of the Holy Spirit, and extended in its salvific value to all humanity and to the entire universe: "No one, therefore, can enter into communion with God except through Christ, by the working of the Holy Spirit."[258]

III. UNICITY AND UNIVERSALITY OF THE SALVIFIC MYSTERY OF JESUS CHRIST

13. The thesis which denies the unicity and salvific universality of the mystery of Jesus Christ is also put forward. Such a position has no biblical foundation. In fact, the truth of Jesus Christ, Son of God, Lord and only Savior, who through the event of his incarnation, death and resurrection has brought the history of salvation to fulfilment, and which has in him its fullness and center, must be *firmly believed* as a constant element of the Church's faith.

The New Testament attests to this fact with clarity: "The Father has sent his Son as the Savior of the world" (1 John 4:14); "Behold the Lamb of God who takes away the sin of the world" (John 1:29). In his discourse before the Sanhedrin, Peter, in order to justify the healing of a man who was crippled from birth, which was done in the name of Jesus (cf. Acts 3:1–8), proclaims: "There is salvation in no one else, for there is no other name under heaven given among men by which we must be saved" (Acts 4:12). St. Paul adds, moreover, that Jesus Christ "is Lord of all," "judge of the living and the dead," and thus "whoever believes in him receives forgiveness of sins through his name" (Acts 10:36, 42, 43).

Paul, addressing himself to the community of Corinth, writes: "Indeed, even though there may be so-called gods in heaven or on earth—as in fact there are many gods and many lords—yet for us there is one God, the Father, from whom are all things and for whom we exist, and one Lord, Jesus Christ, through whom are all things and through whom we exist" (1 Cor. 8:5–6). Furthermore,

John the apostle states: "For God so loved the world that he gave
his only Son, so that everyone who believes in him may not perish
but may have eternal life. God did not send his Son into the world
to condemn the world, but in order that the world might be saved
through him" (John 3:16–17). In the New Testament, the universal salvific will of God is closely connected to the sole mediation
of Christ: "[God] desires all men to be saved and to come to the
knowledge of the truth. For there is one God; there is also one
mediator between God and men, the man Jesus Christ, who gave
himself as a ransom for all" (1 Tim. 2:4–6).

It was in the awareness of the one universal gift of salvation
offered by the Father through Jesus Christ in the Spirit (cf. Eph.
1:3–14), that the first Christians encountered the Jewish people, showing them the fulfilment of salvation that went beyond
the Law and, in the same awareness, they confronted the pagan
world of their time, which aspired to salvation through a plu-
rality of saviors. This inheritance of faith has been recalled recently by the Church's Magisterium: "The Church believes that
Christ, who died and was raised for the sake of all (cf. 2 Cor.
5:15) can, through his Spirit, give man the light and the strength
to be able to respond to his highest calling, nor is there any other
name under heaven given among men by which they can be
saved (cf. Acts 4:12). The Church likewise believes that the key,
the center, and the purpose of the whole of man's history is to be
found in its Lord and Master."[259]

14. It must therefore be *firmly believed* as a truth of Catholic
faith that the universal salvific will of the One and Triune God
is offered and accomplished once for all in the mystery of the
incarnation, death, and resurrection of the Son of God.

Bearing in mind this article of faith, theology today, in its
reflection on the existence of other religious experiences and
on their meaning in God's salvific plan, is invited to explore if
and in what way the historical figures and positive elements of
these religions may fall within the divine plan of salvation. In
this undertaking, theological research has a vast field of work
under the guidance of the Church's Magisterium. The Second

Vatican Council, in fact, has stated that "the unique mediation of the Redeemer does not exclude, but rather gives rise to a manifold cooperation which is but a participation in this one source."[260] The content of this participated mediation should be explored more deeply but must remain always consistent with the principle of Christ's unique mediation: "Although participated forms of mediation of different kinds and degrees are not excluded, they acquire meaning and value *only* from Christ's own mediation, and they cannot be understood as parallel or complementary to his."[261] Hence, those solutions that propose a salvific action of God beyond the unique mediation of Christ would be contrary to Christian and Catholic Faith.

15. Not infrequently it is proposed that theology should avoid the use of terms like "unicity," "universality," and "absoluteness," which give the impression of excessive emphasis on the significance and value of the salvific event of Jesus Christ in relation to other religions. In reality, however, such language is simply being faithful to revelation, since it represents a development of the sources of the faith themselves. From the beginning, the community of believers has recognized in Jesus a salvific value such that he alone, as Son of God made man, crucified and risen, by the mission received from the Father and in the power of the Holy Spirit, bestows revelation (cf. Matt. 11:27) and divine life (cf. John 1:12, 5:25–26, 17:2) to all humanity and to every person.

In this sense, one can and must say that Jesus Christ has a significance and a value for the human race and its history, which are unique and singular, proper to him alone, exclusive, universal, and absolute. Jesus is, in fact, the Word of God made man for the salvation of all. In expressing this consciousness of faith, the Second Vatican Council teaches: "The Word of God, through whom all things were made, was made flesh, so that as perfect man he could save all men and sum up all things in himself. The Lord is the goal of human history, the focal point of the desires of history and civilization, the center of mankind, the joy of all hearts, and the fulfilment of all aspirations. It is he whom the Father raised from the dead, exalted and placed at his right hand, constituting him judge of the living and the dead."[262] "It is precisely this uniqueness of Christ which gives him an absolute and universal significance whereby, while belonging to history, he remains history's center and goal: 'I am the Alpha and the Omega, the first and the last, the beginning and the end' (Rev. 22:13)."[263]

IV. UNICITY AND UNITY OF THE CHURCH

16. The Lord Jesus, the only Savior, did not only establish a simple community of disciples, but constituted the Church as a *salvific mystery:* he himself is in the Church and the Church is in him (cf. John 15:1ff.; Gal. 3:28; Eph. 4:15–16; Acts 9:5). Therefore, the fullness of Christ's salvific mystery belongs also to the Church, inseparably united to her Lord. Indeed, Jesus Christ continues his presence and his work of salvation in the Church and by means of the Church (cf. Col. 1:24–27),[264] which is his body (cf. 1 Cor. 12:12–13, 27; Col. 1:18).[265] And thus, just as the head and members of a living body, though not identical, are inseparable, so too Christ and the Church can neither be confused nor separated, and constitute a single "whole Christ."[266] This same inseparability is also expressed in the New Testament by the analogy of the Church as the *Bride* of Christ (cf. 2 Cor. 11:2; Eph. 5:25–29; Rev. 21:2,9).[267]

Therefore, in connection with the unicity and universality of the salvific mediation of Jesus Christ, the unicity of the Church founded by him must be *firmly believed* as a truth of Catholic faith. Just as there is one Christ, so there exists a single body of Christ, a single Bride of Christ: "a single Catholic and apostolic Church."[268] Furthermore, the promises of the Lord that he would not abandon his Church (cf. Matt. 16:18, 28:20) and that he would guide her by his Spirit (cf. John 16:13) mean, according to Catholic faith, that the unicity and the unity of the Church—like everything that belongs to the Church's integrity—will never be lacking.[269]

The Catholic faithful *are required to profess* that there is an historical continuity—rooted in the apostolic succession[270]—

between the Church founded by Christ and the Catholic Church: "This is the single Church of Christ . . . which our Savior, after his resurrection, entrusted to Peter's pastoral care (cf. John 21:17), commissioning him and the other apostles to extend and rule her (cf. Matt. 28:18ff.), erected for all ages as 'the pillar and mainstay of the truth' (1 Tim. 3:15). This Church, constituted and organized as a society in the present world, subsists in (*subsistit in*) the Catholic Church, governed by the Successor of Peter and by the Bishops in communion with him."[271] With the expression *subsistit in,* the Second Vatican Council sought to harmonize two doctrinal statements: on the one hand, that the Church of Christ, despite the divisions which exist among Christians, continues to exist fully only in the Catholic Church, and on the other hand, that "outside of her structure, many elements can be found of sanctification and truth,"[272] that is, in those Churches and ecclesial communities which are not yet in full communion with the Catholic Church.[273] But with respect to these, it needs to be stated that "they derive their efficacy from the very fullness of grace and truth entrusted to the Catholic Church."[274]

17. Therefore, there exists a single Church of Christ, which subsists in the Catholic Church, governed by the Successor of Peter and by the Bishops in communion with him.[275] The Churches which, while not existing in perfect communion with the Catholic Church, remain united to her by means of the closest bonds, that is, by apostolic succession and a valid Eucharist, are true particular Churches.[276] Therefore, the Church of Christ is present and operative also in these Churches, even though they lack full communion with the Catholic Church, since they do not accept the Catholic doctrine of the Primacy, which, according to the will of God, the Bishop of Rome objectively has and exercises over the entire Church.[277]

On the other hand, the ecclesial communities which have not preserved the valid Episcopate and the genuine and integral substance of the Eucharistic mystery,[278] are not Churches in the proper sense; however, those who are baptized in these communities are, by Baptism, incorporated in Christ and thus are in a certain communion, albeit imperfect, with the Church.[279] Baptism in fact tends per se toward the full development of life in Christ, through the integral profession of faith, the Eucharist, and full communion in the Church.[280]

"The Christian faithful are therefore not permitted to imagine that the Church of Christ is nothing more than a collection—divided, yet in some way one—of Churches and ecclesial communities; nor are they free to hold that today the Church of Christ nowhere really exists, and must be considered only as a goal which all Churches and ecclesial communities must strive to reach."[281] In fact, "the elements of this already-given Church exist, joined together in their fullness in the Catholic Church and, without this fullness, in the other communities."[282] "Therefore, these separated Churches and communities as such, though we believe they suffer from defects, have by no means been deprived of significance and importance in the mystery of salvation. For the spirit of Christ has not refrained from using them as means of salvation which derive their efficacy from the very fullness of grace and truth entrusted to the Catholic Church."[283]

The lack of unity among Christians is certainly a *wound* for the Church; not in the sense that she is deprived of her unity, but "in that it hinders the complete fulfilment of her universality in history."[284]

V. THE CHURCH: KINGDOM OF GOD AND KINGDOM OF CHRIST

18. The mission of the Church is "to proclaim and establish among all peoples the kingdom of Christ and of God, and she is on earth, the seed and the beginning of that kingdom."[285] On the one hand, the Church is "a sacrament—that is, sign and instrument of intimate union with God and of unity of the entire human race."[286] She is therefore the sign and instrument of the kingdom; she is called to announce and to establish the kingdom. On the other hand, the Church is the "people gathered by the unity of the Father, the Son

and the Holy Spirit;"[287] she is therefore "the kingdom of Christ already present in mystery"[288] and constitutes its *seed* and *beginning*. The kingdom of God, in fact, has an eschatological dimension: it is a reality present in time, but its full realization will arrive only with the completion or fulfilment of history.[289]

The meaning of the expressions *kingdom of heaven, kingdom of God*, and *kingdom of Christ* in Sacred Scripture and the Fathers of the Church, as well as in the documents of the Magisterium, is not always exactly the same, nor is their relationship to the Church, which is a mystery that cannot be totally contained by a human concept. Therefore, there can be various theological explanations of these terms. However, none of these possible explanations can deny or empty in any way the intimate connection between Christ, the kingdom, and the Church. In fact, the kingdom of God which we know from revelation, "cannot be detached either from Christ or from the Church. . . . If the kingdom is separated from Jesus, it is no longer the kingdom of God which he revealed. The result is a distortion of the meaning of the kingdom, which runs the risk of being transformed into a purely human or ideological goal and a distortion of the identity of Christ, who no longer appears as the Lord to whom everything must one day be subjected (cf. 1 Cor. 15:27). Likewise, one may not separate the kingdom from the Church. It is true that the Church is not an end unto herself, since she is ordered toward the kingdom of God, of which she is the seed, sign and instrument. Yet, while remaining distinct from Christ and the kingdom, the Church is indissolubly united to both."[290]

19. To state the inseparable relationship between Christ and the kingdom is not to overlook the fact that the kingdom of God— even if considered in its historical phase—is not identified with the Church in her visible and social reality. In fact, "the action of Christ and the Spirit outside the Church's visible boundaries" must not be excluded.[291] Therefore, one must also bear in mind that "the kingdom is the concern of everyone: individuals, society and the world. Working for the kingdom means acknowledging

and promoting God's activity, which is present in human history and transforms it. Building the kingdom means working for liberation from evil in all its forms. In a word, the kingdom of God is the manifestation and the realization of God's plan of salvation in all its fullness."[292]

In considering the relationship between the kingdom of God, the kingdom of Christ, and the Church, it is necessary to avoid one-sided accentuations, as is the case with those "conceptions which deliberately emphasize the kingdom and which describe themselves as 'kingdom centered.' They stress the image of a Church which is not concerned about herself, but which is totally concerned with bearing witness to and serving the kingdom. It is a 'Church for others,' just as Christ is the 'man for others.' . . . Together with positive aspects, these conceptions often reveal negative aspects as well. First, they are silent about Christ: the kingdom of which they speak is 'theocentrically' based, since, according to them, Christ cannot be understood by those who lack Christian faith, whereas different peoples, cultures, and religions are capable of finding common ground in the one divine reality, by whatever name it is called. For the same reason, they put great stress on the mystery of creation, which is reflected in the diversity of cultures and beliefs, but they keep silent about the mystery of redemption. Furthermore, the kingdom, as they understand it, ends up either leaving very little room for the Church or undervaluing the Church in reaction to a presumed 'ecclesiocentrism' of the past and because they consider the Church herself only a sign, for that matter a sign not without ambiguity."[293] These theses are contrary to Catholic faith because they deny the unicity of the relationship which Christ and the Church have with the kingdom of God.

VI. THE CHURCH AND THE OTHER RELIGIONS IN RELATION TO SALVATION

20. From what has been stated above, some points follow that are necessary for theological reflection as it explores the relationship of the Church and the other religions to salvation.

Above all else, it must be *firmly believed* that "the Church, a pilgrim now on earth, is necessary for salvation: the one Christ is the mediator and the way of salvation; he is present to us in his body which is the Church. He himself explicitly asserted the necessity of faith and baptism (cf. Mark 16:16; John 3:5), and thereby affirmed at the same time the necessity of the Church which men enter through baptism as through a door."[294] This doctrine must not be set against the universal salvific will of God (cf. 1 Tim. 2:4); "it is necessary to keep these two truths together, namely, the real possibility of salvation in Christ for all mankind and the necessity of the Church for this salvation."[295]

The Church is the "universal sacrament of salvation,"[296] since, united always in a mysterious way to the Savior Jesus Christ, her Head, and subordinated to him, she has, in God's plan, an indispensable relationship with the salvation of every human being.[297] For those who are not formally and visibly members of the Church, "salvation in Christ is accessible by virtue of a grace which, while having a mysterious relationship to the Church, does not make them formally part of the Church, but enlightens them in a way which is accommodated to their spiritual and material situation. This grace comes from Christ; it is the result of his sacrifice and is communicated by the Holy Spirit;"[298] it has a relationship with the Church, which "according to the plan of the Father, has her origin in the mission of the Son and the Holy Spirit."[299]

21. With respect to the *way* in which the salvific grace of God— which is always given by means of Christ in the Spirit and has a mysterious relationship to the Church—comes to individual non-Christians, the Second Vatican Council limited itself to the statement that God bestows it "in ways known to himself."[300] Theologians are seeking to understand this question more fully. Their work is to be encouraged, since it is certainly useful for understanding better God's salvific plan and the ways in which it is accomplished. However, from what has been stated above

about the mediation of Jesus Christ and the "unique and special relationship"[301] which the Church has with the kingdom of God among men—which in substance is the universal kingdom of Christ the Savior—it is clear that it would be contrary to the faith to consider the Church as *one way* of salvation alongside those constituted by the other religions, seen as complementary to the Church or substantially equivalent to her, even if these are said to be converging with the Church toward the eschatological kingdom of God.

Certainly, the various religious traditions contain and offer religious elements which come from God,[302] and which are part of what "the Spirit brings about in human hearts and in the history of peoples, in cultures, and religions."[303] Indeed, some prayers and rituals of the other religions may assume a role of preparation for the Gospel, in that they are occasions or pedagogical helps in which the human heart is prompted to be open to the action of God.[304] One cannot attribute to these, however, a divine origin or an *ex opere operato* salvific efficacy, which is proper to the Christian sacraments.[305] Furthermore, it cannot be overlooked that other rituals, insofar as they depend on superstitions or other errors (cf. 1 Cor. 10:20–21), constitute an obstacle to salvation.[306]

22. With the coming of the Savior Jesus Christ, God has willed that the Church founded by him be the instrument for the salvation of *all* humanity (cf. Acts 17:30–31).[307] This truth of faith does not lessen the sincere respect which the Church has for the religions of the world, but at the same time, it rules out, in a radical way, that mentality of indifferentism "characterized by a religious relativism which leads to the belief that 'one religion is as good as another.'"[308] If it is true that the followers of other religions can receive divine grace, it is also certain that *objectively speaking* they are in a gravely deficient situation in comparison with those who, in the Church, have the fullness of the means of salvation.[309] However, "all the children of the Church should nevertheless remember that their exalted condition results, not

from their own merits, but from the grace of Christ. If they fail to respond in thought, word, and deed to that grace, not only shall they not be saved, but they shall be more severely judged."[310] One understands then that, following the Lord's command (cf. Matt. 28:19–20) and as a requirement of her love for all people, the Church "proclaims and is in duty bound to proclaim without fail, Christ who is the way, the truth, and the life (John 14:6). In him, in whom God reconciled all things to himself (cf. 2 Cor. 5:18–19), men find the fullness of their religious life."[311]

In inter-religious dialogue as well, the mission *ad gentes* "today as always retains its full force and necessity."[312] "Indeed, God 'desires all men to be saved and come to the knowledge of the truth' (1 Tim. 2:4); that is, God wills the salvation of everyone through the knowledge of the truth. Salvation is found in the truth. Those who obey the promptings of the Spirit of truth are already on the way of salvation. But the Church, to whom this truth has been entrusted, must go out to meet their desire, so as to bring them the truth. Because she believes in God's universal plan of salvation, the Church must be missionary."[313] Inter-religious dialogue, therefore, as part of her evangelizing mission, is just one of the actions of the Church in her mission *ad gentes*.[314] *Equality,* which is a presupposition of inter-religious dialogue, refers to the equal personal dignity of the parties in dialogue, not to doctrinal content, nor even less to the position of Jesus Christ—who is God himself made man—in relation to the founders of the other religions. Indeed, the Church, guided by charity and respect for freedom,[315] must be primarily committed to proclaiming to all people the truth definitively revealed by the Lord, and to announcing the necessity of conversion to Jesus Christ and of adherence to the Church through Baptism and the other sacraments, in order to participate fully in communion with God, the Father, Son and Holy Spirit. Thus, the certainty of the universal salvific will of God does not diminish, but rather increases the duty and urgency of the proclamation of salvation and of conversion to the Lord Jesus Christ.

CONCLUSION

23. The intention of the present *Declaration,* in reiterating and clarifying certain truths of the faith, has been to follow the example of the apostle Paul, who wrote to the faithful of Corinth: "I handed on to you as of first importance what I myself received" (1 Cor. 15:3). Faced with certain problematic and even erroneous propositions, theological reflection is called to reconfirm the Church's faith and to give reasons for her hope in a way that is convincing and effective.

In treating the question of the true religion, the Fathers of the Second Vatican Council taught: "We believe that this one true religion continues to exist in the Catholic and Apostolic Church, to which the Lord Jesus entrusted the task of spreading it among all people. Thus, he said to the apostles: 'Go therefore and make disciples of all nations baptizing them in the name of the Father and of the Son and of the Holy Spirit, teaching them to observe all that I have commanded you' (Matt. 28:19–20). Especially in those things that concern God and his Church, all persons are required to seek the truth, and when they come to know it, to embrace it and hold fast to it."[316]

The revelation of Christ will continue to be "the true lodestar"[317] in history for all humanity: "The truth, which is Christ, imposes itself as an all-embracing authority."[318] The Christian mystery, in fact, overcomes all barriers of time and space, and accomplishes the unity of the human family: "From their different locations and traditions all are called in Christ to share in the unity of the family of God's children. . . . Jesus destroys the walls of division and creates unity in a new and unsurpassed way through our sharing in his mystery. This unity is so deep that the Church can say with Saint Paul: 'You are no longer strangers and sojourners, but you are saints and members of the household of God' (Eph. 2:19)."[319]

The sovereign pontiff John Paul II, at the Audience of June 16, 2000, granted to the undersigned Cardinal Prefect of the Congregation for the

Doctrine of the Faith, with sure knowledge and by his apostolic authority, ratified and confirmed this Declaration, adopted in Plenary Session and ordered its publication.

Rome, from the Offices of the Congregation for the Doctrine of the Faith, August 6, 2000, the Feast of the Transfiguration of the Lord.

Joseph Card. Ratzinger
Prefect

Tarcisio Bertone, S.D.B.
Archbishop Emeritus of Vercelli
Secretary

Pope Benedict XVI on St. Paul and the Doctrine of Justification

The following two audiences were given by Pope Benedict XVI in 2008 as part of his catechesis on St. Paul. They deal with the doctrine of justification in St. Paul, how it is to be understood, and how it may be seen in an ecumenical light. For more information, see chapter 8.

BENEDICT XVI
GENERAL AUDIENCE

St. Peter's Square
Wednesday, 19 November 2008

Saint Paul (13):
The Doctrine of Justification: From Works to Faith.

Dear Brothers and Sisters,
On the journey we are making under St. Paul's guidance, let us now reflect on a topic at the center of the controversies of the century of the Reformation: the question of justification. How does man become just in God's eyes? When Paul met the Risen One on the road to Damascus he was an accomplished man; irreproachable according to the justice deriving from the Law (cf. Phil. 3:6), Paul surpassed many of his contemporaries in the observance of the Mosaic Law and zealously upheld the traditions of his fathers (cf. Gal. 1:14). The illumination of Damascus radically changed his life; he began to consider all merits acquired in an impeccable religious career as "refuse," in comparison with the sublimity of knowing Jesus Christ (cf. Phil. 3:8). The Letter

to the Philippians offers us a moving testimony of Paul's transition from a justice founded on the Law and acquired by his observance of the required actions, to a justice based on faith in Christ. He had understood that what until then had seemed to him to be a gain, before God was, in fact, a loss; and thus he had decided to stake his whole existence on Jesus Christ (cf. Phil. 3:7). The treasure hidden in the field and the precious pearl for whose purchase all was to be invested were no longer in function of the Law, but Jesus Christ, his Lord.

The relationship between Paul and the Risen One became so deep as to induce him to maintain that Christ was no longer solely his life but also his very living, to the point that to be able to reach him death became a gain (cf. Phil. 1:21). This is not to say he despised life, but that he realized that for him at this point there was no other purpose in life and thus he had no other desire than to reach Christ as in an athletics competition to remain with him for ever. The Risen Christ had become the beginning and the end of his existence, the cause and the goal of his race. It was only his concern for the development in faith of those he had evangelized and his anxiety for all of the Churches he founded (cf. 2 Cor. 11:28) that induced him to slow down in his race towards his one Lord, to wait for his disciples so they might run with him towards the goal. Although from a perspective of moral integrity he had nothing to reproach himself in his former observance of the Law, once Christ had reached him he preferred not to make judgments on himself (cf. 1 Cor. 4:3–4). Instead he limited himself to resolving to press on, to make his own the One who had made him his own (cf. Phil. 3:12).

It is precisely because of this personal experience of relationship with Jesus Christ that Paul henceforth places at the center of his Gospel an irreducible opposition between the two alternative paths to justice: one built on the works of the Law, the other founded on the grace of faith in Christ. The alternative between justice by means of works of the Law and that by faith in Christ thus became one of the dominant themes that run through his Letters: "We ourselves, who are Jews by birth and not Gentile sinners, yet who know that a man is not justified by works of the law but through faith in Jesus Christ, even we have believed in Christ Jesus in order to be justified by faith in Christ, and not by works of the law; because by works of the law no one will be justified" (Gal. 2:15–16). And to the Christians of Rome he reasserts that "all have sinned and fall short of the glory of God, they are now justified by his grace as a gift, through the redemption which is in Christ Jesus" (Rom. 3:23–24). And he adds "we hold that a man is justified by faith apart from works of the law" (ibid., v. 28). At this point Luther translated: "justified by faith alone." I shall return to this point at the end of the Catechesis. First, we must explain what is this "Law" from which we are freed and what are those "works of the Law" that do not justify. The opinion that was to recur systematically in history already existed in the community at Corinth. This opinion consisted in thinking that it was a question of moral law and that the Christian freedom thus consisted in the liberation from ethics. Thus in Corinth the term "πάντα μοι ἔξεστιν" (I can do what I like) was widespread. It is obvious that this interpretation is wrong: Christian freedom is not libertinism; the liberation of which St. Paul spoke is not liberation from good works.

So what does the Law from which we are liberated and which does not save mean? For St. Paul, as for all his contemporaries, the word "Law" meant the Torah in its totality, that is, the five books of Moses. The Torah, in the Pharisaic interpretation, that which Paul had studied and made his own, was a complex set of conduct codes that ranged from the ethical nucleus to observances of rites and worship and that essentially determined the identity of the just person. In particular, these included circumcision, observances concerning pure food and ritual purity in general, the rules regarding the observance of the Sabbath, etc., codes of conduct that also appear frequently in the debates between Jesus and his contemporaries. All of these observances that express a social, cultural and religious identity had become uniquely important in the time of Hellenistic culture, starting from the third century B.C. This culture which had become the universal culture of that time and was a seemingly rational culture; a polytheistic culture, seemingly tolerant constituted a strong pressure for cultural uniformity and thus threatened the identity of Israel, which was politically constrained to enter into this common identity of the Hellenistic culture. This resulted in the loss of its own identity, hence also the loss of the precious heritage of the faith of the Fathers, of the faith in the one God and in the promises of God.

Against this cultural pressure, which not only threatened the Israelite identity but also the faith in the one God and in his promises, it was necessary to create a wall of distinction, a shield of defense to protect the precious heritage of the faith; this wall consisted precisely in the Judaic observances and prescriptions. Paul, who had learned these observances in their role of defending God's gift, of the inheritance of faith in one God alone, saw this identity threatened by the freedom of the Christians; this is why he persecuted them. At the moment of his encounter with the Risen One he understood that with Christ's Resurrection the situation had changed radically. With Christ, the God of Israel, the one true God, became the God of all peoples. The wall as he says in his Letter to the Ephesians between Israel and the Gentiles, was no longer necessary: it is Christ who protects us from polytheism and all of its deviations; it is Christ who unites us *with* and *in* the one God; it is Christ who guarantees our true identity within the diversity of cultures. The wall is no longer necessary; our common identity within the diversity of cultures is Christ, and it is he who makes us just. Being just simply means being with Christ and in Christ. And this suffices. Further observances are no longer necessary. For this reason Luther's phrase: "*faith alone*" is true, if it is not opposed to faith in charity, in love. Faith is looking at Christ, entrusting oneself to Christ, being united to Christ, conformed to Christ, to his life. And the form, the life of Christ, is love; hence to believe is to conform to Christ and to enter into his love. So it is that in the Letter to the Galatians in which he primarily developed his teaching on justification St. Paul speaks of faith that works through love (cf. Gal. 5:14).

Paul knows that in the twofold love of God and neighbor the whole of the Law is present and carried out. Thus in communion with Christ, in a faith that creates charity, the entire Law is fulfilled. We become just by entering into communion with Christ who is Love. We shall see the same thing in the Gospel next Sunday, the Solemnity of Christ the King. It is the Gospel of the judge whose sole criterion is love. What he asks is only this: Did you visit me when I was sick? When I was in prison? Did you give me food to eat when I was hungry, did you clothe me when I was naked? And thus justice is decided in charity. Thus, at the end of this Gospel we can almost say: love alone, charity alone. But there is no contradiction between this Gospel and St. Paul. It is the same vision, according to which communion with Christ, faith in Christ, creates charity. And charity is the fulfilment of communion with Christ. Thus, we are just by being united with him and in no other way.

At the end, we can only pray the Lord that he help us to believe; really believe. Believing thus becomes life, unity with Christ, the transformation of our life. And thus, transformed by his love, by the love of God and neighbor, we can truly be just in God's eyes.

BENEDICT XVI
GENERAL AUDIENCE

Paul VI Audience Hall
Wednesday, 26 November 2008

Saint Paul (14):
The Doctrine of Justification: The Apostle's Teaching on Faith and Works

Dear Brothers and Sisters,
In the Catechesis last Wednesday I spoke of how man is justified before God. Following St. Paul, we have seen that man is unable to "justify" himself with his own actions, but can only truly become "just" before God because God confers his "justice"

upon him, uniting him to Christ his Son. And man obtains this union through faith. In this sense, St. Paul tells us: not our deeds, but rather faith renders us "just." This faith, however, is not a thought, an opinion, an idea. This faith is communion with Christ, which the Lord gives to us, and thus becomes life, becomes conformity with him. Or to use different words faith, if it is true, if it is real, becomes love, becomes charity, is expressed in charity. A faith without charity, without this fruit, would not be true faith. It would be a dead faith.

Thus, in our last Catechesis, we discovered two levels: that of the insignificance of our actions and of our deeds to achieve salvation, and that of "justification" through faith which produces the fruit of the Spirit. The confusion of these two levels has caused more than a few misunderstandings in Christianity over the course of centuries. In this context it is important that St. Paul, in the same Letter to the Galatians radically accentuates, on the one hand, the freely given nature of justification that is not dependent on our works, but which at the same time also emphasizes the relationship between faith and charity, between faith and works: "In Christ Jesus neither circumcision nor uncircumcision counts for anything, but only faith working through love" (Gal. 5:6). Consequently, there are on the one hand "works of the flesh," which are "immorality, impurity, licentiousness, idolatry. . . ." (Gal. 5:19–20): all works that are contrary to the faith; on the other, there is the action of the Holy Spirit who nourishes Christian life, inspiring "love, joy, peace, patience, kindness, goodness, faithfulness, gentleness, self-control" (Gal. 5:22–23). These are the fruits of the Spirit that blossom from faith.

Agape, love, is cited at the beginning of this list of virtues and self-control at the conclusion. In fact, the Spirit who is the Love of the Father and the Son pours out his first gift, *agape*, into our hearts (cf. Rom. 5:5); and to be fully expressed, *agape*, love, requires self-control. In my first Encyclical, *Deus Caritas Est*, I also treated of the love of the Father and the Son which reaches us and profoundly transforms our existence. Believers know that reciprocal love is embodied in the love of God and of Christ, through the Spirit. Let us return to the Letter to the Galatians. Here St. Paul says that by bearing one another's burdens believers are fulfilling the commandment of love (cf. Gal. 6:2). Justified through the gift of faith in Christ, we are called to live in the love of Christ for neighbor, because it is on this criterion that we shall be judged at the end of our lives. In reality Paul only repeats what Jesus himself said and which is proposed to us anew by last Sunday's Gospel, in the parable of the Last Judgment. In the First Letter to the Corinthians St. Paul pours himself out in a famous eulogy of love. It is called the "hymn to love": "If I speak in the tongues of men and of angels, but have not love, I am a noisy gong or a clanging cymbal. . . . Love is patient and kind; love is not jealous or boastful; it is not arrogant or rude. Love does not insist on its own way" (1 Cor. 13:1, 4–5). Christian love is particularly demanding because it springs from Christ's total love for us: that love that claims us, welcomes us, embraces us, sustains us, to the point of tormenting us since it forces each one to no longer live for himself, closed into his own selfishness, but for him "who for their sake died and was raised" (2 Cor. 5:15). The love of Christ makes us, in him, that new creation (cf. 2 Cor. 5:17), which comes to belong to his Mystical Body that is the Church.

Seen in this perspective, the centrality of justification without works, the primary object of Paul's preaching, does not clash with faith that works through love; indeed, it demands that our faith itself be expressed in a life in accordance with the Spirit. Often there is seen an unfounded opposition between St. Paul's theology and that of St. James, who writes in his Letter: "as the body apart from the spirit is dead, so faith apart from works is dead" (James 2:26). In reality, while Paul is primarily concerned to show that faith in Christ is necessary and sufficient, James accentuates the consequential relations between faith and works (cf. James 2:24). Therefore, for both Paul and James, faith that is active in love testifies to the freely given gift of justification in Christ. Salvation received in Christ needs to be preserved and witnessed to "with fear and trembling. For God is at work in you, both to will and to work for his good pleasure. . . . Do all things without grumbling or questioning . . . holding fast the word of life," St. Paul was to say further, to the Christians of Philippi (cf. Phil. 2:12–14, 16).

We are often induced to fall into the same misunderstandings that characterized the community of Corinth; those Christians thought that since they had been freely justified in Christ through faith, "they could do as they pleased." And they believed and it often seems that today's Christians also think this that it is permissible to create divisions in the Church, the Body of Christ, to celebrate the Eucharist without looking after the neediest of our brothers, to aspire to better charisms without being aware that each is a member of the other, and so forth. The consequences of a faith that is not manifested in love are disastrous, because it reduces itself to the arbitrariness and subjectivism that is most harmful to us and to our brothers. On the contrary, in following St. Paul, we should gain a new awareness of the fact that precisely because we are justified in Christ, we no longer belong to ourselves but have become a temple of the Spirit and hence are called to glorify God in our body with the whole of our existence (cf. 1 Cor. 6:19). We would be underselling the inestimable value of justification, purchased at the high price of Christ's Blood, if we were not to glorify him with our body. In fact, our worship at the same time reasonable and spiritual is exactly this, which is why St. Paul exhorts us "to present [our] bodies as a living sacrifice, holy and acceptable to God" (Rom. 12:1). To what would a liturgy be reduced if addressed solely to the Lord without simultaneously becoming service to one's brothers, a faith that would not express itself in charity? And the apostle often places his communities in confrontation with the Last Judgment, on the occasion of which: "we must all appear before the judgment seat of Christ, so that each one may receive good or evil, according to what he has done in the body" (2 Cor. 5:10; cf. also Rom. 2:16). And this idea of the Last Judgment must illumine us in our daily lives.

If the ethics that Paul proposes to believers do not deteriorate into forms of moralism and prove themselves timely for us, it is because, each time, they start from the personal and communal relationship with Christ, to be realized concretely in a life according to the Spirit. This is essential: the Christian ethic is not born from a system of commandments but is a consequence of our friendship with Christ. This friendship influences life; if it is true it incarnates and fulfills itself in love for neighbor. For this reason, any ethical decay is not limited to the individual sphere but it also weakens personal and communal faith from which it derives and on which it has a crucial effect. Therefore let us allow ourselves to be touched by reconciliation, which God has given us in Christ, by God's "foolish" love for us; nothing and no one can ever separate us from his love (cf. Rom. 8:39). We live in this certainty. It is this certainty that gives us the strength to live concretely the faith that works in love.

BONUS MATERIALS
VII

Glossary of Terms

The many terms that apply to the study of salvation are often unfamiliar. The reader should be aware that, while each word does convey a slightly different notion, the terms are used by the writers of the Bible in an overlapping, often interchangeable manner.

The reader should also be aware that each definition given below is meant to convey the basic, root idea of a term rather than the complete theology associated with it. For example, justify is defined as "to make right (just) with God." This conveys the root idea but does not examine whether justification occurs only at the beginning of the believer's life, whether it can be lost, how it is received, or whether it involves one's receiving legal or actual righteousness or both. For that kind of information, see the preceding chapters of this book.

Atone: To reconcile by making amends or compensation (noun: *atonement*).

Attrition: Sorrow for our sins based on any supernatural motive other than charity.

Charity: The theological virtue whereby we love God above all things for his own sake and whereby we love our neighbor as ourselves for God's sake.

Contrition: Sorrow for our sins, which is divided into perfect contrition and imperfect contrition (attrition).

Expiate: To make amends or provide compensation (noun: *expiation*).

Faith: The theological virtue whereby we believe all that God reveals because it is revealed by God.

Formed faith: The theological virtue of faith made active by the virtue of charity.

Hope: The theological virtue whereby we trust God for all the grace that is needed for our salvation.

Justify: To make right (just) with God (noun: *justification*).

Merit: (1) Something that is given as a reward, (2) something for which a reward is given.

Perfect contrition: Sorrow for our sins that is based on charity, including repentance and the will to do what is needed to be reconciled with God.

Redeem: To buy back (e.g., from slavery to sin, from death, from danger of going to hell) (noun: *redemption*).

Repent: (1) To turn from a particular sin and firmly resolve not to do it in the future, (2) to turn from sins generally, firmly resolving to live according to God's law in accord with the conditions of this life.

Righteousness: The quality of a person who has been justified, or made right with God. Righteousness may be actual (ontological), legal, or behavioral.

Sanctify: To make holy (noun: *sanctification*).

Satisfy: To reconcile by providing adequate compensation (noun: *satisfaction*).

Save: To rescue, whether from temporal dangers (such as the danger of dying in battle) or eternal dangers (such as the danger of going to hell). In Greek and Latin, often carries the idea of health or a restoration to health (noun: *salvation*).

Soteriology: The branch of theology concerned with the doctrine of salvation.

Notes

1. Thus John MacArthur's Grace To You ministry Web site states, "True saving faith involves repentance from one's sin and a complete trust in the work of Christ to save from sin and make one righteous" ("What is the nature of true saving faith?" online at gty.org, retrieved May 16, 2014).
2. Unfortunately, Wesleyans place this event some time *after* initial justification, which is not correct.
3. In addition to these passages in Hebrews, see Rom. 12:2, 13:14; see also 2 Cor. 4:16 and Eph. 4:21–25.
4. In many Bibles this is given as an alternate translation, but the common version reading "we have peace" is based on inferior manuscripts.
5. By definition, justification involves the bestowal of legal, actual, or behavioral righteousness.
6. The Greek word here is *dikaiosune*, which translates as "righteousness" or "justification." In either case, the text points to a future bestowal of righteousness and thus a future justification.
7. *Word Biblical Commentary* (vol. 38a): *Romans 1–8* (Dallas: Word Books, 1988), 153.
8. *The Theology of Martin Luther* (Philadelphia: Fortress, 1966), 226.
9. *Disputation on Justification*, thesis 23, in *Luther's Works* 34:152.
10. *D. Martin Luthers Werke. Kritische Gesamtausabe* (Weimar, 1883), 39I:252 (cited in Althaus, 237 n. 63).
11. Greek, *hoti*, which translates as "because," "since," "that," "for."
12. Trent, session 25, *Decree on Indulgences*.
13. The Latin terms for these liabilities are *reatus culpae* and *reatus poena*.
14. See also Eph. 5:26–27, Acts 22:16, 1 Cor. 6:11, 1 John 1:7, and Rev. 7:13–14.
15. See also Matt. 12:36 and Rom. 2:16.
16. See also Matt. 21:2, 2 Thess. 1:9, and Rev. 14:11.
17. See 2 Sam. 12:7–12 for a list.
18. Here a confessor is not a priest but one who confessed the Christian faith before the state during a persecution. Confessors, like martyrs, pleased God in a special way by holding to their faith at the risk of their lives.

19. This kind of argument, of the form "If X is the case, then how much more is Y the case," is called an *a fortiori* argument. *A fortiori* arguments were often used by Jesus and Paul: See Matt. 7:11, 10:25, 12:12, Luke 11:13, 12:24, 28, Rom. 11:12, 24, and 1 Cor. 6:3.

20. *Indulgentiarum Doctrina*, 3.

21. The Old Testament sin sacrifices dealt only with the temporal atonement for sins, "for it is impossible that the blood of bulls and goats should take away (the eternal punishment for) sins" (Heb. 10:4).

22. This is one reason the Church cannot simply "empty purgatory," as Martin Luther suggested it should. Because it lacks jurisdiction, the earthly Church can only pray for those there.

23. Some parties may be one and the same person. The person who provides the basis for an indulgence may request one and apply it to another; the person who requests an indulgence may ask it for himself or someone else. One limit under current canon law is that one may not obtain an indulgence for another living person (although it is possible to do so in principle, as the case of the early penitents shows).

24. These rewards are metaphorically referred to as "the treasury of the Church," or sometimes as "the treasury of merits." A merit is anything that pleases God and moves him to issue a reward, not things that earn "payment" from God. Strictly speaking, human beings cannot earn anything from God, though by his grace they can please him in a way he chooses to reward. Picturing the saints' acts under a single, collective metaphor (such as a treasury) finds precedent in the Bible: "It was granted her (the Bride) to be clothed with fine linen, bright and pure" (Rev. 19:8). John, the author of Revelation, tells us that "the fine linen is the righteous deeds of the saints." Here the righteous deeds of the saints are pictured under the collective metaphor of clothing on the Bride of Christ, the Church. Jewish theology recognizes an analogous concept. Jewish theologians speak of the collective "merits of the fathers"—the idea being that the patriarchs pleased God and inherited certain promises as a reward. God fulfills these promises and ends up treating later Jews more gently than he would have otherwise.

25. *Indulgentiarum Doctrina* 11.

26. For example, it does not offend Christ for a fireman to pull a child out of a burning building. The idea of one human saving another from temporal misfortune does not diminish the victory of Christ.

27. Morris, L., *The Atonement* (Downers Grove: InterVarsity, 1983), 151.

28. *Wycliff Bible Encyclopedia* (Chicago: Moody, 1975), 1:578.

29. It explains, for instance, that expiation differs from propitiation, which "carries in addition the idea of appeasing an offended person, of regaining the favor of a higher individual" (ibid.). Thus expiation and propitiation both focus on fixing things after a wrong has been committed, but the former focuses on the wrong itself whereas the latter focuses on the one offended by the wrong.

30. In biblical quotations containing the phrase "works of Torah," unless otherwise indicated the translation we use will continue to be the RSV:CE but with the word "Torah" replacing "law."

31. Even if it is implicit faith.

32. A case could be made that Paul would acknowledge the coming of a post-Temple, post-synagogue age in which Jewish Christians should not continue certain rites.

33. There is also such a thing as human positive law—laws decreed by human government—but here we are concerned with divine positive law—i.e., laws proclaimed by God in special revelation.

34. Also known as the *Catechism of the Council of Trent*; not the same as the *Catechism of the Catholic Church*.

35. See 1 Cor. 9:15, 15:31; 2 Cor. 2:12, 14, 7:4, 14, 8:24, 9:2–4, 10:8, 13–16, 11:10, 2 Thess. 1:4. See also 2 Cor. 10:16–17, Rom. 15:17, 1 Cor. 1:31, 3:21, 2 Cor. 5:12.

36. Frequently, this passage is used to argue that things such as repentance and baptism are not necessary for salvation. However, Paul's opponents are Jewish Christians who are telling Gentile Christians that they must become Jews. The controversy is thus taking place in a post-baptismal context and does not address the subject of how one becomes a Christian. The people Paul is trying to keep from being circumcised had already repented and been baptized. The question at hand is: For Gentile Christians, is it enough simply to continue having faith in Christ, or do they need to be circumcised as well? Because the context is post-repentance, post-baptism, this text cannot be used to deny things Scripture elsewhere says about repentance and baptism (e.g., Matt. 3:7–10, 1 Pet. 3:21).

37. Many translations render v. 1 as saying "since we are justified by faith, *we have peace* with God." This translation is sometimes used to claim that peace with God is an automatic consequence of justification that can never be lost. In most manuscripts, however, what Paul says is this: "Therefore, since we are justified by faith, *let us have*

peace with God." Justification provides the basis of our relationship with God and does make our initial peace with God, but we must continue to live at peace with God and at war with sin rather than sliding back into grave sin. Even if the minority reading were correct, it would not imply that justification cannot be lost but simply that those who are currently justified are currently at peace.

38. "A German pope heads for the Land of Luther," *National Catholic Reporter*, Sept. 2, 2011, online at *ncronline.org*.

39. Ibid.

40. Ibid.

41. *The Condemnations of the Reformation Era: Do They Still Divide?*, Karl Lehmann and Wolfhart Pannenberg, eds. (Minneapolis: Fortress Press, 1990).

42. Specifically, Canons 2, 4–13, 16, 24, and 32. This list was not exhaustive. Other canons in Trent's Decree were never thought to apply to Lutherans. Canon 1, for example, condemns those who say we can be justified by our own works, while Canon 3 condemns those who would say we do not need the grace of the Holy Spirit to be justified—both of which were as firmly condemned by Lutherans as by Catholics.

43. The omission of the term *sanctifying grace* in favor of the term *charity* is not to an endorsement of the Scotist view. The document is not intended to settle questions that are still open for Catholics; much less is it intended to endorse the less common of two views.

44. In Latin, the phrase corresponding to "so that thus he understands" is *ita ut intelligat*. The term *intelligat* can also be translated as "perceives" or "feels." This construction in Latin serves to explain which understanding of the term "faith alone" is being condemned.

45. In conciliar documents, such as those of Trent, the term *anathema* does not mean damned by God. It referred to a canon law penalty in which a bishop used a particular ceremony to perform an excommunication. Such excommunications were not automatic, and they came to be employed only rarely. The penalty no longer exists, having lapsed with the promulgation of the 1983 *Code of Canon Law*. However, the doctrinal value of canons using this term remains (that is, any doctrinal or moral proposition rejected in such canons is still infallibly rejected).

46. Pontifical Council for Promoting Christian Unity and Lutheran World Federation, *From Conflict to Communion: Lutheran-Catholic Common Commemoration of the Reformation in 2017*, 82.

47. Fitzmyer, Joseph A., *Romans (The Anchor Yale Bible Commentaries),* (New Haven: Yale University Press, 1993), 360.
48. *The Church's Confession of Faith: A Catholic Catechism for Adults* (San Francisco: Ignatius Press, 1987), 200; emphasis in original.
49. Mal. 4:2.
50. Heb. 12:2.
51. John 14:26.
52. Rom. 5:12, 1 Cor. 15:22.
53. Isa. 64:6.
54. Eph. 2:3.
55. Rom. 6:17.
56. 2 Cor. 1:3.
57. Gal. 4:4.
58. See Gal. 5:4.
59. Rom. 9:30.
60. Rom. 3:25.
61. 1 John 2:2.
62. 2 Cor. 5:15.
63. Col. 1:12–14.
64. Introduced by way of digression or comment.
65. Rom. 5:21.
66. Titus 3:5.
67. John 3:5.
68. I.e., the grace of God *going before.* This is an old use of the verb *prevent,* used as a translation of *prævenire.*
69. Zach. 1:3.
70. Lam. 5:21.
71. Rom. 10:17.
72. Rom. 3:24.
73. Cf. Sess. xiv, 4.
74. Heb. 11:6.
75. Matt. 9:5.
76. Eccles. 1:21.
77. Acts 2:38.
78. Matt. 28:19.
79. 1 Sam. 7:3.
80. Titus 3:7.
81. 1 Cor. 6:11.
82. Eph. 1:13, 14.

83. Rom. 5:10.
84. Eph. 2:4.
85. Eph. 4:23.
86. 1 Cor. 12:11.
87. Rom. 5:6.
88. James 2:20.
89. Gal. 5:6, 6:15.
90. Matt. 19:17.
91. Luke 15:22.
92. Rom. 3:24, 28.
93. Heb. 11:6.
94. Rom. 11:6.
95. Eph. 2:19.
96. Ps. 83:8 (84:7).
97. 2 Cor. 4:16.
98. Col. 3:5.
99. Rom. 6:13, 19.
100. Rev. 22:11.
101. Eccles. 18:22. "do not wait until death to be released".
102. James 2:24.
103. Thirteenth Sunday post Pentecost.
104. See St. Augustine, De Natura et Gratis, c. 43.
105. 1 John 5:3.
106. Matt. 11:30.
107. John 14:15.
108. Literally, "debts"; Matt. 6:12.
109. Rom. 6:18.
110. Titus 2:12.
111. Rom. 5:2.
112. Rom. 8:17.
113. Latin, consummatus.
114. Heb. 5:8, 9.
115. 1 Cor. 9:24, 26, 27.
116. 2 Pet. 1:10.
117. See below, Canon 25.
118. See Canon 31.
119. Ps. 118:112 ("to perform thy statutes for ever, to the end," 119:112).
120. Heb. 11:26.
121. Matt. 24:13.

122. See Rom. 14:4.
123. Phil. 1:6; 2:13.
124. 1 Cor. 10:12.
125. Phil. 2:12.
126. Cf. 1 Pet. 1:3.
127. Rom. 8:12, 13.
128. See Hieron. *Ep. ad Demetr* [Jerome, *Letter to Demetrias*].
129. John 20:22, 23.
130. Ps. 50:19 (51:17).
131. Eph. 4:30.
132. 1 Cor. 3:17.
133. Rev. 2:5, "repent and do," & c.
134. 2 Cor. 7:10, "produces a repentance".
135. Matt. 3:2; Luke 3:8.
136. Rom. 16:18.
137. 1 Cor. 6:9, 10.
138. 1 Cor. 15:58.
139. Heb. 6:10.
140. Heb. 10:35.
141. Matt. 10:22.
142. 2 Tim. 4:8.
143. John 4:13, 14.
144. Rom. 10:3.
145. Matt. 10:42.
146. 2 Cor. 4:17.
147. 1 Cor. 1:31, 2 Cor. 10:17.
148. *Ep. Cælest* [*Letter to Celestine*], i., c. 12.
149. James 3:2.
150. 1 Cor. 4:3, 4.
151. 1 Cor. 4:5.
152. Matt. 16:27.
153. Rom. 5:5.
154. See Sess. v. 5, *sub finis* [toward the end].
155. Matt. 24:13.
156. Latin, *reatus*.
157. See Sess. xxv. *sub initium* [toward the beginning].
158. Buckley, T. A. *The Canons and Decrees of the Council of Trent* (London: George Routledge and Co., 1851), 29–46.
159. Rom. 3:22, cf. 6:3–4.

160. Rom. 6:8–11.
161. Cf. 1 Cor. 12, John 15:1–4.
162. St. Athanasius, *Ep. Serap.* [*Letter to Serapion*], 1, 24: PG 26, 585 and 588.
163. Matt. 4:17.
164. Council of Trent (1547): *Decretum de Sacramentis* (DS), 1528.
165. Cf. ibid. 1529.
166. Rom. 3:21–26.
167. Council of Trent (1547): DS 1525.
168. St. Augustine, *In Jo. ev.* [*Tractates on the Gospel of John*], 72, 3: PL 35, 1823.
169. Cf. Rom. 7:22, Eph. 3:16.
170. Rom. 6:19, 22.
171. Cf. John 1:12–18, 17:3, Rom. 8:14–17; 2 Pet. 1:3–4.
172. Cf. 1 Cor. 2:7–9.
173. Cf. John 4:14, 7:38–39.
174. 2 Cor. 5:17–18.
175. St. Augustine, *De Gratia et Libero Arbitrio*, 17: PL 44, 901.
176. St. Augustine, *De Natura et Gratia*, 31: PL 44, 264.
177. St. Augustine, *Confessions*, 13, 36, 51: PL 32, 868; cf. Gen 1:31.
178. Cf. LG 12, Second Vatican Council, Dogmatic Constitution, *Lumen Gentium*, 12.
179. Cf. 1 Cor. 12.
180. Rom. 12:6–8.
181. Cf. Council of Trent (1547): DS 1533–1534.
182. Matt. 7:20.
183. Acts of the trial of St. Joan of Arc.
184. Roman Missal, Prefatio I de Sanctis; Qui in Sanctorum concilio celebraris, et eorum coronando merita tua dona coronas, citing the "Doctor of grace," St. Augustine, *En. in Ps.* [*The Ennarations, or Expositions, on the Psalms*], 102, 7: PL 37, 1321–1322.
185. Council of Trent (1547): DS 1546.
186. Cf. Council of Trent (1547): DS 1548.
187. St. Augustine, *Sermo*, 298, 4–5: PL 38, 1367.
188. St. Thérèse of Lisieux, "Act of Offering" in *Story of a Soul*, John Clarke, tr. (Washington D.C.: ICS, 1981), 277.
189. The Smalcald Articles, II, 1; Book of Concord, 292.
190. "*Rector et Judex Super Omnia Genera Doctrinarum*," Weimar Edition of Luther's Works (WA), 39, I, 205.

NOTES 343

191. It should be noted that some Lutheran churches include only the Augsburg Confession and Luther's Small Catechism among their binding confessions. These texts contain no condemnations about justification in relation to the Roman Catholic Church.

192. Report of the Joint Lutheran-Roman Catholic Study Commission, published in *Growth in Agreement* (New York: Geneva, 1984), 168–189.

193. Published by the Lutheran World Federation (Geneva, 1994).

194. Lutheran and Catholics in Dialogue VII (Minneapolis, 1985).

195. Minneapolis, 1990.

196. *"Gemeinsame Stellungnahme der Arnoldshainer Konferenz, der Vereinigten Kirche und des Deutschen Nationalkomitees des Lutherischen Weltbundes zum Dokument 'Lehrverurteilungen-kirchentrennend?'"* Ökumenische Rundschau 44 (1995): 99–102; see also the position papers that underlie this resolution, in *Lehrverurteilungen im Gespräch, Die ersten offiziellen Stellungnahmen aus den evangelischen Kirchen in Deutschland* (Göttingen: Vandenhoeck & Ruprecht, 1993).

197. The word "church" is used in this Declaration to reflect the self-understandings of the participating churches, without intending to resolve all the ecclesiological issues related to this term.

198. Cf. "Malta Report," paras. 26–30; *Justification by Faith*, paras. 122–147. At the request of the US dialogue on justification, the non-Pauline New Testament texts were addressed in *Righteousness in the New Testament*, by John Reumann, with responses by Joseph A. Fitzmyer and Jerome D. Quinn (Philadelphia: Fortress Press, 1982), 124–180. The results of this study were summarized in the dialogue report *Justification by Faith* in paras. 139–142.

199. "All Under One Christ," para. 14, in *Growth in Agreement*, 241–247.

200. Cf. WA 8:106; American Edition 32:227.

201. Cf. Council of Trent DS 1528.

202. Cf. Council of Trent DS 1530.

203. Cf. Apology II:38–45; Book of Concord, 105f.

204. Cf. Council of Trent DS 1515.

205. Cf. Council of Trent DS 1515.

206. Council of Trent Cf. DS 1545.

207. Cf. DV 5.

208. Cf. DV 5.

209. *Condemnations of the Reformation Era*, 27.

210. Ibid., n. 5 *"einen Konsens in Grundwahrheiten der Rechtfertigungslehre"* (cf. n. 13; 40; 43).

211. Cf. "Joint Declaration," n. 4: *"ein hohes Mass an gemeinsamer Ausrichtung und gemeinsamem Urteil."*
212. Cf. Council of Trent, Decree on original sin (DS 1515).
213. Cf. Council of Trent, Decree on justification, cap. 8: ". . . . *iustificatio.* . . . *quae non est sola peccatorum remissio, sed et sanctificatio et renovatio interioris hominis"* (DS 1528); cf. also can. 11 (DS 1561).
214. Cf. Council of Trent, Decree on Justification, cap. 16 (DS 1546), which quotes John 15:5, the vine and the branches.
215. Cf. ibid. DS 1545; and can. 26 (DS 1576).
216. Ibid., cap. 14 (cf. DS 1542).
217. Cf. ibid., can. 29 (DS 1579); Decree on the sacrament of Penance, cap. 2 (DS 1671); can. 2 (DS 1702).
218. First Council of Constantinople, *Symbolum Constantinopolitanum:* DS 150.
219. Cf. John Paul II, Encyclical Letter *Redemptoris Missio,* 1: *AAS* 83 (1991), 249–340.
220. Cf. Second Vatican Council, Decree *Ad Gentes* and Declaration *Nostra Aetate;* cf. also Paul VI Apostolic Exhortation *Evangelii Nuntiandi: AAS* 68 (1976), 5–76; John Paul II, Encyclical Letter *Redemptoris Missio.*
221. Second Vatican Council, Declaration *Nostra Aetate,* 2.
222. Pontifical Council for Inter-religious Dialogue and the Congregation for the Evangelization of Peoples, Instruction *Dialogue and Proclamation,* 29: *AAS* 84 (1992), 424; cf. Second Vatican Council, Pastoral Constitution *Gaudium et Spes,* 22.
223. Cf. John Paul II, Encyclical Letter *Redemptoris Missio,* 55: *AAS* 83 (1991), 302–304.
224. Cf. Pontifical Council for Inter-religious Dialogue and the Congregation for the Evangelization of Peoples, Instruction *Dialogue and Proclamation,* 9: *AAS* 84 (1992), 417ff.
225. John Paul II, Encyclical Letter *Fides et Ratio,* 5: *AAS* 91 (1999), 5–88.
226. Second Vatican Council, Dogmatic Constitution *Dei Verbum,* 2.
227. Ibid., 4.
228. John Paul II, Encyclical Letter *Redemptoris Missio,* 5.
229. John Paul II, Encyclical Letter *Fides et Ratio,* 14.
230. Council of Chalcedon, *Symbolum Chalcedonense:* DS 301; cf. St. Athanasius *De Incarnatione,* 54, 3: SC 199, 458.
231. Second Vatican Council, Dogmatic Constitution *Dei Verbum,* 4.
232. Ibid., 5.
233. Ibid.

234. Cf. *Catechism of the Catholic Church*, 144.

235. Ibid., 150.

236. Ibid., 153.

237. Ibid., 178.

238. John Paul II, Encyclical Letter *Fides et Ratio*, 13.

239. Cf. ibid., 31–32.

240. Second Vatican Council, Declaration *Nostra Aetate*, 2; cf. Second Vatican Council, Decree *Ad Gentes*, 9, where it speaks of the elements of good present "in the particular customs and cultures of peoples"; Dogmatic Constitution *Lumen Gentium*, 16, where it mentions the elements of good and of truth present among non-Christians, which can be considered a preparation for the reception of the gospel.

241. Cf. Council of Trent, *Decretum de Libris Sacris et de Traditionibus Recipiendis*: DS 1501; First Vatican Council, Dogmatic Constitution *Dei Filius*, cap. 2: DS 3006.

242. Second Vatican Council, Dogmatic Constitution *Dei Verbum*, 11.

243. Ibid.

244. John Paul II, Encyclical Letter *Redemptoris Missio*, 55; cf. 56 and Paul VI, Apostolic Exhortation *Evangelii Nuntiandi*, 53.

245. First Council of Nicaea, *Symbolum Nicaenum*: DS 125.

246. Council of Chalcedon, *Symbolum Chalcedonense*: DS 301.

247. Second Vatican Council, Pastoral Constitution *Gaudium et Spes*, 22.

248. John Paul II, Encyclical Letter *Redemptoris Missio*, 6.

249. Cf. St. Leo the Great, *Tomus ad Flavianum*: DS 294.

250. Cf. St. Leo the Great, Letter to the Emperor Leo I *Promisisse me Memini*: DS 318: ". . .*in tantam unitatem ab ipso conceptu Virginis deitate et humanitate conserta, ut nec sine homine divina, nec sine Deo agerentur humana.*" Cf. also ibid., DS 317.

251. Second Vatican Council, Pastoral Constitution *Gaudium et Spes*, 45; cf. also Council of Trent, *Decretum de Peccato Originali*, 3: DS 1513.

252. Cf. Second Vatican Council, Dogmatic Constitution *Lumen Gentium*, 3–4.

253. Cf. ibid., 7; cf. St. Irenaeus, who wrote that it is in the Church "that communion with Christ has been deposited, that is to say: the Holy Spirit" (*Adversus Haereses*, III, 24, 1: SC 211, 472).

254. Second Vatican Council, Pastoral Constitution *Gaudium et Spes*, 22.

255. John Paul II, Encyclical Letter *Redemptoris Missio*, 28. For the "seeds of the Word" cf. also St. Justin Martyr, *Second Apology*, 8, 1–2; 10, 1–3; 13, 3–6, E.J. Goodspeed, ed., 84, 85, 88–89.

256. Cf. John Paul II, Encyclical Letter, *Redemptoris Missio*, 28–29.

257. Ibid., 29.

258. Ibid., 5.

259. Second Vatican Council, Pastoral Constitution *Gaudium et Spes*, 10. Cf. St. Augustine, who wrote that Christ is the way, which "has never been lacking to mankind. . . . and apart from this way no one has been set free, no one is being set free, no one will be set free" *De Civitate Dei*, 10, 32, 2: CCSL 47, 312.

260. Second Vatican Council, Dogmatic Constitution *Lumen Gentium*, 62.

261. John Paul II, Encyclical Letter *Redemptoris Missio*, 5.

262. Second Vatican Council, Pastoral Constitution *Gaudium et Spes*, 45. The necessary and absolute singularity of Christ in human history is well expressed by St. Irenaeus in contemplating the preeminence of Jesus as firstborn Son: "In the heavens, as firstborn of the Father's counsel, the perfect Word governs and legislates all things; on the earth, as firstborn of the Virgin, a man just and holy, reverencing God and pleasing to God, good and perfect in every way, he saves from hell all those who follow him since he is the firstborn from the dead and Author of the life of God," *Demonstratio Apostolica*, 39: SC 406, 138.

263. John Paul II, Encyclical Letter *Redemptoris Missio*, 6.

264. Cf. Second Vatican Council, Dogmatic Constitution *Lumen Gentium*, 14.

265. Cf. ibid., 7.

266. Cf. St. Augustine, *Enarratio in Psalmos*, Ps. 90, *Sermo*, 2, 1: CCSL 39, 1266; St. Gregory the Great, *Moralia in Iob*, *Praefatio*, 6, 14: PL 75, 525; St. Thomas Aquinas, *Summa Theologiae*, III, q. 48, a. 2 ad 1.

267. Cf. Second Vatican Council, Dogmatic Constitution *Lumen Gentium*, 6.

268. *Symbolum Maius Ecclesiae Armeniacae*: DS 48. Cf. Boniface VIII, *Unam Sanctam*: DS 870–872; Second Vatican Council, Dogmatic Constitution *Lumen Gentium*, 8.

269. Cf. Second Vatican Council, Decree *Unitatis Redintegratio*, 4; John Paul II, Encyclical Letter *Ut Unum Sint*, 11: AAS 87 (1995), 927.

270. Cf. Second Vatican Council, Dogmatic Constitution *Lumen Gentium*, 20; cf. also St. Irenaeus, *Adversus Haereses*, III, 3, 1–3: SC 211, 20–44; St. Cyprian, *Epistal*, 33, 1: CCSL 3B, 164–165; St. Augustine, *Contra Adver. Legis et Prophet.* [*Against the Adversaries of the Law and the Prophets*], 1, 20, 39: CCSL 49, 70.

271. Second Vatican Council, Dogmatic Constitution *Lumen Gentium*, 8.

272. Ibid., cf. John Paul II, Encyclical Letter *Ut Unum Sint*, 13. Cf. also Second Vatican Council, Dogmatic Constitution *Lumen Gentium*, 15, and the Decree *Unitatis Redintegratio*, 3.

273. The interpretation of those who would derive from the formula *subsistit in* the thesis that the one Church of Christ could subsist also in non-Catholic Churches and ecclesial communities is therefore contrary to the authentic meaning of *Lumen Gentium*. "The Council instead chose the word *subsistit* precisely to clarify that there exists only one 'subsistence' of the true Church, while outside her visible structure there only exist *elementa Ecclesiae,* which—being elements of that same Church—tend and lead toward the Catholic Church," Congregation for the Doctrine of the Faith, *Notification on the Book "Church: Charism and Power" by Father Leonardo Boff*: *AAS* 77 (1985), 756–762.

274. Second Vatican Council, Decree *Unitatis Redintegratio*, 3.

275. Cf. Congregation for the Doctrine of the Faith, Declaration *Mysterium Ecclesiae*, 1: *AAS* 65 (1973), 396–398.

276. Cf. Second Vatican Council, Decree *Unitatis Redintegratio*, 14 and 15; Congregation for the Doctrine of the Faith, Letter *Communionis Notio*, 17: *AAS* 85 (1993), 848.

277. Cf. First Vatican Council, Constitution *Pastor Aeternus*: DS 3053–3064; Second Vatican Council, Dogmatic Constitution *Lumen Gentium*, 22.

278. Cf. Second Vatican Council, Decree *Unitatis Redintegratio*, 22.

279. Cf. ibid., 3.

280. Cf. ibid., 22.

281. Congregation for the Doctrine of the Faith, Declaration *Mysterium Ecclesiae*, 1.

282. John Paul II, Encyclical Letter *Ut Nnum Sint*, 14.

283. Second Vatican Council, Decree *Unitatis Redintegratio*, 3.

284. Congregation for the Doctrine of the Faith, Letter *Communionis Notio*, 17; cf. Second Vatican Council, Decree *Unitatis Redintegratio*, 4.

285. Second Vatican Council, Dogmatic Constitution *Lumen Gentium*, 5.

286. Ibid., 1.

287. Ibid., 4. Cf. St. Cyprian, *De Dominica Oratione*, 23: CCSL 3A, 105.

288. Second Vatican Council, Dogmatic Constitution *Lumen Gentium*, 3.

289. Cf. ibid., 9; cf. also the prayer addressed to God found in the *Didache* 9, 4: SC 248, 176: "May the Church be gathered from the ends of the earth into your kingdom" and ibid., 10, 5: SC 248, 180: "Remember, Lord, your Church . . . and, made holy, gather her together

from the four winds into your kingdom which you have prepared for her."

290. John Paul II, Encyclical Letter *Redemptoris Missio*, 18; cf. Apostolic Exhortation *Ecclesia in Asia*, 17: *L'Osservatore Romano* (November 7, 1999). The kingdom is so inseparable from Christ that, in a certain sense, it is identified with him (cf. Origen, In Mt. Hom. [*Commentary on Matthew*], 14, 7: PG 13, 1197; Tertullian, *Adversus Marcionem*, IV, 33, 8: CCSL 1, 634.

291. John Paul II, Encyclical Letter *Redemptoris Missio*, 18.

292. Ibid., 15.

293. Ibid., 17.

294. Second Vatican Council, Dogmatic Constitution *Lumen Gentium*, 14; cf. Decree *Ad Gentes*, 7; Decree *Unitatis Redintegratio*, 3.

295. John Paul II, Encyclical Letter *Redemptoris Missio*, 9; cf. *Catechism of the Catholic Church*, 846–847.

296. Second Vatican Council, Dogmatic Constitution *Lumen Gentium*, 48.

297. Cf. St. Cyprian, *De Catholicae Ecclesiae Unitate* 6: CCSL 3, 253–254; St. Irenaeus, *Adversus Haereses*, III, 24, 1: SC 211, 472–474.

298. John Paul II, Encyclical Letter *Redemptoris Missio*, 10.

299. Second Vatican Council, Decree *Ad Gentes*, 2. The famous formula *Extra Ecclesiam, nullus omnino salvatur* is to be interpreted in this sense (cf. Fourth Lateran Council, Cap. 1. *De Fide Catholica*: DS 802). Cf. also the *Letter of the Holy Office to the Archbishop of Boston*: DS 3866–3872.

300. Second Vatican Council, Decree *Ad Gentes*, 7.

301. John Paul II, Encyclical Letter *Redemptoris Missio*, 18.

302. These are the seeds of the divine Word (*semina Verbi*), which the Church recognizes with joy and respect (cf. Second Vatican Council, Decree *Ad Gentes*, 11; Declaration *Nostra Aetate*, 2).

303. John Paul II, Encyclical Letter *Redemptoris Missio*, 29.

304. Cf. ibid., *Catechism of the Catholic Church*, 843.

305. Cf. Council of Trent, *Decretum de Sacramentis*, can. 8, *De Sacramentis in Genere*: DS 1608.

306. Cf. John Paul II, Encyclical Letter *Redemptoris Missio*, 55.

307. Cf. Second Vatican Council, Dogmatic Constitution *Lumen Gentium*, 17; John Paul II, Encyclical Letter *Redemptoris Missio*, 11.

308. John Paul II, Encyclical Letter *Redemptoris Missio*, 36.

309. Cf. Pius XII, Encyclical Letter *Mystici Corporis*: DS 3821.

310. Second Vatican Council, Dogmatic Constitution *Lumen Gentium*, 14.

311. Second Vatican Council, Declaration *Nostra Aetate*, 2.

312. Second Vatican Council, Decree *Ad Gentes*, 7.

313. *Catechism of the Catholic Church*, 851; cf. also 849–856.

314. Cf. John Paul II, Encyclical Letter *Redemptoris Missio*, 55; Apostolic Exhortation *Ecclesia in Asia*, 31.

315. Cf. Second Vatican Council, Declaration *Dignitatis Humanae*, 1.

316. Ibid.

317. John Paul II, Encyclical Letter *Fides et Ratio*, 15.

318. Ibid., 92.

319. Ibid., 70.